Confidentiality and Mental Health

of related interest

**Ethical Practice and the Abuse of Power
in Social Responsibility**
Edited by Helen Payne and Brian Littlechild
ISBN 1 85302 743 X

Crime, Psychodynamics and the Offender Patient
Edited by Christopher Cordess and Murray Cox
ISBN 1 85302 634 4
Forensic Focus 1

**Community Care Practice and the Law,
Second Edition**
Michael Mandelstam
ISBN 1 85302 647 6

**Good Practice in Risk Assessment
and Risk Management 1 and 2**
Edited by Jacki Pritchard and Hazel Kemshall
ISBN 1 85302 552 6
Two volume set

**Working with Sex Offenders in Prisons
and through Release to the Community**
A Handbook
Alec Spencer
Forensic Focus 15

Risk Assessment in Social Care and Social Work
Edited by Phlyllida Pasloe
ISBN 1 85302 689 1
Research Highlights in Social Work 36

Confidentiality and Mental Health

Edited by
Christopher Cordess

Jessica Kingsley Publishers
London and Philadelphia

Appendix I, *Confidentiality: Protecting and Providing Information* (2000) © General Medical Council, is reproduced in full with the kind permission of the General Medical Council.

First published in the United Kingdom in 2001 by
Jessica Kingsley Publishers Ltd
116 Pentonville Road
London N1 9JB, England
and
325 Chestnut Street,
Philadelphia, PA19106, USA

www.jkp.com

Copyright © 2001 Jessica Kingsley Publishers Ltd
The Paradoxes of Confidentiality: A Philosophical Introduction © 2001 Bill (K.W.M.) Fulford

Library of Congress Cataloging in Publication Data
A CIP catalog record for this book is available from the Library of Congress

British Library Cataloguing in Publication Data
A CIP catalogue record for this book is available from the British Library

ISBN 1-85302-860-6 pb
ISBN 1-85302-859-2 hb

Printed and Bound in Great Britain by
Athenaeum Press, Gateshead, Tyne and Wear

Contents

The Paradoxes of Confidentiality

A Philosophical Introduction

Bill (K.W.M.) Fulford

Keep a diary and one day it will keep you. (Mae West, Hollywood, 1937)

Our culture, as Christopher Cordess writes in the opening chapter of this book, is a 'culture of disclosure' (p.27). But it is also a culture of confidentiality. Health professionals thus find themselves caught in a double bind. On the one hand, as Cordess describes, they are subject to growing pressures to reduce the threshold of disclosure. Yet at the same time they are the target of increasingly stringent ethical and legal controls aimed at protecting the confidentiality of their clients and patients.

This double bind on healthcare practice – to disclose *and* to keep secret, to expose *and* to hide – is the first of the paradoxes of confidentiality revealed by this book.[1] It is a paradox, moreover, which is nowhere more evident than in the area of healthcare with which this book is particularly concerned, namely *mental* health. There are many reasons for this: the recent historical shift from closed institutions to the open framework of modern community care (Chapter 3); the organisation of community mental health into multi-agency teams (extending beyond healthcare to social services and other non-clinical agencies, Chapter 8); the growing importance of issues of dangerousness (e.g. in situations of dual responsibility, Chapter 6; and in relation to child abuse, Chapter 5); the self-revelatory nature of many forms of psychotherapy (Chapter 7); and a host of other factors, have all combined to make deep dilemmas of disclosure and confidentiality a fact of daily life for everyone concerned with mental health, professionals and users alike.

Small wonder, then, that in the conference from which this book sprang, as Julian Stern describes in his report on the break-out groups (Chapter 13), the call was for clarification. More detailed professional codes were urgently needed, many felt, and tighter legal rules; or perhaps a specialised ethics committee, a statutory body on the lines of the Human Fertilization and Embryology Authority (HFEA) with responsibility for the regulation of practice in this difficult area.

---

1   This is of course not a strict or linguistic paradox like the classical paradox of the liar ('this statement is a lie' is true if false and is false if true).

The demand from health professionals for rules and regulation is understandable. But is it realistic? Professionals have always needed rules to play by (Fulford and Bloch, forthcoming). But would an even larger rulebook, would regulation by yet another tier of ethics committee, make matters better or worse?

In this Philosophical Introduction I will argue that the 'rules and regulation' approach could well make matters worse. This is a second paradox, then. Dilemmas about professional confidentiality are quintessentially ethical dilemmas. But this book, as we will see, contains many examples of situations, in both clinical work and research, in which the rules and regulation approach of traditional bioethics, although helpful in the past, has now reached the point of diminishing returns.

Rules and regulation, let me repeat, will always have a place. In the first section of this chapter I will indeed spell out some of the many ways in which bioethics, as traditionally conceived,[2] has and will continue to have, an important contribution to make in relation to the dilemmas about confidentiality and disclosure (I will call these 'disclosure dilemmas') raised by healthcare practice. But more is not necessarily better. Bioethics, traditionally conceived, is helpful up to a point. But we need to balance up the ethical agenda: instead of yet more rules, ethical and legal, we should look rather to the *processes* by which, in the circumstance of modern healthcare, clinical decisions are made; and instead of yet another ethics committee, regulating practice from above, we should look rather to the *values of our clients and patients*.

Professional confidentiality as a problem for traditional bioethics

Philosophers are professional sceptics. At first glance, though, it may seem gratuitously contrary-minded, even by the standards of sceptical philosophy, to take an anti-bioethics line on a problem which, as I noted a moment ago, is quintessentially a *bioethical* problem. In seeking to expand the ethical agenda, therefore, we must be careful to avoid throwing out the baby with the bathwater. The bathwater, as we will see, is an over-reliance on rules and regulation; but the baby is the wide range of both ethical and legal theories on which bioethics, traditionally conceived, can draw.

This book includes many examples of such theories, notably the principles approach and both utilitarian and deontological arguments (all introduced by Cordess in Chapter 1 and noted by a number of other authors), and virtue theory (see in particular the philosopher, Paul Cain's, Chapter 9). Absent from this book but well worth exploring are a range of more recent ethical theories which, in one way or another, make relationships, rather than individuals, the centre of the ethical action. Confidentiality, after all, as Cain (among others in this book) argues, is a function of relationships. Hence communitarian ethics (e.g. Mike Parker's Health Care Ethics, 1999), feminist ethics (introduced by Carol Gilligan In a Different Voice, 1982, and applied to mental health by, among others, Gwen Adshead 2000), and Donna Dickenson's neo-Hegelian property ethics (1997), are all relevant in principle to the disclosure dilemmas of healthcare practice.

2   There are of course many individual bioethicists who have emphasised the limitations of rules and regulation. For example, Stephen Toulmin's *The Tyranny of Principles* (1981) draws a distinction relevant to mental health, between the value of rules within an intimate community and their dangers in regulating our relationships with strangers.

The utilitarian calculus, the 'greatest good of the greatest number', illustrates the practical value of ethical theory. Utilitarianism, as Cordess (Chapter 1) and others describe, analyses the problems of professional confidentiality in terms of the balance of utilities between confidentiality and disclosure. If professionals are to profess, it is said, if they are to be in a position to do the job they are there to do, their clients must be willing to confide in them. This depends on trust. Professionals must be trusted to keep confidential the confidences confided in them by their clients. Hence, it is said, while third parties (relatives, the public at large, or the state) may have an interest in disclosure, the balance of utilities dictates that the threshold for disclosure by a professional should be set at a high level. Nonetheless, the utility of confidentiality is not absolute. It must always be weighed in a given case against other utilities attaching to disclosure.

The utilitarian calculus, it is true, is difficult to apply in practice: it depends on an imaginative identification with the wishes, interests and beliefs of others, an identification which is notoriously unreliable. Notwithstanding this difficulty, though, utilitarianism clearly does offer one way of tackling the disclosure dilemmas of professional practice.

Other ethical theories advanced in this book may also be helpful practically. The principles approach, for example, seeks to resolve disclosure dilemmas by balancing competing prima facie principles, e.g. the principle of autonomy (of patient choice) against the principle of beneficence (guiding professional interventions). A deeper treatment of autonomy, derived from Immanuel Kant, analyses disclosure dilemmas in terms of people treating each other as 'ends in themselves' rather than as a means to someone else's ends. Virtue theory, on the other hand, as Cain persuasively argues (Chapter 9), shows the importance of good character: the virtue of discretion, for example, is central to good practice. Deontology frames ethical issues in terms of duties, rights and responsibilities: the professional owes a duty to his or her client; the client has a right to confidentiality; the professional a responsibility to protect that right; and so on. Much of medical law is shaped deontologically. In the UK, as McClelland and Hale (Chapter 2) note, confidentiality is a *general* right. It is a right, moreover, that will be strengthened by incorporation of the European Convention on Human Rights.[3]

Ethical theory, then, offers a range of theoretical resources for tackling the disclosure dilemmas which arise in healthcare practice. So why the anti-bioethics line? The reasons for this start to emerge when we look at how these ethical theories, reasonable as they may seem, and helpful as they have been in the past, work out in the context of modern mental health practice.

Traditional bioethics as a problem for healthcare professionals

This book gives at least three clear signals that, positive and important as the role of bioethics has been in relation to problems of professional confidentiality in the past, it has now reached the point of diminishing returns.

---

[3]   Section 6.1 of the Convention specifies that '*everyone* has the right to respect for his private and family life, his home and his correspondence', cited by Andrew Hall, Chapter 10, p. 148, emphasis added.

First signal: bioethics begs many of the key questions

Adarsh Kaul's review of dual role issues (Chapter 6) illustrates how, on the really tricky issues, the prescriptions of medical ethics and law often do no more than beg the key questions.

As with many other areas of ethical concern, the question-begging nature of traditional bioethics is especially apparent in mental health. For example, neither the General Medical Council nor the Royal College of Psychiatrists[4] have yet provided psychiatrists with substantive guidance which would cover the really critical and difficult individual situation. The new Mental Health Act for England and Wales, apparently, will not cover research. (I return to research below.) The law generally, as both Andrew Hall (Chapter 10) and Anthony Harbour (Chapter 11) point out, is ad hoc and inconsistent in this area. Hall hopes for clarification from the European Convention on Human Rights. Practitioners similarly, are inclined to place their hopes in European law (e.g. Kaul, Chapter 6; and his reference to Adshead 1999). But a closer look at the wording of the Convention suggests that, far from being helpful, it may deepen the health professional's dilemmas over disclosure: how, for example, will healthcare professionals deal with the Convention's inclusion of the 'protection of morals' among the grounds for disclosure?[5]

Second signal: bioethics is becoming impractical

A number of authors in this book note that as ethicists and lawyers continually 'up the ante' on professional confidentiality, so the standards they set are becoming increasingly out of touch with the contingencies of day-to-day practice.

George Szmukler and Frank Holloway, for example, argue that the GMC's guidance on confidentiality, although developed (in part) by and for doctors, is 'unrealistic' (Chapter 3, pp. 53–54) in the context of the teamwork on which modern community-based mental healthcare depends. Figure 3.1 lists no less than 23 different agencies typically involved in any one case. In Chapter 4, similarly, Sue Bailey records that NHS managers are regularly in touch with over 30 different professional groups. Jacki Pritchard actually calls Chapter 8, on social work practice, The *Myth* of Confidentiality (emphasis added).

Ever higher standards of confidentiality could be a legitimate response to the growing pressure on professionals for disclosure. To an extent they *are* a legitimate response. Strict professional codes can certainly give power to the arm of professionals working in adverse regimes. The American psychiatrists, Al Freedman and A Halpern, have recently made a strong plea for the American Psychiatric Association to strengthen its code on the involvement of psychiatrists in executions on precisely these grounds (Freedman and Halpern 1998). All the same, it is far from clear, given that professionals are already finding existing ethical and legal codes impractical, that even stricter codes are or will prove helpful in the present case.

---

4   A Royal College of Psychiatrists' working party has recently produced a set of detailed guidelines under the Chairmanship of Professor R. McClelland.

5   This is only insofar as such disclosure is consistent with law – but then, as the Finnish case of Z *v. Finland [1997]* reported in Chapter 10 shows, if the law is inconvenient it can always be changed!

Someone may say, but if there is a gap between theory and practice here, surely professionals should raise their standards rather than expecting ethicists and lawyers to lower theirs. Cordess, reflecting this attitude, writes of a 'rhetoric of observance which belies an actual erosion' (Chapter 1, p 26). Perhaps, then, the social workers described in Watson's empirical study (Watson 1999, cited by Cordess, Chapter 1), who were found to be regularly in breach of their own professional code of conduct, need retraining to meet the increased demands of modern practice. But this begs the question of whose standards are actually the higher – those of ethicists and lawyers on the one hand or those of healthcare practitioners on the other! For many contributors to this book, the widening gap between theory and practice reflects the growing extent to which ethical (and legal) codes of confidentiality are perceived by healthcare practitioners not as ratcheting up standards of practice, but as a restraint, as a drag-anchor, holding them back.

Third signal: bioethics may even be counterproductive

That bioethics may be, not merely question begging, nor even just impractical, but actually counterproductive is perhaps the clearest signal that, in its present form at least, bioethics has reached the point of diminishing returns.

In a recent review, David Osborn (1999) has shown that the criteria of consent to a research procedure nowadays demanded by ethicists and lawyers, are perceived by many researchers as unrealistic. This is well illustrated by the problems of confidentiality in research. Mike Ferriter and Martin Butwell (Chapter 12) give a number of clear examples of the ways in which unrealistic demands for confidentiality may directly compromise good research practice and hence put progress at risk. This is especially so in mental health. In medical research, participants are normally able to give their explicit consent, this being the most secure ground for breaching confidentiality. But in mental health research, those most in need of the results of good research, for example people with major psychotic illnesses or severe learning disability, are also those most likely to lack the capacity for consent (Dickenson and Fulford forthcoming, Ch.10).

Similar problems are raised by audit, by teaching, and by some forms of counselling and psychotherapy. In this book, Christopher Bollas (Chapter 7) argues that anything short of absolute confidentiality makes some forms of psychoanalysis literally impossible. Bioethicists, arguing for a balance between confidentiality and disclosure, may regard this as too extreme. But Bollas' point is well made, that the mere *possibility* of disclosure 'in the public interest' invalidates the grounds of certain forms of psychoanalysis. Hence, he says, rather than hiding behind an anodyne mask of 'reasonableness', we should face up honestly to the fact that these forms of therapy will no longer be possible. We should therefore call a spade a spade, and rename them social therapies.

In all these areas, then, healthcare professionals increasingly feel that, on questions of confidentiality, bioethicists have gone a principle too far. This has been apparent for some time to many in the user movement. Priscilla Alderson, now Chair of the patient-advocacy group, CERES (Consumers for Ethics in Research), was among the first to point out that users, already disenfranchised by lack of expert knowledge, were at risk of becoming as she put it 'doubly disenfranchised' by the rise of bioethics as a new expert discipline (Alderson 1990). Suzanne Alford, similarly, a social worker with wide experience in the area of mental health, has pointed out the extent to which in identifying with their professional 'codes of ethics', healthcare professionals are at risk of adopting a defensive persona, of slipping into a Sartrean 'bad faith' which may be directly contrary to the interests of their clients (Alford 2000). Certainly, professionals and users alike are aware of the growing dangers of practice becoming excessively legalistic: how many patients will feel well served by a consultation which begins, as one reading of the General Medical Council and the Royal College of Psychiatrists' proposals (cited by Cordess, Chapter 1, p.41) will require consultations to begin, with a 'bill of rights'.

None of this is what most health professionals want. None of this is what most clients and patients want. In the past, health professionals have been at fault for assuming that 'doctor knows best'. Traditional bioethics, therefore, rightly insisted on a shift from paternalism ('doctor knows best') to autonomy ('patient knows best'). The problem nowadays, though, is that, as professionals and users alike, we are faced with an ethos of 'ethicist knows best'.

Professional confidentiality as a problem for professionals

If there is a divergence between bioethicists and healthcare professionals over issues of confidentiality, if indeed bioethicists are getting it wrong, then perhaps professionals should take back the territory! This will require a qualitative shift in the way we think about confidentiality itself as an aspect of professional expertise. In this section I will first sketch this key shift and then set it out in a little more detail.

First, then, the sketch. In the standard medical model, a professional's expertise is assumed to be primarily to matters of scientific fact. Bioethics reflects this model in taking confidentiality, along with other ethical issues, to be concerned merely with the regulation of practice (Fulford 1994). On this standard model, ethics come in only at the point of regulating how a professional applies his or her technical knowledge and skills. Taking back the territory, however, means that professionals have to accept that judgements of confidentiality, although essentially ethical rather than scientific in nature, are an integral part of, rather than external to, their expertise. Judgements of confidentiality, then, on this new model, are (partly) *constitutive*, rather than (merely) *regulative*, aspects of professional expertise.

That is the sketch. Now for more detail.[6] One route to seeing that judgements of confidentiality (as *ethical* judgements) are not merely regulative but constitutive aspects of professional practice is by way of a deeper understanding of what is involved in exercising professional expertise. The standard medical model corresponds with what the courts (in the UK) have traditionally called a 'man of science': someone who is an expert to a defined corpus of objective facts, which, granted only certain technical competences, can in principle be fully and explicitly set out. It is this model which, for

---

6   I give a more detailed argument for the general claim that ethical judgements are (partly) constitutive of professional expertise in Fulford (1994). I develop this further in relation to professional judgements of confidentiality in *Eight Paradoxes of Confidentiality* (Fulford, forthcoming a).

example, prioritises the results of meta-analyses of double-blind cross-over studies in the 'evidence hierarchy' of evidence-based medicine. The model is indeed well matched to certain areas of professional expertise. One can be an expert in this sense, for example, to the likely course of the median nerve in the arm; or to the probable physiological effects of a given drug in a given population.

Expertise of this kind, expertise on explicit knowledge of facts, is vitally important in healthcare. Indeed it is to expertise of this kind that we owe much of the success of modern medical science. There is a second strand to professional expertise, however. This has been identified, variously, by Aristotle as praxis, by modern writers as intuitive or craft knowledge, or as 'knowing how' as distinct from 'knowing that'. I will call it here, following the terminology current in philosophy, implicit (as distinct from explicit) knowledge. As an aspect of professional expertise, implicit knowledge is knowledge which professionals display without being able to explain fully *how* they do it.

There is nothing in itself mysterious or other-worldly about implicit knowledge. Recognising faces, for example, or riding a bicycle, both involve implicit (as well as explicit) knowledge. Such knowledge, furthermore, as these examples show, is not peculiar to professional expertise. It has been the focus of much recent research interest, not only in the human sciences but in artificial intelligence. It is the basis of at least one approach to medical ethics education (Hope, Fulford and Yates 1996). Work in the philosophy of science, moreover, suggests that implicit knowledge is important even in areas of scientific expertise which, in the past, have been assumed to rely only on explicit knowledge (see, e.g. Michael Polanyi's classic work, 1958). Philosophers of mind, more radically still, though with important implications for professional practice, have identified the irreducibility of implicit knowledge with the very grammar of mental content.[7]

That professional expertise depends on implicit as well as explicit knowledge surely comes as no surprise to the practitioner. Yet in these days of evidence-based practice we are encouraged to think that 'knowing what you are talking about' means, paradigmatically, being able to 'define your terms'. It is this explicit knowledge model, too, which is behind the belief that the ethical issues of professional confidentiality would be resolved if only we had a sufficiently clear and comprehensive set of rules. Yet as we have seen, there are clear signals that this approach, by way of rules and regulation, helpful as it has been in the past, has now reached the point of diminishing returns. Since, therefore, professional expertise depends on implicit as well as explicit knowledge, we need to widen the agenda of bioethics. Instead of continuing to chase after ever more detailed criteria of confidentiality, we should look rather to the *processes* by which, drawing on *implicit* knowledge, professional judgements of confidentiality are actually made.[8]

---

7   See, for example, the Warwick philosopher, Michael Luntley's application of his neo-Fregean philosophy of mind (1999) to professional expertise in school teachers (Luntley 2000).

8   I justify the step from explicit to implicit knowledge here on the grounds that both kinds of knowledge are, as a matter of fact, essential to professional expertise. A more theoretically grounded approach is possible by way of the expertise shown by professionals in the use of concepts. This is especially important in mental health because of the key ethical role of difficult concepts like capacity and rationality. (See my *Eight Paradoxes of Confidentiality*, forthcoming a.)

Widening the bioethical agenda

1. From criteria to process

What would a shift from criteria to process mean in practice? A full answer to this question would take us well beyond the scope of this chapter. The shift would have at least three specific consequences, however.

FIRST CONSEQUENCE: REHABILITATION OF CASE LAW

A shift from criteria to process would reinforce the value of case law. As Andrew Hall (Chapter 10) describes, there are major inconsistencies in the case law on confidentiality, notably between the Family and Criminal Courts. By the standards of explicit knowledge this is a criticism; and case law, in its potential for producing idiosyncratic decisions, certainly carries dangers of its own. But if professional judgements of confidentiality turn as much on implicit as explicit knowledge, then the (apparent) inconsistencies in case law could actually reflect genuine, though not readily codifiable, differences between cases. The example (noted earlier) of face recognition applies. The distinctions we make between faces, to the extent that such distinctions are based on intuitive knowledge, accurately reflect genuine, though not readily codifiable, differences. We do it (expertly) without being able (wholly) to explain *how* we do it. Implicit knowledge can thus be used to identify differences between concrete cases which are (in practice and sometimes in principle) impossible to distinguish by explicit criteria.

SECOND CONSEQUENCE: RE-ESTABLISHMENT OF PROFESSIONAL PEER REVIEW (BUT NOW IN PARTNERSHIP WITH USERS)

A second practical effect of the shift from criteria to process would be to give us back our confidence in professional peer review. In medicine, the Bolam principle, according to which professional competence is defined by the opinion of any group of competent co-professionals, has been under increasing attack from medical law and ethics. But like case law, the ad hoc, embedded, concrete character of peer review, on the Bolam model, is well tuned to the legitimate differences of opinion by which implicit knowledge, applied by professionals in a professional context, is characterised. As with case law, Bolam-type processes allow us to access the resources of implicit knowledge.

Bioethical criticisms of Bolam, it is true, are not so much of inconsistency, like Andrew Hall's criticisms of case law. The criticisms are concerned rather with professional self-interest. The Bolam test is said to be a licence for professional self-protection to masquerade as professional self-regulation. There is clearly a danger of professions becoming self-protective. But professions depend for their effective functioning (in their *clients'* interests) on mutual support (Fulford and Bloch, forthcoming). The criteria-to-process lesson, therefore, that we should take from the danger of mutual support slipping to mutual self-interest is not, as many in medical ethics and law have supposed, that we should substitute for peer review a set of externally imposed explicit regulations. It is rather that the review process itself should more accurately reflect the nature of the particular kind of knowledge relevant to judgements of confidentiality.

What kind of knowledge is relevant, then? The Bolam test, as it stands, is well tuned to judgements which turn more or less exclusively on the corpus of (implicit as well as explicit) knowledge to which a professional is expert. Scientific knowledge is of this kind. Here, then, a Bolam-type peer review which is limited to the professionals concerned, is sufficient. But confidentiality, as Cain (Chapter 9) and others argue, is located in the *relationship* between client and professional. In respect of judgements of confidentiality, then, users of services (patients and carers) are as much relevant experts as professionals (Fulford 1998a). What is needed, then, if the shift from criteria to process is accepted, is not less Bolam but more. What is needed is a Bolam-type process of review which more accurately tracks the *shared* expertise on which professional judgements of confidentiality depend.[9]

THIRD CONSEQUENCE: REINFORCEMENT OF CASUISTRY IN BIOETHICS

A third practical consequence of a shift from criteria to process concerns ethical reasoning itself. This consequence is a shift from principles reasoning, of the kind noted earlier, and other forms of top-down ethical reasoning, to casuistry or case-based reasoning.

Casuistry, as I have argued elsewhere (Fulford and Bloch, forthcoming), depends on and reflects implicit knowledge. Where most forms of substantive ethics – utilitarianism, deontology and so forth – involve applying general theory to particular cases, casuistry works the other way round; it focuses on the details of particular cases and eschews general theory. The strength of this approach, as the two American philosophers who reintroduced it into bioethics, Albert Jonsen and Stephen Toulmin (1988), argued, is that it allows us to tap directly into ethical intuitions.[10] Such intuitions, they noted, are often shared between people with quite different overt ethical principles. As with other areas of implicit knowledge, then, people often agree about *what* ought to be done while being largely unable to agree about *why*. Casuistry thus gives substantive ethics a powerful method for exploring ethical issues by accessing the resources of implicit knowledge.

Widening the bioethical agenda

2. From regulation by committees to the values of clients and patients

The three consequences just outlined of a shift in medical ethics and law from criteria to process, all leave open the possibility of radical differences of view on ethical issues. From the perspective of traditional bioethics, to the extent that this aims at rules and regulation, it may seem that such differences of view are a considerable downside to widening the bioethical agenda. The point of bioethics, as traditionally conceived, is to

---

9   Again, I set out this move, from a professional-alone to a professional-plus-client Bolam test, more fully in my *Eight Paradoxes of Confidentiality* (forthcoming).

10   The term casuistry, in modern usage, has come to have pejorative associations. It implies a cynical manipulation of cases. In calling their book, *The Abuse of Casuistry*, Jonsen and Toulmin emphasised that this is not how case-based ethical reasoning should be used.

provide ethical guidance. It is such guidance, as I noted at the start of this article, that professionals expect from bioethics.

Looked at from the other end, though, from the reality of practice rather than from the objectives of bioethics, radical differences of ethical view are the norm. This is especially so in the area of mental health. Every chapter in this book illustrates, in one way or another, the extent to which radical differences of view over judgements of confidentiality in mental health arise both between professionals and their clients, and between the very different kinds of professional involved in multi-agency teams.

In the traditional model of bioethics, these radical differences of view are taken to be a reflection of an incomplete or immature ethical theory, much as the corresponding radical differences of view on causal theories in psychiatry are taken to be a reflection of an incomplete or immature scientific theory. Work in philosophical value theory, however, notably by R.M. Hare (1963), J.O. Urmson (1950) and G.J. Warnock (1971), suggests, to the contrary, that these radical differences of view are a reflection, no more and no less, of the particularly *wide diversity of human values* in the areas of human experience and behaviour with which we are concerned in mental health. That is to say, the peculiar ethical difficulties we face in mental health practice are driven not by immaturity of ethical theory but by differences in human values. These differences, moreover, are *legitimate* differences, between one person and another, between cultures, and between different historical periods.[11]

It is worth emphasising this point because it reflects an important respect in which mental health differs from and is ethically more difficult than high-tech areas of medicine. Thus, a heart attack, for example, is, in itself, a bad condition for anyone. Similarly, pain, dizziness, nausea, collapse, indeed all those areas of human experience and behaviour with which physical medicine is typically concerned, whatever their instrumental value as a means to some other end, are in themselves bad experiences for (nearly) everyone. In respect of such experiences, then, human values are broadly convergent. But in mental health, by contrast, we are concerned with areas of human experience and behaviour – emotions, beliefs, desires, motivations and so forth – in which human values are highly divergent. In areas such as these, in contrast to the areas with which physical medicine is concerned, human values differ widely and legitimately.[12]

The practical importance of the diversity of human values in mental health is well illustrated by the problems of risk assessment. Risk assessment, as several chapters in this book illustrate, is at the heart of some of our most difficult judgements of confidentiality.

11   I have set out this point in detail in my *Moral Theory and Medical Practice* (1989, Ch. 3–5).
12   The difference here between bodily medicine and psychiatry, the difference in diversity of human values, is of course a difference of degree only. Paul Cain gives an arresting example of how unexpectedly diverse people's values are in general, not just in mental health: he was (understandably) surprised to find that some of his students regarded the colour of their carpets at home as 'personal and sensitive' information (Chapter 9).

It is also important to add that developments in technology are driving physical medicine increasingly into areas of human experience and behaviour in which, as in psychiatry, human values differ widely and legitimately. Assisted reproduction is a case in point. In this respect, then, in factoring the diversity of human values into its ethical thinking, psychiatry could well be beating a path which the rest of medicine will soon have to follow.

Risk is partly a matter of fact (the probability of this or that outcome), partly a matter of values (the utilities, negative and positive, of the different outcomes). Both sides, fact and value, are important. On the fact side, estimates of probable outcomes for dangerous behaviours are, in the present state of our scientific knowledge, considerably less reliable than estimates of the outcomes of dangerous heart conditions.[13] On the value side, though, the diversity of human values in mental health's area of concern means that, however accurate our estimates of probabilities become in the future, judgements of professional confidentiality will always remain more difficult in mental health than in areas like cardiology.

Radical differences of ethical view, therefore, are and will remain a feature of ethical practice in mental health. This is why a shift from criteria to process, in widening the agenda of bioethics, brings with it a shift from regulation by committees to the values of clients and patients. In an area like high-tech medicine, to the extent that human values are convergent, bioethics may draw conclusions with which most people will identify. In an area in which human values are convergent, that is to say, bioethics will be able to please most of the people most of the time. Hence the relative success of bioethics in high-tech medicine. Not so, though, where human values are divergent. Where human values are divergent, a given ethical conclusion, in coinciding with the values of some of those concerned, will, of necessity, diverge from the values of others. Where human values are divergent, therefore, bioethics, just in that it is successful in drawing a given ethical conclusion, will *fail* to please most of the people most of the time.

The diversity of values in mental health, then, means that the harder ethicists press for a particular ethic, the more carefully they try to tie things down, the more comprehensive their regulations and the more precise their rules, the more counterproductive they will become clinically. The danger, noted earlier, of 'ethicist knows best' is thus at its most extreme in an area like mental health where human values differ widely and legitimately.

Judgements of professional confidentiality in practice

From (hopes of) certainty to (acceptance of) uncertainty

Where, though, does all this leave healthcare practitioners on judgements of confidentiality? Are they left up an ethical creek without an ethical paddle?

First, let me repeat, the arguments presented here are not for the negative conclusion that we should abandon rules and regulation. They are rather for the positive conclusion that we need to balance rules and regulation, as the dominant modus operandi of traditional bioethics, with an approach which focuses: 1) on the diversity of individual values, and 2) on the processes through which this diversity of values can be incorporated into sound ethical judgements in the contingencies of particular concrete clinical situations.

Balancing up the bioethical agenda in this way would have a wide range of effects on clinical practice. In this section I look briefly at three such effects:

---

13   Though of course there may be considerable uncertainty even over the outcome of bodily diseases.

- an enlarged role for communication skills;

- a shift in the aims of ethical reasoning from consensus to dissensus;

- a recognition of the positive clinical value of uncertainty.

COMMUNICATION SKILLS

One directly practical consequence of balancing up the bioethical agenda, then, is to reinforce the importance of good communication as a key practice skill for ethical reasoning. The diversity of human values in mental health means that the healthcare professional, as an expert, must have the knowledge and skills to understand the perspectives of their patients as unique individuals. A balanced ethical agenda thus puts the patient firmly at the centre of the ethical action (Fulford 1995). Where values clash, though, the professional must also have the knowledge and skills required for shared decision making, for drawing on the rich variety of perspectives represented by the different agencies involved in mental health services. This gives a distinctive and important new role to the multi-agency team. In the traditional model the multi-agency team has a role in providing a variety of skills concerned with management. In this new model, the multi-agency team also provides a balance of different perspectives on disputed questions of value (Fulford 1999).

Good communication skills are thus central to ethical decision making in mental health. This has important implications for ethics education in healthcare (Hope, Fulford and Yates 1996). The diversity of values in mental health, however, means that, as I noted in the last section, it is radical differences of view, rather than consensus, which may emerge from 'good communication'. Such differences of view will not always be reconcilable. The values of the client or patient may be at odds with those of other people – their family, the professionals involved, the wider society. In its most extreme form, differences of values may amount to psychopathology (some delusions of guilt, for example, take the form of delusional value judgements rather than delusions as to matters of fact (Fulford 1991). Even, though, leaving aside these extreme cases, differences of values, as this book illustrates, will commonly go beyond what I have called elsewhere 'the limits of tolerance' (Fulford 1996).

Such differences of view, however, if the need for a shift from criteria to process is accepted, should be dealt with primarily, as I noted earlier, not by setting up ever more detailed rules and regulations, but by extending the review process to allow the concrete details of the particular disputed case to be exposed to a wider range of relevant expertise. An extended review process of this kind, rather than seeking inappropriately to substitute explicit knowledge for implicit knowledge, aims to exploit the available implicit knowledge to the full. In the case of mental health, analogously with the Bolam-plus test suggested above, the different agencies involved in community mental healthcare, including those representing users and carers, provide a particularly rich resource of relevant implicit knowledge. Good communication skills are the key to unlocking this implicit knowledge.

FROM CONSENSUS TO DISSENSUS

An extended review process of this kind, it should immediately be said, certainly carries dangers of its own. In the first place, just in that cases are resolved by a wider range of parties having access to the 'concrete details' of a given case, the process itself raises issues of confidentiality.[14] In the second place, to the extent that it aims at resolving differences by consensus, the review process is at risk of imposing the majority view on minorities (Fulford 1998b). The dangers of consensus, indeed, as the American philosopher Loretta Kopelman (1994) has pointed out, are inherent even in the most process-friendly form of ethical reasoning, casuistry. This was introduced into bioethics primarily as a way of reaching consensus (Jonsen and Toulmin 1988). But casuistry only leads to ethical consensus if the ethical intuitions to which it gives access are shared. Where these intuitions are not shared, the danger is that the intuitions of the majority will be imposed on those of dissenting minorities.

There is no easy way with either of these dangers, the danger of compounding the problems of confidentiality, and the danger of an abusive imposition of majority values. It is important, though, to recognise that these dangers are inherent, too, in the rules and regulation approach of bioethics and medical law. Any review process, whether by peers or by committees and courts of law, necessarily extends the range of those who have access to confidential information about the case in question. Any method of ethical decision making, whether by multidisciplinary teams or by reference to 'higher' authority (the doctor of the old medical paternalism, the ethicist or lawyer of the new bioethical paternalism), necessarily risks the abusive imposition of one set of values over another.

These dangers, however, if unavoidable, are at least mitigated in a process-based approach which recognises and acknowledges legitimate differences of values. Thus casuistry, as we have seen, although introduced originally as a means of reaching consensus, has an equally important role in helping to make transparent *differences* of ethical view. This is especially important in mental health, in which, as we have also seen, our ethical intuitions are indeed characteristically and legitimately different. A similar point applies to the extended peer review, the Bolam-plus process, suggested above. There are different ways in which such a process might work and these would have to be tested out in practice. But the aim would be to create a process in which *differences* of view are clarified and respected.

The dangers of abusive consensus, then, in such a system, although still present, are considerably less than in a system which relies on the imposition by an ethics committee of a set of regulations which reflect ethical intuitions external to the context of the client–professional relationship. Regulation, it is worth adding, does have a role here (Fulford and Hope 1993). But the proper role of regulation in this respect, whether ethical or legal, is not to impose consensus. It is rather to guarantee a structure within which the processes of ethical review remain sensitive to, and allow full expression of, diversity of opinion (Fulford 1999).

14   I owe this point to one of my MA students at Warwick University, Debbie Osborn.

A POSITIVE ROLE FOR UNCERTAINTY

All this will not guarantee a simple or unproblematic way forward! But then we know that these are not simple or unproblematic situations. So far as diversity of values is concerned, tolerance of uncertainty is, anyway, among the key skills required of mental healthcare professionals (Fulford forthcoming, b). In mental health, moreover, the lesson of history is that it is from misplaced certainty, rather than from uncertainty, that we have most to fear. Time after time in psychiatry the most abusive practices have been driven not by evil will but by well-intentioned convictions. Psychiatry, like any other area of medicine, has its share of plain malpractice. But it seems peculiarly vulnerable to what the eighteenth-century political philosopher, and founder of British Empiricism, John Locke, called 'enthusiasms' – values, not in themselves mistaken, but overblown.

High profile abuses, arising from political 'enthusiasms' in the former USSR, for example, are well recognised (Fulford, Smirnoff and Snow 1993). More insidious, but of no less importance clinically, are the low profile generic abuses of day-to-day practice. We have only to read the increasingly influential 'user literature' to see that, for all the new enlightenment of patient autonomy, the values of those on the receiving end of healthcare continue to be eclipsed by the values of those providing it (Campbell 1996). While as to the political uses of psychiatry, the dangers we face from current enthusiasms are writ large on every page of this book. The pressure for disclosure, the presence as Bollas (Chapter 7) puts it of the state in the very consultation, is driven, not by the needs of an intrusive executive (though no doubt it will be exploited to that end) but by 'public interest'. Jack Straw, the present Home Secretary, launching the UK government's plans to make psychiatry responsible for dangerous people, made this political enthusiasm explicit: 'The safety of the public is our prime concern,' he said (Straw 1999).

The lesson, then, of history is that the healthcare professional's answer to the diversity of values in mental health should not be a retreat to the false certainties of the standard medical and bioethical model. It should rather be to build up our competencies in the aspects of practice that have been devalued in the standard model – implicit knowledge, good process and the communication skills to recognise and work within rather than against the rich diversity of human values. This is why, as I said at the start of this chapter, the calls by healthcare practitioners, recorded by Stern (Chapter 13), for more rules and regulation, were understandable but misplaced. The message of this book is the paradox that the enthusiasm from which mental health practitioners are most at risk, on ethical issues of professional confidentiality, is ethics itself.

Conclusion

The paradoxes of confidentiality

The paradoxes we have encountered in this Philosophical Introduction are not strict or linguistic paradoxes (see footnote 1). They are, rather, observations or conclusions which are surprising in that they contradict expectations. Like strict paradoxes, though, these paradoxes of confidentiality, just in that they contradict expectations, have opened up new lines of enquiry.

The paradox from which we began, and which is at the heart of the concerns explored in this book, is the double bind of the incompatible demands for confidentiality and disclosure in which health professionals are increasingly caught. This led us to question whether the entirely understandable call by health professionals for more rules and regulation, was realistic. A second paradox then emerged. This was to the effect that, although problems of professional confidentiality are essentially ethical in nature, traditional bioethics, far from helping, has in some respects been making matters worse. Correspondingly, therefore, health professionals had to take back the territory. This was paradoxical from the perspective of the standard scientific medical model according to which ethical issues are regulative rather than constitutive of professional expertise. It led, nonetheless, to two further conclusions which, although paradoxical from the perspectives equally of standard bioethics and of the standard medical model, bore directly on practice: first, that alongside ethical criteria (the rules of practice), we should be concerned with the processes by which judgements of professional confidentiality are made – case law, Bolam-type peer review (incorporating users equally with professionals) and casuistry, would all be important in this respect; second, that alongside ethics committees (regulating practice from above), we should be concerned equally with the values of individual users (clients, patients and carers).

This opened up the possibility of radical differences of view, a result at odds with the thrust of modern bioethics and law to the extent that these have been concerned to provide rules for the regulation of practice. Mental health though, as I argued, is concerned with areas of experience and behaviour in which human values are characteristically and legitimately diverse. In mental health, then, we had the further paradox that regulation, insofar as it is concerned with imposing ethical rules reflecting a given set of values, will necessarily be experienced as abusive by many of those concerned, users and professionals alike. Indeed the lesson of history, the historical counterpart of this ethical paradox, is that in mental health it is from the misplaced certainties of ideological conviction, rather than from being open to diversity of values, that we have most to fear.

This is not to say, let me emphasise again, that we can do without rules and regulation altogether. To the contrary, in a properly balanced system, they have an important role to play. But it is to say that rules and regulation are not sufficient. Our final conclusion, then, our response to the radical differences of ethical view inherent in mental health, was that, instead of yet more rules and regulation, we should build up our competencies in the aspects of practice which have been neglected equally by the standard medical model and by much of traditional bioethics – implicit knowledge, good process, and communication skills.

There is a Chinese proverb which says, put a frog in hot water and it will immediately jump out; but put a frog in warm water and gently bring it to the boil and your frog will not try to jump out until it is too late. Healthcare professionals are already in bioethical hot water but it is not too late to jump out!

Acknowledgements

I am grateful to Mark Bratton, Paul Cain, Christopher Cordess, Sue Chetwynd, Michael Luntley, Roy McClelland and Debbie Osborn, for their detailed comments and help in developing this chapter.

References

Adshead, G. (2000) 'A different voice in psychiatric ethics.' In M.Parker and D.Dickenson [eds] *The Cambridge Workbook in Medical Ethics*. Cambridge: Cambridge University Press.

Alderson, P. (1990) *Choosing for Children: Parents' Consent to Surgery*. Oxford: Oxford University Press.

Alford, S, (2000) 'Philosophical conflicts in the ethics of involuntary psychiatric treatment.' Unpublished MA essay.

Campbell, P. (1996) 'What we want from crisis services.' In J. Read and J. Reynolds (eds) *Speaking Our Minds: An Anthology*. Basingstoke: Macmillan/Open University, pp.180–183.

Dickenson, D. (1997) *Property, Women, and Politics: Subjects or Objects?* Cambridge: Polity Press.

Dickenson, D. and Fulford, K.W.M. (forthcoming) 'The three 3's of research ethics.' In D.Dickenson and K.W.M Fulford (eds) *In Two Minds: A Casebook of Psychiatric Ethics*. Oxford: Oxford University Press.

Freedman, A. and Halpern, A. (1998) 'The psychiatrist's dilemma: a conflict of roles in legal executions.' *Australian and New Zealand Journal of Psychiatry 33*, 629–635.

Fulford, K.W.M. (1989) *Moral Theory and Medical Practice*. Cambridge: Cambridge University Press.

Fulford, K.W.M. (1991) 'Evaluative delusions: their significance for philosophy and psychiatry.' *British Journal of Psychiatry 159*, 108–112, Supplement 14, Delusions and Awareness of Reality.

Fulford, K.W.M. (1994) 'Medical education: knowledge and know-how.' In R. Chadwick (ed) *Ethics and the Professions*. Aldershot: Avebury Press.

Fulford, K.W.M (1995) 'Concepts of disease and the meaning of patient-centred Care.' In K.W.M. Fulford, S. Ersser and T. Hope(eds) *Essential Practice in Patient-centred Care*. Oxford: Blackwell.

Fulford, K.W.M. (1996) 'Religion and psychiatry: extending the limits of tolerance.' In D. Bhugra (ed) *Psychiatry and Religion: Context, Consensus and Controversies*. London: Routledge and Kegan Paul.

Fulford, K.W.M. (1998a) 'Replacing the Mental Health Act 1983? How to change the game without losing the baby with the bath water or shooting ourselves in the foot. Invited commentary on: G. Szmukler and F. Holloway "Mental health legislation is now a harmful anachronism".' *Psychiatric Bulletin 22*, 666–670.

Fulford, K.W.M. (1998b) 'Dissent and dissensus: the limits of consensus formation in psychiatry.' In H.A.M.J. ten Have and H.M. Saas (eds) *Consensus Formation in Health Care Ethics*. Lancaster: Kluwer, pp.175–192.

Fulford, K.W.M. (1999) 'From culturally sensitive to culturally competent: a seminar in philosophy and practice skills.' In K. Bhui and D. Olajide (eds) *Mental Health Service Provision for a Multi-cultural Society*. London: Saunders.

Fulford, K.W.M. (forthcoming, a) *Eight Paradoxes of Confidentiality*. London: Jessica Kingsley Publishers.

Fulford, K.W.M. (forthcoming, b) 'Schizophrenia and religious experience: value judgements in psychiatric diagnosis and the impact of the DSM's new criterion B on the differential diagnosis of psychotic experiences.' *Advances in Psychiatric Treatment*.

Fulford, K.W.M. and Hope, R.A. (1993) 'Psychiatric ethics: a bioethical ugly duckling?' In R. Gillon and A. Lloyd (eds) *Principles of Health Care Ethics.* Chichester: Wiley.

Fulford, K.W.M., Smirnoff, A.Y.U. and Snow, E. (1993) 'Concepts of disease and the abuse of psychiatry in the USSR.' *British Journal of Psychiatry 162*, 801–810.

Fulford, K.W.M., Yates, A. and Hope, T. (1997) 'Concepts of disease and the paradox of patient power.' Paper presented at the Practice Skills Project Conference: Patient Centred Care. Green College, Oxford.

Fulford, K.W.M. and Bloch, S. (forthcoming) 'Psychiatric ethics: codes, concepts and clinical practice skills.' In M.G Gelder, J. López-Ibor and N. Andreasen (eds) *New Oxford Textbook of Psychiatry.* Oxford: Oxford University Press.

Gilligan, C. (1982) *In a Different Voice: Psychological Theory and Women's Development.* Cambridge MA: Harvard University Press.

Hare, R.M. (1963) 'Descriptivism.' *Proceedings of the British Academy 49*, 115–134. Reprinted in R.M. Hare (1972) *Essays on the Moral Concepts.* London: Macmillan.

Hope, T., Fulford, K.W.M. and Yates, A. (1996) *Manual of the Oxford Practice Skills Project.* Oxford: Oxford University Press.

Jonsen, A.R. and Toulmin, S. (1988) *The Abuse of Casuistry: A History of Moral Reasoning.* Berkeley: University of California Press.

Kopelman, L.M. (1994) 'Case method and casuistry: the problem of bias.' *Theoretical Medicine 15*, 1, 21–38

Luntley, M. (1999) *Contemporary Philosophy of Thought.* Oxford: Blackwell.

Luntley, M. (2000) 'Performance, pay and professionals.' Impact Pamphlet no.2. London: Philosophy of Education Society of Great Britain.

Montgomery, J. (1995) 'Patients first: the role of rights.' In K.W.M. Fulford, S. Ersser and T. Hope (eds) *Essential Practice in Patient-centred Care.* Oxford: Blackwell.

Osborn, D. (1999) 'Research and ethics: leaving exclusion behind.' *Current Opinion in Psychiatry 12*, 5, 601–604.

Parker, M. (1999) 'Health care ethics: liberty, community or participation.' In M.Parker (ed) *Ethics and Community in the Health Care Professions.* London: Routledge.

Polanyi, M. (1958) *Personal Knowledge.* London: Routledge.

Straw, J. (1999) Cited in Central Office of Information (COI), 221, 19.7.1999. In a report on the launch of the government's consultative paper 'Managing dangerous people with severe personality disorder'.

Toulmin, S. (1981) *The Tyranny of Principles. Hastings Center Report.* New York: Hastings Center.

Urmson, J.O. (1950) 'On grading.' *Mind 59*, 145–169.

Warnock, G.J. (1971) *The Object of Morality.* London: Methuen.

Watson, F. (1999) 'Overstepping our boundaries.' Practice Focus. *Professional Social Work*, pp.14–15

Confidentiality
and Contemporary Practice
Christopher Cordess

Introduction

Ethical issues have always been essential in the practice of medicine. In recent decades there has been a massive increase in the complexities of clinical practice and research across all fields of health. In no field has this been greater than in mental health. Ethics perforce are increasingly in a position of centrality. Some of the problems are reflected in rapidly changing civil and criminal legislation and the consequent explosion of guidelines and position statements from professional bodies and government departments. To take two examples of legal changes, the incorporation of the European Convention of Human Rights into the law of England and Wales (see Hall, Chapter 10) and developments in the funding of medical negligence cases (the so-called 'No win no fee' deals), will inevitably produce fundamental changes in many aspects of clinical practice. The benefits of increased patient rights (and means of enforcing them) will be hedged by the encouragement of a culture of complaint and compensation, and of necessarily defensive medical practice. Issues of information sharing of hitherto confidential clinical information pose increasingly difficult dilemmas.

Since ethical questions in mental healthcare involve the application of moral theory, there are necessarily certain core values and principles, which are however subject to changing interpretations in the light of these new situations. There may be a tension between different interests with regard to information sharing for the benefit of any one particular individual. More commonly, the interests of one individual or group may impinge on, or be in frank opposition to those of others. There can be no clearer example of this than the changes brought in expectation and practice by the Children Act 1989. With the emphasis on the paramountcy of the welfare of the child came consequences for the whole basis of adult mental health practice and of sharing information, particularly in relation to third party protection. These effects have been fully traced by Bollas and Sundelson (1995) among others. There have been numerous other changes, too, which have impacted on time-honoured practices of confidentiality and contributed to its incremental erosion. These include increasingly dominant models of multidisciplinary working; the often politically driven policies of inter-agency working (including the so-called multi-agency risk panels where clinicians and police officers frequently find themselves sitting within the same 'patient-centred' conference); increased emphasis on 'health management' – precursor, possibly, of managed care, US style; the depredations of the now defunct 'internal market' within the NHS, and, of course, the means, via information technology, to store information and disseminate it almost instantaneously. Clinical information that would previously have been considered confidential is freely shared. We now live in a society where expectations of clinical information sharing are continually on the increase.

What has become clear to this writer is that: confidentiality has been taken for granted by the clinical professions; and the introduction of a great deal of new statute law, especially of guidelines for practice relating to this law, has paid little attention to clinical traditions of confidentiality. Where issues of confidentiality have been acknowledged there is frequently a rhetoric of observance which belies an actual erosion.

The concept and practice of confidentiality within the doctor–patient relationship is grounded upon several foundations. The first is deontological, based upon the principle of respecting the autonomy of the individual. The second is utilitarian; there is acknowledgement that in certain circumstances a patient/client will not divulge information (which for health reasons he needs to do) unless confidentiality is assured. There is, also, the conflicting and more usual interpretation of the utilitarian position as one of the greatest possible good for the greatest number; this is an ongoing tension which arises in many different clinical situations. Is the greater public good served by disclosure to all, or by maintaining preserves of privacy? Third, and overlapping with the preceding, are professional codes of practice, first adumbrated in the Hippocratic Oath (WMA, 1995), and encoded now, among other rewrites, in *Duties of a Doctor – Confidentiality* (GMC, 1995). Finally, there is the legal foundation – which is covered in Chapter 10 (Hall) and Chapter 11 (Harbour).

Related to the concept of confidentiality is that of 'privacy' and, at one remove, that of 'secrecy' (Warwick 1989) – a more paranoid conceptualisation.

Lined up against such concepts is the general principle of openness, within society and its institutions, and as a prime general principle of the delivery of justice. A Law Lord has quoted Jeremy Bentham:

> In the darkness of secrecy, sinister interest and evil in every shape have full swing. Only in proportion as publicity has a place can any of the checks applicable to judicial justice operate. Where there is no publicity there is no justice ... publicity is the very soul of justice. It is the keenest spur to exertion and the surest of all grounds against improbity. It keeps the judge himself while trying under trial. (Shaw 1913)

The issue of openness versus privacy, of freedom versus withholding of information, is topical now in UK politics, but should always be topical in any democracy. This chapter, and this book, seeks to address a very particular aspect of this wider scene – that of confidentiality within the mental health system. Lord Bingham, a lawyer, puts the general case, as it were, for the limits of openness:

> So familiar is this principle of openness to those of us brought up in the common law that we sometimes forget how contrary it is to the principles on which the rest of our

lives are conducted. It is very hard to think of any professional relationship which does not have a duty of confidence as one of its ingredients, probably a legal duty but certainly an ethical duty. Doctors, lawyers, accountants, bankers, social workers, probation officers, spiritual counsellors, officers of government would all recognise a clear obligation to preserve the confidentiality of matters imparted to them in confidence... And to some extent we respect the same rules in our private lives, looking askance at those who betray the confidences of their friends and acquaintances, even when they do not earn money by doing so. We do not, most of us, run our lives on a basis of total disclosure. (Bingham 1996)

I have prefaced what follows in this chapter with these introductory comments since what I see as an incremental erosion of confidential practice, at least within my own spheres of psychiatry, forensic psychiatry and psychotherapy, must be seen within a societal context; on the one hand of enforced 'openness', albeit invariably about others (the 'culture of disclosure') and, on the other, of a perceived increase in the tendency of the Executive to withhold information (the 'culture of secrecy') – for example, the much diluted proposed Freedom of Information Act. There is a danger that inequalities of power breed inequalities of rights, including those of privacy and confidentiality.

Our relatively specialised area of concern does need to be seen within a contemporary climate of suspiciousness of professionals and their practice (spurred for medicine by the perceived failures at Bristol Children's Hospital in 1998 among others). The introduction of Clinical Governance (DoH 1998, 1999) focuses 'on a fundamental shift required to enable good clinical quality'. While admirable in itself, encouraging greater multidisciplinary team working, increased accountability and reporting, and integrated planning based upon access to clinical and research information, it necessarily challenges hitherto accepted boundaries of information sharing. There is a complex interrelation between patient autonomy, and professional self-regulation and autonomy on the one hand, and greater centralised control on the other; privacy and confidentiality are necessarily part of this tension.

Recently introduced legislation adds to expectations of disclosure, for example, the Public Interest Disclosure Act 1998. It has been dubbed the 'whistle-blowers' charter'. Those covered under the Act are defined as 'workers', including all employees as well as the self-employed who provide services under contract. We are invited to make disclosures of colleagues' likely commission, or commission, of a criminal offence; actual, or likely, failure to comply with a legal obligation; behaviour which might lead to a miscarriage, or likely miscarriage, of justice, or actual, or likely, danger to the health and safety of a person; behaviour which might lead to actual, or likely, damage to the environment, or finally to the concealment of any of these. Although it is expected that whistle-blowers should act in good faith, it is anticipated that: (a) general whistle-blowing will be encouraged; (b) malicious whistle-blowing will increase, as also will (c) targeted whistle-blowing (i.e. for vengeful purposes). A substantial risk of being reported to the Inland Revenue by colleagues (fellow 'workers') for suspected tax evasion has been predicted.

Questions arise about the whole conception of such enactments in law, but also of the type of thinking which underpins them. Is this not a paranoid state of thinking, which may induce paranoid thinking in others, in the name of beneficence and equity? May not the foreseeable 'advantages' be outweighed by their likely opposite? Are not some of these policies likely to backfire, by way of further morale reduction, if, indeed, this legislation is ever much used? Is it too homely to suggest that parental exhortations to children 'not to tell tales' (or, significantly, not to blame others for what one might have some responsibility for oneself) had their place in a recognition of honour among children? May one not suggest, even, that the prohibition against 'grassing', one prisoner to another, does recognise some human necessity for 'honour among thieves'? The point, of course, is not to condone the practice of inadequate or neglectful medicine – and there are now ample guidelines and advice in addition to the introduction of clinical governance (e.g. *Maintaining Good Practice*, GMC 1998; *Supporting Doctors, Protecting Patients*, DoH 1999) concerning the appraisal and maintenance of clinical standards, and actions to be taken when concern arises about a colleague's practice. Such, however, is the present 'political correctness' of policies of surveillance and reporting (branded 'snitch laws' and resisted in the USA, Stone 1984) that there is a risk of being seen to be supporting, colluding with, or covering up bad practice, by questioning too aggressive an enactment of such policies. The problem is that multiple and increasing encouragements to disclose more and more information about clients, patients, colleagues and fellow 'workers' in the 'public interest' over-ride the individual moral dilemmas which such decisions may entail, and may in the longer term have massive downsides – many of which are addressed in this chapter and this volume. There is a balance to be preserved and that balance is rapidly changing. This same dilemma has been prominent in US professional practice for some decades and is well covered by Stone (1984). Stone discusses the public perception of confidentiality providing a cloak to hide professional incompetence of, say, the sexually offending therapist. He also writes of the difficulties of deciding when to act by informing on a deficient colleague, when the basis will most likely be that of only partial information or frequently in the form of vague rumours. These dilemmas seem to have received relatively little discussion in this country for such a major cultural shift of such consequential import.

The maintenance of the duty of confidence by a doctor to his patient was traditionally partly justified as not only for the patient's private interest, but for the public interest; that it is in the interests of all patients, present and future, to expect the medical profession to respect their confidences for the sake of the preservation of the general concept of the confidential doctor–patient relationship. This same argument has protected priests, lawyers (outside child care and family law), psychoanalysts, certain government departments, e.g. MI6 (where absolute confidentiality for security is deemed necessary) and, to some extent, journalists and their sources. Andrew Hall in Chapter 10 shows that those very same arguments which have sustained legal professional privilege (at least for criminal lawyers) have been used to force doctors and other health workers into greater disclosure, especially with the advent of increased concerns for public protection, where 'public interest' has come to be interpreted as a justification for disclosure, rather than an argument against such sharing of sensitive information.

Forensic psychiatry

Forensic psychiatry differs from other psychiatric or medical specialities in concerning itself directly with the law (the Latin 'forum', hence 'forensic'). Its activities may be divided into:

1. The provision of treatment, in whatever setting – outpatient or inpatient – with the establishment of a doctor–patient relationship, albeit most commonly with an expressed criminal justice interest.

2. The provision of expert opinion for courts or other agencies without the establishment of any such relationship.

Ethical arguments and position statements in medicine are generally based upon the treatment relationship – (1) above. Clearly there need to be different guidelines for the role of the expert acting, for example, in a 'one-off' assessment. There are other special situations, too, where an adaptation of ethical position possibly needs to be made. These include the so-called roles of dual responsibility – for example, participation in court diversion schemes, and work within prisons as a prison psychiatrist, where allegiances are divided between duty to the patient and those of one's official role. These matters are addressed by Kaul in Chapter 6. A special contemporary difficulty arises in cases where forensic psychiatrists or other professionals work in a ' psychological profiling' or other detective capacity for the police. They may easily be seduced into a dilution of their usual ethical standards, or police may use information gained clinically for their own non-clinical purposes. Referring particularly to the USA, Appelbaum (1997) sees the whole of forensic psychiatry as fundamentally one of dual role or dual agency.

Actually, the simple division given above could be misleading. We should not under-estimate the power which the role of 'doctor' or 'psychiatrist' brings with it. The mere fact that it is a psychiatrist interviewing a patient, rather than a lawyer or policeman may tend towards disclosure. We as doctors or clinicians in other specialities are emblematic holders of the power of the healing arts. In psychodynamic terms there is an immediate 'transference' set up between the examinee and the doctor which is likely to tend towards dependence and information sharing, and we abuse this to the peril of our art and science. In addition, psychiatrists and psychotherapists (hopefully) have particular skills in engaging patients, including engaging their trust. It is a fine and debatable line that has to be observed in making an expert assessment, between the conducting of a comprehensive interview, yet not lulling the examinee into a therapeutic assumption or dependent position, where the rules are different – and thereby to implicate or damn him/herself. Eastman (2000) has addressed these problems in terms of 'confidentiality contracts' between clinician and interviewee allowing the latter to take his own 'confidentiality risks'. This does not, however, solve the problem for people in positions of stress, the poorly educated, the mentally ill and, for example, those with learning disabilities, who can easily, wittingly or unwittingly, be manipulated in this situation. Repeated statements during an interview of the true position of lack of confidentiality – indeed of the likely disclosure of anything significant – can often be 'forgotten' or ignored by those being assessed, to their own detriment. This is but one aspect of the dubious ethical position of the expert within the criminal justice system, and the psychiatric expert in particular, which has sometimes earned him the label of 'professional prostitute'.

Ideally, the ethic of maintaining patient privacy and maintaining the health of the public should not be seen as necessarily in opposition (Vandenbroucke 1998), although clearly tensions may arise between the interests of the health of the individual and the interests of the health of the public. A quite different matter obtains where the issue at stake is that between the interests of the individual and the disclosure of information for the sake of the *safety* of the public, for example, to protect them from possible future violence. This will be fully dealt with later in this chapter.

In matters of the protection of those who are victims of neglect or abuse, the General Medical Council (GMC) has for years endorsed the principle that clinical information about patients may be disclosed '*in the public interest*' (GMC 2000). No problem arises if the patient consents. However, 'if you believe a patient to be a victim of neglect or physical, sexual or emotional abuse and that the patient cannot give or withold consent to disclosure, you should give information promptly to an appropriate responsible person or statutory agency, where you believe that the disclosure is in the patient's best interests' (GMC 2000). The possible causes of a patient being judged incapable are immaturity, illness or mental incapacity. What is significant is that this is *guidance* – albeit pretty strong – and discretionary, and not mandatory. The brave clinician still has room to weigh the overall dangers and benefits, for example, in an incest case the greater trauma to the child of a consequentially fragmented family.

In other jurisdictions, notably the vast majority of the states in the USA, notification to the appropriate authorities is mandatory – taking all the ethical onus, and legal liability, for a breach of confidentiality away from the doctor, whose role becomes fact finding rather than protective. There is considerable pressure for the same mandate in the Republic of Ireland but not so far in the UK (Hoyte 1998).

The publication of numerous and updated guidelines of good clinical practice for psychiatrists is a necessary and welcome assistance to decision making in general, and informs deliberations over any individual case. New guidelines from the GMC (2000), the Royal College of Psychiatrists (2000) and the British Medical Association (1999) are examples of acknowledgement of the complexities which are an inevitable part of contemporary practice and research. The shift towards duties to provide information (and no longer just to protect it) is reflected in the title of the GMC guidance, *Confidentiality: Protecting and Providing Information* (2000). Other clinical professions are in the process of providing their own updated guidelines. However, the current picture is one of rapid change and in the difficult case – where context is all important, and while (at least for medical practitioners) discretion is still allowed – the clinician must be prepared not only to make judgements on a 'case by case' basis, but also potentially to be the subject of a 'test case' in law.

Forensic psychiatrists have an interestingly contrasting experience of demands for disclosure and for maintenance of confidentiality. On the one hand they are especially cautious as a result of their work at the psychiatric–legal interface. On the other they are especially used to treatment arenas where little or no confidentiality can exist – for example within secure institutions where, in my view, one starts from the premise that confidentiality hardly exists, if it exists at all.

Important distinctions for the practising psychiatrist are those between:

1. The 'right' to breach confidentiality – as, for example, expressed in *Egdell* v. *W* [1990] (albeit expressing a high threshold for disclosure) (see Kaul, Chapter 6 and Harbour, Chapter 11) and *R* v. *Crozier* [1988], both of which are also given detailed analysis in Hall (Chapter 10), and the 'duty' to breach in the public interest where a failure to disclose information may expose 'the patient or others to risk of death or serious harm' set out in the GMC guidance (2000).

2. A patient in treatment where the treatment is for the patient's benefit, and the client under assessment within the criminal justice system where the assessment is unlikely to be primarily for his advantage, but rather for that of society.

3. The guiding principle of the child's welfare in the family courts, contrasted with the principle of justice within the criminal courts.

4. The breaching of confidentiality on grounds of public interest implying consequent possible legal or penal sanction against a patient/client, and that on the basis of 'need to know' among fellow professionals (or 'right to know' of professionals or a possible future victim) implying the possibility of preventative action (see also Harbour, Chapter 11). Depending upon which agency receives such information, this distinction between 'need to know' and 'right to know' may become blurred as appears to have been the case in the recommendations contained in the Ritchie Report of the Christopher Clunis case. The much quoted case of Tarasoff (pp.33–34 of this chapter) which applies to certain US jurisdictions – where there was a finding of duty to breach confidentiality for the purposes of third party protection is the exemplar of many of the critical issues. It contrasts with the situation in the UK where no such absolute duty (yet) exists.

Case example 1

A teacher of previous blameless record is concerned for his own welfare, his job, and his family, but unable to resist escalating, dangerous, sexual contact with young adolescent pupils in the school where he teaches. Prosecutable behaviour has already occurred but has not yet been divulged. To whom should he turn? He is, indeed, faced with a dilemma. Perhaps it would be more true to say that if he only knew it, he is faced with a fait accompli. He would be 'safe' in going to seek the help of a priest, and possibly most psychoanalysts (see Chapter 7 by Bollas, this volume), although probably not the medical analysts (who are covered by GMC guidelines), and some psychotherapists. He might trust a friend, or possibly even a journalist, practising within his professional ethic. If he went to a general practitioner he would, at best, be referred on to a psychiatrist who (like the general practitioner), under present GMC guidelines, 'should disclose information promptly to an appropriate person or authority' where there is a risk of serious harm. He would, in short, quite likely be at risk of being prosecuted and if found guilty of a sexual offence find himself on the new 'Sexual Offender Register' pursuant to the Sex Offenders Act 1997. He may find himself sentenced to prison. He would necessarily be suspended from his job, at least initially. Is that predicament good for anyone? Is this reflex series of events helpful? Does it not provide a powerful disincentive to the troubled person/offender seeking help? Is this beneficial to the potential or actual offender patient or, indeed, to possible future victims? I think not, yet such are the likely and logical consequences of this aspect of a 'culture of informing'.

For the clinician – psychiatrist, psychologist, forensic psychiatrist, psychotherapist or other – in such a case, there would be a dilemma concerning the likely risk, and degree, of harm. But at its most basic (and assuming that the teacher declined to tell others or take further advice, e.g. voluntary removal from school), the crucial question for the clinician would be: 'Do I "shop" this patient, and probably lose him as a patient to help, or do I keep confidence, accept the risk, and hope to help him and his potential victims?'

The reference above to the distinction between medical psychoanalysts or therapists and non-medical raises the question of whether a psychotherapist (or anyone else) practises under the rule of his original, or adopted, discipline or a combination of both. It seems clear that, for those who are doctors and come under the statutory requirements of the GMC, that code of ethics is binding in whatever clinical practice.

By way of informing this example, it is of interest that the 'Draft guidance on the Disclosure of Information about Sex Offenders' (Home Office 1999) appears to have taken note of the complexities of such a predicament. It states that the 'disclosure of information on its own does not in itself reduce the risk to the public, and in some cases inappropriate or irresponsible disclosure could actually increase that risk'. In some cases even, 'notification might lead the offender to act irrationally'. For example, he might reoffend because he feels trapped by the system, or abscond.

In an annex to this guidance, headed 'legal considerations', considerable attention is given, too, to the law on defamation. This introduces the other side of the coin as it were, and its dangers to the professional in matters of disclosure to third parties. It is emphasised that clinicians must be as certain as possible of the reliability of their data before it is imparted, even though in the real, clinical, emergency situation certitude is unlikely. It states, 'accuracy of information to be shared with "fellow agencies" or third parties is paramount', and continues, 'a person who communicates information about another person, which is untrue and likely to damage the reputation of that person, is defamatory and may lead to a claim in damages'. However, 'where a person communicates information in order to discharge a duty, or in the public interest, they may be able to claim qualified privilege', by way of a defence. The clinician, indeed, has a dilemma and is vulnerable either way.

Case example 2

A young psychiatrist, Dr Joseph de Masi, in training to be a child psychiatrist at New York Medical College and also in training to be a psychoanalyst, revealed to his analyst, Dr Douglas Ingram, that he felt himself to have in everyday parlance paedophilic desires. However, he did not say whether he intended to act on his paedophilic wishes.

Dr Ingram, with the agreement of the patient, therefore stopped the analysis (and thereby the training analysis) but offered Dr de Masi 'generalised therapy' – in an attempt to 'challenge Dr de Masi's thinking, manage his stress and thus try to make sure that he did not act on his desires'. He did not take steps to report Dr de Masi to the Medical College authorities, nor any other steps to remove him from the child psychiatry training. Soon after this Dr de Masi apparently sexually assaulted a young boy patient, then 10 years old (for which he has now been found guilty). All this happened some ten years prior and the plaintiff at the time of trial was aged 21 years. The case arose since a lawsuit was filed against Dr Ingram and New York Medical College claiming that more should have been done to prevent the abuse (*New York Times* 1998).

The main questions which arise are:

1. Did Dr de Masi pose a clear threat to others (at the time he was in treatment with Dr Ingram)?

2. Was there a readily identifiable victim or class of victims for Dr Ingram to protect?

The case clearly raises issues concerning *whether, when*, and *what* to report, and to *whom*. It may be instructive briefly to review the decision-making process in this case, using a deceptively simple three-part model of the 'Tarasoff obligation' first described by Appelbaum (1985) – especially since our example occurred within a Tarasoff jurisdiction. The, by now well-known Tarasoff case has been especially well covered from the legal and clinical points of view by Anfang and Appelbaum (1996) and by Lipson and Mills (1998). I shall describe the case briefly. A graduate student of the University of California, Prosenjit Poddar, developed a pathological belief system of obsessional 'love' for a young woman, Tatiana Tarasoff – along with developing elements of destructiveness, as she did not comply with his romantic desires. He sought psychiatric help and, although he was at first diagnosed as suffering from a paranoid schizophrenic illness and treated with anti-psychotic medication, the diagnosis was later changed to that of borderline personality disorder.

Poddar had made death threats concerning Tatiana and these were known to the evaluating psychiatrist and to the psychologist to whom he was subsequently referred. The threats increased in force and frequency (including a decision to buy a gun) and the psychologist discussed the matter with the assistant director of psychiatry with a view to compulsory admission to hospital. The assistance of the police was solicited. However, committal did not happen because of a failure in the procedural system. When the director of psychiatry returned, he considered that the psychologist had over-reacted and ordered that the correspondence to the police be returned. Further (and damningly) he ordered the psychologist to 'falsify clinic records by expunging all references to the divulgence of confidential information and threats that promulgated its divulgence' (Myers 1986).

A short time later Poddar fatally shot Tatiana Tarasoff and multiply stabbed her. Poddar was convicted of second degree murder, later reduced to manslaughter, and served five years in prison.

It is the consequences of the civil proceedings, however, which concern us here. The Supreme Court ruling in *Tarasoff v. Regents of the University of California* [1974] ('Tarasoff I') was unprecedented. They ruled that 'when a doctor or psychotherapist, in the exercise of his professional skill and knowledge, determines, or should determine, that a warning is essential to avert a danger rising from a medical or psychological condition of a patient, he incurs a legal obligation to give that warning'. There was outcry from professionals – including protest that this imposition would lead inevitably to many false positive predictions (such are the vagaries of risk assessment) and loss of the therapist–client relationship. It was pointed out that patients generally would not be free to disclose violent fantasies and that all psychotherapy and other clinical practice would thereby be sabotaged.

Under pressure the Supreme Court agreed to review the case. This time, however, the court ruled that 'when a therapist determines, or pursuant to the standard of his profession should determine, that his patient presents a serious danger of violence to another, he incurs an obligation to use reasonable care to protect the intended victim against such danger' (so-called 'Tarasoff II'). It will be noted that in the initial ruling – Tarasoff I – the duty was 'to warn' the relevant third party. In the Tarasoff II ruling this was extended to that of a duty 'to protect', i.e. to follow up and check that warnings have been acted upon. The Tarasoff doctrine has subsequently been adopted by many states in the USA as well as California, but even after nearly thirty years the Tarasoff doctrine 'continues to confuse and confound' (Anfang and Appelbaum 1996). It should be noted that there is no legal requirement similar to the Tarasoff obligation in British jurisdictions. Whether there will be in the future depends upon how far public protection issues continue to be prioritised.

The three steps described by Appelbaum (1985) are:

1. *Assessment.* This includes: (a) 'gathering data relevant to an evaluation of dangerousness'; (b) a determination on the basis of those data.

   It would appear that Dr Ingram did not gather the necessary data to carry out any sort of detailed risk assessment. He relied on what he was told within the psychoanalytic setting. Many psychoanalysts would defend this position. Certainly, ten years ago this was within the spirit of how I was taught and how I would have practised. Indeed, Dr Ingram's defence includes the reasonable argument that it was unlikely Dr de Masi would admit any sexual abuse of children because he (Dr Ingram) 'had warned him that such a disclosure would supersede confidentiality'.

   The predicament raises questions of the extent to which it is feasible, from such a context, to fulfil the Tarasoff obligation 'to gather data for the assessment of the patient's potential dangerousness in the same manner as would a reasonably careful practitioner'. It is easier at the assessment stage, but far more difficult if the situation arises mid-therapy. Dr Ingram made a determination of risk, based upon what some would say was inadequate data. He clearly saw a problem of psychopathology, but maintains (through his defence lawyer) that 'short of clairvoyance he had no business to know that the plaintiff would be harmed by de Masi'.

2. *Selecting a course of action.* Dr Ingram's selected course of action was to stop the training analysis, but to continue to try to influence Dr de Masi's proclivities in 'general therapy', while not reporting him to the Child Psychiatric Training Board, or to any other official body. This is the major area of dispute.

3. *Implementation.* There is little to say about this in this case since it concerned no action involving any third parties.

This is a tale from our times and may send some shivers through a number of professional spines. Dr Ingram was, in fact, found to have been negligent. There is the strong implication in the criticism of Dr Ingram that others, including the Medical College authorities and possibly hospitals where Dr de Masi would work, should have been informed and warned by Dr Ingram.

Inter-agency working

Concern arises – from the point of view of the perceived importance of confidential relationships – from the current and burgeoning practice of multidisciplinary and inter-agency work. Which agencies are to be included? Inter-agency protection panels, for example, now include mental health professionals alongside the police. Szmukler and Holloway (in Chapter 3, this volume) have referred to these difficulties, giving the apparently innocuous example of the local housing department having access to certain clinical information. My experience is of a general but uncritical assumption of beneficence by the different agencies which come together in inter-agency work. It behoves psychiatrists and other clinicians constantly to be alert to too easy compliance in such seemingly innocuous, even 'cosy', sharing of information. The dynamic can tend towards a polarity of the professionals 'ganged up' on one side, against the dependant/patient/offender on the other. Doctors, social workers, housing officers and police officers have different roles and different role expectations. Blurring or transgressing ethical boundaries in particular cases according to individual judgements may be good or bad practice; eroding these boundaries by statute or onerous guideline is likely to lead to a 'dumbing down' of clinical practice – from an understandable 'dumbing', or silencing, of the patients' willingness to impart confidences. It is, of course, the case that – contrary to the rhetoric of beneficence – those who will suffer most from this enforced sharing of information will be those least able to protect their own rights.

New expectations of disclosure and reporting are presently negating the efforts of drug treatment services and those offering services to people who include drug misuse among their problems. The need for residential rehabilitation and structured day care and prescribing programmes is acknowledged. They have been shown to be capable of having a major impact on drug use, health, offending and social integration. However, a recent court case has massive implications for those in the community working with groups such as homeless and young people who might come into contact with drugs. By extension, it impinges, too, on community mental health teams and hospital psychiatric services. The director and project manager of a day centre for the homeless in Cambridge were recently found guilty of allowing the supply of heroin on their premises. Although they had banned some clients for suspected dealing, they were deemed not to have taken all 'reasonable' steps to stamp out drugs. They were reprimanded by the judge for 'not installing close circuit television and mirrors to observe clients and for failing to close the centre down when they thought dealing may be going on' (*Guardian* 1999). This culture of control has generally been predicted only to increase over future decades. This case has been seen as emblematic and has provoked something of a furore: 'There will be more Orwellian policing...more CCTV surveillance and police databases' (Adams 1999) – as if an extended form (into the community) of Jeremy Bentham's panopticon proposals is coming to awful fruition. In the Cambridge case police had asked for a copy of the centre's 'banned book' which listed those who had been barred from the centre. The request was refused because of concerns over breach of confidentiality. The two defendants also received censure from the court for this principled decision. The five years sentence that each of these senior staff received reflects the risks of censure that working in such already unpopular service areas now presents. As a consequence of this conviction, Release has had to update its report *Room for Drugs* (1999) with *Additional Guidelines for Direct Access Services after the Wintercomfort Trial* (Release 2000), urging organisations to look closely at their management and staff training policies and to take a more proactive role in supervising buildings. However, the reported comments of the project manager of Release strike a by now familiar chord: 'There's a balance to be struck because if people don't feel they can go to an agency and talk to staff openly, you just won't get them into the service.' It is also to be noted that if the harsh criteria of drug use monitoring and prevention applied in this case were extended generally, psychiatric hospitals and units in metropolitan areas (where drug misuse is rife and impossible totally to prevent) and, indeed, prisons, may look vulnerable at the very least to censure, and possibly to prosecution. At the time of writing this case is under consideration by the Court of Appeal.

Patient information

The advent of the NHS net may well offer an answer to the overwhelming amounts of paperwork which doctors currently handle. There are obvious advantages to having 'fully computerised medical records available to all doctors twenty-four hours a day ... we have to recognise that online technology is part of every day experience' (Frank Dobson, Health Secretary, October 1998). Also, plans are in place for the use of e-mail for referrals (especially for GPs), and for the communication of test results. However, leaving poorly controlled systems aside, there are real fears that hackers will be able to break into even competent systems, as has happened in some US healthcare companies. Such is the concern at the misuse of computerised healthcare records – including health insurance companies and credit companies excluding those they know to be suffering from a range of illnesses – that a Bill is presently before Congress to make such uses of health records illegal.

There is common misuse of information gathered for strictly clinical purposes and of clinical databases, for ulterior purposes. This may include the automatic use of anonymised, or sometimes identifiable, patient data for the purposes of audit, health service planning, research or, in some cases, for pharmaceutical industry interests. These issues are currently the subject of much official concern and discussion (see, for example, Chapter 12 on research). A test case was the Latham/Source Informatics Ltd case in which the Court of Appeal (21 December 1999) (The Times Law Reports 18 January 2000, pp.17–18) overturned a High Court ruling (28 May 1999) that the use of anonymised patient data breached confidentiality. The specific issue involved and involves the General Practice Research Database, run by the Medicines Control Agency, and the UK primary care database, formerly run by Source Infomatics but now owned by IMS Health, a commercial company that supplies information to pharmaceutical companies. The data held by IMS Health alone, the smaller of the two databanks, are on 2 million patients. While the ruling allows legitimate epidemiological and genetic research and drug safety evaluation to continue as before, the possibility of misuse of data for commercial purposes continues. The legal issue has been clarified, but the ethical one remains. These effects may be considered broadly to be the negative consequences of the potentially beneficial culture of information availability.

Even though there is a commitment to maintaining 'the highest standards' of confidentiality, it should not need a forensic psychiatric/psychotherapist to warn against those few prepared to use their sophistication and knowledge to pervert the aimed-for benefits. Medical, and particularly mental health, records are valuable property for those who wish to misuse them. Anderson (1995) gave an early warning of what he dubbed the 'wide and slippery slope', highlighting the dangers of aggregation of knowledge – well known, according to Anderson, to the military, banking and health insurance – and providing terrifying examples of the latter in the USA. Second, he warned against the sheer technical impossibility of maintaining adequate security for records which, by their nature, are meant to have wide availability within the healthcare system. Anderson (1995) also criticises the language of the proposed 'constituency' for the NHS net, which has been described as the 'extended NHS community'. For Anderson this 'is officialese for social workers, insurance companies, and the police'. Proposed controls include the signing of 'a code of connection' – effectively, Anderson continues, 'a declaration that they will behave themselves – backed by neither a credible security policy nor by the prospect of punishment for transgressors'. It is noteworthy that it is not a criminal offence in England and Wales to sell private records, as it is in some other jurisdictions – see comments above on new legislation being introduced in the USA.

An example of the concern about the ways in which patient information is used in the NHS led to the *Report on the Review of Patient-identifiable Information* (Department of Health 1997). This review covered 'all patient-identifiable information which passes from National Health Service organisations in England to other NHS or non NHS bodies for purposes other than direct care, medical research, or where there is a statutory requirement for information'. The committee which prepared the review mapped 'flows' of patient-identifiable information relating to a wide range of planning, operational and monitoring purposes. The report concluded (surprisingly) that 'within the context of current policy all the flows identified were for justifiable purposes'. However, the report added that 'a number of the flows currently use more patient-identifiable information than is required' – like names and addresses where a code would suffice. The report recommended that 'a programme of work should be established to reinforce awareness of confidentiality and information security requirements among all staff within the NHS', and that a 'guardian' of patients' information be nominated in each health organisation. This is a step in the right direction, but probably vests too much responsibility – for what is likely to become a growing role, placing increasingly difficult decision making – in one individual.

Publication of case studies

Psychoanalysis, psychotherapy and psychiatry have traditionally placed case studies and illustrative case histories at the centre of exegeses of their conceptual and theoretical base (Patterson 1999). In recent times, however, there has been an increasing concern that such publication can make an individual identifiable and impinge upon patients' fundamental rights. Forensic psychiatry is a special case where publication of case histories of extreme cases was considered to be prohibited by their infamy (or relative 'celebrity') and therefore their identifiability. Contemporary culture on the one hand tends towards greater disclosure – especially of a prurient nature – in the name of freedom of information, and on the other seeks to protect privacy and individual rights to confidentiality.

While such publication should still be resisted, certainly without the 'meaningful consent' (Joseph and Over 1991) of the patient, there are far more stark modern-day circumstances where even the figleaf of protection of patient confidentiality has been blown away. Thus, a series of statutory and non-statutory inquiries into apparent and real failures of mental healthcare have included highly personal clinical case material – including that previously gathered on a basis of confidentiality – within public documents offered for general sale, sometimes even in novelettish form (see, e.g. Blom-Cooper, Hally and Murphy 1994).

Statutory and non-statutory inquiries

There are two aspects which I will take in turn. First, that of the lack of confidentiality of the content of an inquiry and, second, expectations of information sharing which some inquiries have come to assume. In no area of the administration and management of mental healthcare has the obliteration of the concept of confidentiality been so apparent as in that of the 'inquiry' – aimed ostensibly to further public perceptions of 'accountability'. The sheer numbers of such inquiries and their relative failure to generate new findings have been reported by a number of authors, and are presently the subject of their own analyses. What has not been emphasised is the extraordinarily public nature of the way the hitherto confidential clinical documentation is dealt with in these inquiries. It has now become a commonplace that just about the whole personal and clinical record of the subject of many of these inquiries becomes available for public consumption, despite the fact that the patient (and future offender) has given this information under different degrees of consent for the purposes of clinical and related care. If he/she becomes the subject of an inquiry, there seems to be no limit upon how this information is used: it then becomes public property, and is effectively used against him/her. It seems to have become assumed that patients in these circumstances have lost all rights to any degree of privacy.

Major questions about the shifting balance towards disclosure of health information about prospective and current healthcare employees in particular have been brought to a focus by two recent and major inquiries. The *Report of the Independent Inquiry into the Major Employment and Ethical Issues arising from the Events leading to the Trial of Amanda Jenkinson* (the so-called 'Bullock Report' 1997) concerned the employment procedures adopted and later disciplinary action against, and dismissal of, a nurse who was believed to have 'tampered with equipment and put patients at risk' on an intensive care unit. The nurse was later convicted of one serious criminal charge. This report referred in some detail to recommendations made in another and earlier inquiry (the Allitt Inquiry 1991) subtitled *Independent Inquiry Relating to Deaths and Injuries on the Children's Ward at Grantham and Kesteven General Hospital during the period February to April 1991* (Clothier, Macdonald and Shaw 1994).

The Allitt Inquiry in making its thirteen recommendations broadly recognised the difficulties and limitations for 'civilised society' in protecting itself from the exceptional and rare malevolent or misguided actions of healthcare professionals, or, as the report put it, providing a 'defence against aimless malice of a deranged mind'. It made practical suggestions concerning formal health screening, mental health information sharing and related matters prior to the employment and later during the employment of health service personnel (in this case nurses). Yorker (1996), however, commented that the recommendations were 'so stringent that some would not be permissible in the United States'. The Bullock Report, by contrast, considered that the recommendations of the Allitt Report were 'now less precise than we feel are necessary given the general developments in employment practice and (these specific) incidents'. In its turn, it made a total of 29 recommendations concerning recruitment practices and health information sharing which would greatly reduce healthcare employees' rights to confidentiality in relation to their employer. The details are less important here than the fact that the recommendations are argued from positions of (albeit understandable) alarm at a very rare occurrence, and aim to reduce an extremely small risk to a smaller one. There is a major shift towards disclosure and against employees' rights to confidentiality of their mental health records in the short duration between the publication of these two reports. Were the Bullock recommendations to be adopted, the changes would imperil hitherto accepted good practice between employer and employed across the whole nursing, occupational health, and other clinical fields. This report has been roundly criticised as essentially advocating greater bureaucratic, more punitive and less confidential approaches – in this particular case, towards medical and nursing staff with mental health problems themselves. It is essentially stigmatising of mental ill health. It seems very much of its time, both in the spirit of the 'control' it advocates, and the likely major backfiring against any benefit which its adoption might involve. All medical records, and specifically mental health consultations of the past would be required to be shared with the employer. The fact that its declared aim is 'beneficence' should not obscure the fact that such piecemeal policy recommendations, if adopted, can become a force for maleficence. The guidance contained in the Bullock Report has placed occupational health officers in untenable positions.

Professional implications and responsibilities

A medical philosopher (Kessel 1998) regards confidentiality as an 'overvalued concept' in the modern world. He writes (somewhat puzzlingly) that this overvaluation 'has arisen through the influence of bioethics (its emphasis on principles and especially respect for patient autonomy) together with somewhat anachronistic medical codes which still strongly imbue western medical culture'. Is it time then to abandon the pretence of the confidential patient–doctor (or clinician) relationship altogether, or is there still time to try to rescue some important aspects of it? The question could hardly be more important for future clinical practice.

The dangers of incrementally forcing mental health professionals into positions where the sensitive balance between individual health interests are regularly trumped by public safety interests have been well described by Glancy, Regehr and Bryant (1998) in the Canadian setting: 'Psychiatrists must carefully consider their positions on issues of duty to inform and advocate for policies that consider all aspects of the issue and are relevant to psychiatric practice.' If they do not, these authors write, they will become agents of social control with little autonomy to provide safe treatment and to ameliorate tendencies towards violence through psychotherapeutic changes.

One example of a 'logical' extension of this failure to understand, or certainly to protect, the legitimate privacy of patients within mental health and to enforce public protection policies above all others is one of seismic shift – that of the current proposals for preventative detention of people with so-called 'dangerous severe personality disorder' (DSPD). There is an invitation to psychiatrists and mental health workers to become implicated (a) in 'enforced' risk assessment, and (b) possible unlimited detention – based on the outcome of the risk assessment of people suspected of posing a risk to the public. The current practice that to 'trigger' an assessment there should be (a) some evidence, at least, of offending behaviour or that the subject should have actually offended and (b) some evidence of mental illness or personality disorder would not necessarily obtain. Also, for indeterminate detention the fulfilment of some criterion of 'treatability' would no longer apply. Thus, the underlying policy of primacy of public protection over individual civil or patient rights becomes clear: far worse, the psychiatric profession is expected to be the agent of what is clearly not a health intervention but one driven overwhelmingly by 'public protection'. It may be that there is a genuine misunderstanding by politicians and policy makers of the significance of different professional roles and their respective ethics; or it may be that there is understanding, but nonetheless a wish to coerce practitioners into positions in which they are ethically compromised. Confidentiality would be but one victim. These proposals are likely to meet insurmountable opposition, or be introduced in much curtailed form. Some of these issues are addressed by Adshead (1999). For the proposed new policies for DSDP to be introduced, it seems that a 'medical expert' would need to declare such people of 'unsound mind' in order to comply with the European Law on Human Rights (Article 5). It is to be hoped that no psychiatrists will so collude. Where, one may ask, are the considerations of confidentiality issues in this proposed legislation? Answer: they appear not to exist; nor could they when third party protection is the dominant aim.

It is to the credit of the GMC and the Royal College of Psychiatrists that in their new guidelines in both cases there is an emphasis on the duty of doctors to ensure that their patients understand that information will be shared, to whom and why:

> Patients with mental disorder are often insufficiently aware of their rights with regard to privacy, or of the kinds of purpose for which information about them is used, or the people to whom such information may need to be passed ... we should therefore seek to ensure that there is an active policy about informing patients in all settings where we practice. (Royal College of Psychiatrists 2000, p.4)

It is the submission of this author, however, that patients and potential patients (i.e. the public) need to be appraised of current day realities, as well as of the principles and best practice; they need to know the increasing likelihood of sensitive information being disclosed widely for which they have not given their consent.

Put more strongly, my submission is that we as clinicians have been ineffective, even supine, as a profession in resisting the incremental erosion of clinical confidentiality by statute law, official guidelines, multidisciplinary team, and interdisciplinary team working, the requirement of exchange of information for the purchaser–provider split, and now the information explosion and particularly the NHS net. If we no longer take confidentiality seriously as an essential component in clinical practice (or merely regret its passing), we can at least take seriously the communication of these facts to the general public and to our individual patients in the name of preserving our own integrity.

If this is considered too gloomy a view, there is, at least, a need for research of the views of patients/users and of clinicians in different roles, and of the way that confidentiality is treated in practice. Watson (1999), for example, studied the responses of community nurses and social workers to dilemmas of disclosure represented by clinical vignettes involving confidential information for which the patients/clients had requested *strict confidentiality*. The questions informing the study were: 'How frequently do professionals disclose information against clients' wishes? How is this justified? And, can a common practice standard be determined?' What was striking was the high level of breaching of confidentiality overall, for what seemed, at that time, like compelling or at least understandable reasons. It included inter-professional communication which may now, in the light of multi-professional and multi-agency work, not be considered a breach at all – although it flew in the face of the expressed patient/client demand. It also included a high rate of disclosure to members of family, and also non-health or welfare agencies. The author of this study comments: 'What is most striking is the enormous disparity between the decisions made by participants and the ethic of confidentiality expressed by the BASW (British Association of Social Work) and the UKCC (United Kingdom Central Council for Nursing, Midwifery and Health Visiting).' Whereas 'these Codes of Ethics suggest that confidentiality is maintained more than it is breached', this research suggested quite the opposite. It seems, at least, likely that this would be true, too, of other clinical professions. The author questions 'the introducing of a code of ethics whose working espouses a standard of confidentiality so far removed from day to day practice. This creates a dangerous situation wherein clients expect far stricter confidentiality than actually occurs'. She concludes that this 'double standard' effectively 'leads to client mistrust, and loss of professional credibility'. From a purely ethical point of view, too, it is clearly unacceptable. For myself, I wonder if any patient or client who really thinks about it now anticipates the observance of confidential clinical practice by any mental health workers. But the system appears largely to rely upon patients' or clients' lack of awareness, their acquiescence, and therefore their potential exploitation – albeit, from the professionals' point of view, unwitting and with the best of intentions.

Conclusion

Confidentiality issues in contemporary practice may be considered largely as part of general ethical questions concerning the tension between responsibility for the health and welfare of the individual patient and that of information sharing with the aim of enhancing the greater public good. The interests of the individual have given way in contemporary clinical practice to the assumed benefit of all, driven by the exigencies of an increased concern, particularly about 'risk' assessment and management and of public protection.

Aside from the aspects of merely bad or sloppy practice, e.g. gossip or leaving case notes or databases unsecured, there are more positive dangers. Sometimes wittingly, often unwittingly, and under a range of pressures from many different sources, there is a tendency to share information that is 'loaded' and clearly of consequence. We have moved towards a culture of disclosing rather than withholding clinical information where there is information that really matters. In such situations the proliferating 'exceptions' which are explicit within contemporary guidelines are invoked and have become the rule. Indeed, at least one author, a GP and ethicist (Warwick 1989) has argued that confidentiality in healthcare is no longer tenable and should be abandoned, and that a principle of 'non-confidentiality' should be substituted instead. The argument hinges upon the patient taking responsibility for anything he divulges and an expectation of that information being freely available. It does seem to avoid, however, the crucial issues of the vulnerable and especially of the mentally ill and those under degrees of coercion, which have been addressed earlier in this chapter.

Medical and other clinical professional trainings in Britain have not traditionally included ethics and the philosophical issues which are intrinsic to clinical practice in their curricula. More significantly, there are few appointed ethicists or clinical ethics committees in mental health practice that would complement research ethics committees – which are rightly regarded to be essential. It is surely time for such developments within clinical mental health practice to help clinicians, to inform, and possibly to form the basis of a bulwark against day-to-day conveniences of clinical and management practice which add up to a major erosion of patients' rights. It seems ironical that issues of confidentiality had hitherto remained rather private – and unaddressed – based loosely upon general assumptions in the spirit of versions of the Hippocratic expectations (see, for example, *Declaration of Geneva*, World Medical Association 1995). Now it appears that increasingly there are demands from government, policy makers, and from particular interest groups, for clear codes and guidelines of good practice. While cloaked in a rhetoric of maintaining confidentiality, in effect, they mostly tend towards the disclosure of patients' healthcare information.

In order to protect confidentiality specifically for psychoanalysts, Bollas and Sundelson (1995) suggest a division of labour into 'social therapists' and 'psychoanalysts'. The former would deal with situations requiring intervention and disclosure (e.g. child abuse), and the latter would declare themselves bound by rules of absolute confidentiality. It may be that similar divisions might be adopted more generally so that ethical, statutory and legal distinctions could be made between, on the one hand, professionals who may disclose information and attempt to represent the client and public protection at least in equal part, and separate categories of practitioners who are under no duty or obligation to disclose information except to their clients (and to the courts, if required).

Further, it may be that psychiatric experts, within their limited role in court, should be allowed some of that 'public interest immunity' which criminal lawyers have preserved. Overall, what needs development is the concept of diverse and different roles for those working in, and in relation to, mental health, and consequent different expectations of disclosure. This is the case too within clinical specialities. The role of the child psychiatrist and that of the forensic psychiatrist, for example, representing different interests, as they often do – of child, on the one hand, and adult abuser, on the other – are likely finally not to be reconcilable. This difference should be acknowledged and not blurred.

The boundaries of clinical information sharing and confidentiality – changing and under threat as they are – need marshalling and nurturing. Alternatively, if the boundaries are regarded as beyond resuscitation in contemporary practice, they at least need to be honestly addressed – dissociating ourselves from the beliefs of our historic past. This chapter and this volume seek to raise consciousness among practitioners in order to do that, and to address many of the contemporary and very pressing issues which arise in the rapidly changing practices within mental healthcare.

References

Adams, J. (1999) 'On the fast track to nowhere.' *Guardian* 15 December, 6–7.

Adshead, G. (1999) 'Duties of psychiatrists – treat the patient or protect the public?' *Advances in Psychiatric Treatment 5*, 321–328.

Anderson, R. (1995) 'NHS-wide networking and patient confidentiality.' Editorial. *British Medical Journal 311*, 5–6.

Anfang, S. and Appelbaum, P. (1996) 'Twenty years after Tarasoff: reviewing the duty to protect.' *Harvard Review of Psychiatry*, 4, 2, 67–76.

Appelbaum, P.S. (1985) 'Tarasoff and the clinician: problems in fulfilling the duty to protect.' *American Journal of Psychiatry 142* 4, 425–429.

Appelbaum, P. (1997) 'A theory of ethics for forensic psychiatry.' *Journal of American Psychiatry and Law 25*, 233–247.

Bingham of Cornhill, Lord (1996) '"Confidentiality"- an inter-disciplinary issue?' The Inaugural Spring Lecture. Family Law, 315. *National Council for Family Proceedings*, pp.2–8.

Blom-Cooper, L., Hally, H. and Murphy, E. (1994) *The Falling Shadow. One Patient's Mental Health Care 1978–1993*. London: Duckworth.

Bolam *v.* Friern Hospital Management Committee [1957] 1 WLR 582; [1957] 2 All ER 118.

Bollas, C. and Sundelson, D. (1995) *The New Informants: Betrayal of Confidentiality in Psychoanalysis and Psychotherapy*. London: Karnac.

British Medical Association (BMA) (1999) *Confidentiality and Disclosure of Health Information*. London: BMA Medical Ethics Committee.

Bullock, R., Edwards, C. and Farrand, I. (1997) *Report of the Independent Inquiry into the Major Employment and Ethical Issues arising from the Events leading to the Trial of Amanda Jenkinson*. North Nottinghamshire Health Authority.

Clothier, C., MacDonald, A. and Shaw, D. (1994) *The Allitt Inquiry – Independent Inquiry. Relating to Deaths and Injuries on the Children's Ward at Grantham and Kesteven General Hospital during the period February to April 1991*. London: HMSO.

Department of Health (DoH) (1996) *The Protection and Use of Patient Information. Guidance from the Department of Health*. London: DoH.

Department of Health (DoH) (1997) *Report on the Review of Patient-identifiable Information* (The Caldicott Committee). London: DoH.

Department of Health (DoH) (1998) *A First Class Service: Quality in the New NHS*. London: DoH. HSC 1998/113.

Department of Health (DoH) (1999) *Supporting Doctors, Protecting Patients*. London: DoH.

Department of Health (DoH) (1999) *Clinical Governance: Quality in the New NHS*. London: DoH. HSC 1999/065.

Eastman, N. (2000) 'Ethical and policy implications of legal and administrative developments since enactment of the Mental Health Act (1983).' Unpublished MD thesis, University of London.

Edgell *v.* W [1990] 1 AC 109.

General Medical Council (GMC) (1992) *Professional Conduct and Discipline: Fitness to Practice*. London: GMC.

General Medical Council (GMC) (2000) *Confidentiality: Protecting and Providing Information*. London: GMC.

General Medical Council (GMC) (1995) *Duties of a Doctor – Confidentiality*. London: GMC.

General Medical Council (GMC) (1998) *Maintaining Good Practice*. London: GMC.

Glancy, G., Regehr, C. and Bryant, A. (1998) 'Confidentiality in crisis: Part I – The duty to inform.' *Canadian Journal of Psychiatry 43*, 1001–1005.

Guardian (1999) 'A poke in the blind eye' by Janet Snell, 15 December, 5–6.

Home Office (1999) *Draft Guidance on the Disclosure of Information about Sex Offenders who may present a Risk to Children and Vulnerable Adults*. Police Science and Technology Unit. London: HMSO.

Hoyte, P. (1998) 'Confidentiality in child protection.' *The Journal of the Medical Defence Union 14*, 3, 14–16.

Joseph, D. and Over, J. (1991) 'Confidentiality in psychiatry.' In S. Bloch and P. Chodoff (eds) *Psychiatric Ethics*, 2nd edn. Oxford: Oxford Medical Publications, pp.313–340.

Kessell, A. (1998) 'Confidentiality may be overvalued.' Commentary in: Education and Debate. *British Medical Journal 316*, 56–57.

Lipson. G. and Mills, M. (1998) 'Stalking, erotomania, and the Tarasoff cases.' In J.R. Meloy *The Psychology of Stalking: Clinical and Forensic Perspectives*. San Diego: Academic Press.

Myers, C.J. (1986) 'The legal perils of psychotherapeutic practice: the further reaches of the duty to warn.' In L. Everstine and D. Everstine (eds) *Psychotherapy and the Law*. New York: Grune and Stratton.

New York Times (1998) 'Child psychiatrist and paedophile.' 19 April, 35, 40.

Patterson, A. (1999) 'The publication of case studies and confidentiality – an ethical predicament.' *Psychiatric Bulletin 23*, 562–564.

R *v.* Crozier [1988] 8 BMLR 128.

Release (1999) *Room for Drugs*. London: Release Publications.

Release (2000) *Additional Guidelines for Direct Access Services after the Wintercomfort Trial*. London: Release Publications.

Richards, T. (2000) 'Court sanctions use of anonymised patient data.' *British Medical Journal 320*, 77.

Royal College of Psychiatrists (2000) *Good Practice Guidance on Confidentiality (Council Report CR85)*. London: Royal College of Psychiatrists.

Shaw, Lord of Dunfermline (1913) Scott *v.* Scott [1913] AC 477.

Stone, A. (1984) *Law, Psychiatry and Morality Essays and Analysis*. Washington DC: American Psychiatric Press.

Vandenbroucke, J. (1998) 'Maintaining privacy and the health of the public should not be seen in opposition.' Editorial. *British Medical Journal 316*, 1331–1332.

Warwick, S. (1989) 'A vote for no confidence.' *Journal of Medical Ethics 15*, 183–185.

Watson, F. (1999) 'Overstepping our boundaries.' Practice Focus. *Professional Social Work*, September, pp. 14–15.

World Medical Association (WMA) (1995) *Declaration of Geneva*. London: WMA.

Yorker, B. (1996) 'Hospital epidemics of factitious disorder by proxy.' In M. Feldman and S. Eisendrath (eds) *The Spectrum of Factitious Disorders*. Washington DC: American Psychiatric Press.

2

The Doctor–Patient
Consultation and Disclosure
Roy McClelland and Rob Hale

*The patient/doctor relationship should be a partnership of mutual trust with the personal consulta-
tion remaining the bedrock of medical practice.* (Core Values for the Medical Profession BMA
1995)

The status of confidentiality

Throughout the Western world there has been a significant shift from a paternalistic
'best interests' argument towards dominance of patients' rights and respect for
individual autonomy (McClelland 1996). From a duty perspective the ethical basis of
confidentiality is grounded in the principle of respect for autonomy. Doctors explicitly
or implicitly promise their patients that they will keep confidential the information
confided to them – keeping promises is a way of respecting people's autonomy. There
are also consequentialist arguments supporting keeping a confidence, for without
promises of confidentiality patients are far less likely to share private and sensitive
information required for their care.

From a professional perspective the requirement of confidentiality appears as early as
the Hippocratic oath which contains the vow: 'What I may see or hear in the course of
treatment or even outside the treatment in regard to the life of men which on no account
one must spread abroad, I will keep to myself holding such things shameful to be spoken
about.' The World Medical Association in its Declaration of Geneva (1948) (in *Psychiatric Ethics* 1991, p.518) affirmed the rule of confidentiality and in its International Code
of Medical Ethics (1949) (BMA 1988) promoted confidentiality as an absolute requirement: 'Doctors shall preserve absolute secrecy on all he knows about his patient because
of the confidence entrusted in him'. In the UK the principle of confidentiality is a matter
of professional conduct and as the GMC states 'patients have a right to expect that information about them will be held in confidence by their doctors' (GMC 2000).

One of the clearest statements on confidentiality is given in the Scottish Home and
Health Code of Practice on Confidentiality of Personal Health Information: 'Information about the health and welfare of a patient is confidential in respect of that patient and

to those providing that patient with healthcare or directly concerned with the social welfare and aftercare of that patient' (Scottish Home and Health Department 1995). It is again reflected in the guidance from the Department of Health on the protection and use of patient information: 'This guidance is based on patients' expectations that information about them will be treated as confidential' (DoH 1996).

Confidentiality is also a legal matter and the relationship of the doctor and the patient carries with it legal obligations of confidence as well as moral ones. In *AG* v. *Guardian* [1988] the judge ruled that a 'duty of confidence arises when confidential information comes to the knowledge of a person (the confidant) in circumstances where he has notice, or is held to have agreed, that the information is confidential, with the effect that it would be just in all the circumstances that he should be precluded from disclosing the information to others'. It is worth noting the status of confidentiality in the lawyer–client relationship. On legal professional privileges the House of Lords concluded in an Appeal Judgement that if a balancing exercise were called for in evaluating competing public interests 'it was performed once for all in the 16th Century and since then has applied across the board in every case, irrespective of the clients individual merits'. 'There may be cases where the principle will work hardship on a third party seeking to assert his innocence. But in the overall interests of the administration of justice it is better that the principle should be preserved intact' (*Regina* v. *Derby Magistrates Court* [1996]).

The most comprehensive judicial statement on medical confidentiality is to be found in *Duncan* v. *Medical Practitioners' Disciplinary Committee* [1986]:

> Without trust, a doctor/patient relationship would not function so as to allow freedom for the patient to disclose all manner of confidences and secrets in the practical certainty that they would repose with the doctor. There rests with the doctor a strong ethical obligation to observe a strict confidentiality by holding inviolate the confidences and secrets he receives in the course of his professional ministerings.

It is worth noting that there are two spheres of accountability – professional and legal. Infringement of professional rules is likely to lead to disciplinary action. Infringement of legal rules will lead to associated legal penalties and probably also professional disciplinary action.

Limits of confidentiality

Nevertheless there are limits to medical confidentiality. Before considering infringements it is important to note that the DoH (1996) guidance *Protection and Use of Patient Information* advises a shift towards explicit consent for the sharing of healthcare information on a 'need to know basis' in the NHS. 'This should be achieved through an active policy for informing patients of the kind of purposes for which information about them is collected and the categories of people or organisations to which information may need to be passed' (DoH 1996). Of significance for the duty of confidentiality the Guidance states: 'if a patient wishes information to be withheld from someone who might otherwise have received it in connection with his/her care or treatment, the patient's wishes should be respected, unless there are overriding considerations to the contrary'.

If one follows the Department's guidance then the confidentiality rule is upheld with respect to the sharing, within the clinical practice, of health-related information.

The duty of confidentiality exists within a wider social context in which other moral obligations may compete. It must be noted however that the duty of confidentiality is a prima facie obligation and decisions to breach confidentiality would only be morally justified if a competing obligation trumps it. It should also be noted that in such circumstances the duty of confidentiality is not just neutralised, it is replaced. If disclosure is judged to be justified there is an obligation to disclose (Beauchamp and Childress 1989).

The competing moral appeals for the sharing of personal healthcare information arise from two sources. The first is patient's best interests (the principle of beneficence). The second is public interest (the principle of justice). The line is often difficult to draw and varies from society to society. It is for these reasons that we need specific UK policy decisions, statute laws and common laws.

Disclosure

The General Medical Council (GMC) identifies a number of situations in which disclosure of information without a patient's consent may be justified:

1. *Disclosure in connection with judicial or other statutory proceedings.* (GMC 2000) Where there is a duty to disclose defined by act of parliament for a doctor to disclose such information a doctor has a statutory responsibility to disclose to the relevant authorities. Where a court orders the disclosure of information a doctor is obligated to disclose only relevant information.

2. *Disclosure in a patient's medical interests.* 'If you believe a patient to be a victim of neglect or physical, sexual or emotional abuse and that the patient cannot give or withhold consent to disclosure, you should give information promptly to an appropriate responsible person or statutory agency, where you believe the disclosure is in the patient's best interests' (GMC 2000)

3. *Disclosure in the interest of others.* Disclosure of personal information without consent may be justified where failure to do so may expose the patient or others to a risk of death or serious harm...you should disclose information promptly to an appropriate person or authority. (GMC 2000)

In the first situation there is an absolute obligation to disclose. Decisions to disclose in the last two situations are matters of judgement and each case must be considered on its merits. From an ethical perspective the disclosure test asks whether the release of information to protect the individual or the public should prevail over the duty of confidence to the patient. From a legal perspective the disclosure test asks whether public interest in disclosure outweighs public interest in maintaining confidentiality. While in civil law there is no general duty to prevent a third party causing damage to another, a duty of care may be owed if there is proximity between one's patient and an identified or identifiable victim (*Palmer* v. *Tees Health Authority* 1999). Even with regard to serious crime there is no law (common or statute) which requires a practitioner to disclose confidential information for the protection of others. However, in *Duncan* v. *Medical Practitioners' Committee* [1986] another element of the judgement states:

> there may be occasions, they are fortunately rare, when a doctor receives information involving a patient that another's life is immediately endangered and urgent action is required. Then the doctor must exercise his professional judgement based upon the circumstances, and if he fairly and reasonably believes that such a danger exists then he must act unhesitatingly to prevent injury or loss of life even if there is to be a breach of confidentiality.

This judgement, while quite specific, applies to a particular set of circumstances. The common law limits on medical confidentiality have been more generally defined in the Court of Appeal Ruling in the case of *W* v. *Egdell* [1990]. Here the Court held that the public interest in the restricted disclosure of the relevant healthcare information to the proper authorities outweighed the public interest that the plaintiff's confidence should be respected: 'Rarely, disclosure may be justified on the ground that it is in the public interest which, in certain circumstances such as, for example, investigation by the police of a grave or very serious crime, might override the doctor's duty to maintain his patient's confidence.'

The General Medical Council gives examples of situations where confidence may be breached:

1. Where a colleague, who is also a patient, is placing patients at risk as a result of illness or other medical condition.

2. Where a patient continues to drive, against medical advice, when unfit to do so. (GMC 2000)

3. Where a disclosure may assist in the prevention, detection or prosecution of a serious crime. (GMC 2000)

4. Where serious harm may occur to a third party for reasons other than a crime, e.g. HIV infection. (GMC 2000)

Decision making

Factors which should be taken into consideration when weighing a decision have been outlined in the Royal College of Psychiatrists *Guidelines on Confidentiality* (2000) and include the following (Figure 2.1):

1. The capacity in which the doctor is working: for example, the threshold for disclosure would be higher when there is a normal doctor–patient therapeutic relationship than when the doctor is preparing a report for a court.

2. On the confidentiality side the benefits and risks both need to be considered. The arguments in favour of maintaining confidentiality have been outlined above. A risk assessment of non-disclosure should include an assessment of the seriousness of the crime or threat. In general disclosure should only be considered when there is a serious risk of death or serious harm including

abuse. The probability of the event occurring also needs to be considered, taking into consideration previous history and current mental state. For example, in situations where possible neglect or abuse of a child is being assessed, the mental health of the parents should be considered. Recent evidence has indicated that a substantial number of parents of abused and neglected children have mental health problems, particularly substance misuse and depression (Reder, P., personal communication, Silent Witness Conference, University of York, 1998).

3. On the disclosure side again the risks and benefits need to be evaluated. Benefits are only likely to accrue if there is adequate information concerning a third party including the ability to identify a potential victim. Risks from disclosure to the public and identified potential victims also need to be considered for there may be occasions when such risks outweigh potential benefits.

Disclosure test

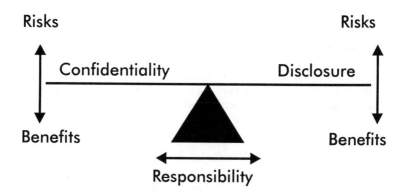

Risks   Risks

Confidentiality   Disclosure

Benefits   Benefits

Responsibility

Figure 2.1 Disclosure test

In all such cases where judgement is involved, it is advisable to discuss the case with colleagues and, if necessary, seek legal or other specialist advice.

In conclusion, the suggestion has been made that different professions, and indeed different divisions of a profession, should operate different thresholds for the disclosure of information, thus defining the role of each profession in relation to the patient. It is instructive that lawyers are required to maintain absolute confidentiality to their clients: it has been argued that we have a public responsibility to protect the patient's individual right to confidentiality. In the UK the clinician must make a considered decision to infringe that right to confidentiality: statute law (e.g. notification of diseases) determines when the clinician must infringe that right and case law when the clinician may do so. In other countries, particularly certain of the USA states, clinicians are statutorily required to disclose whenever there is a danger to a third party. The result is that the clinician is now dubbed 'the new informant for the state'. Difficult and painful as it is to achieve a balance between our duty to the patient and our duty to the public, we must seek to maintain that balance if we are to continue to enjoy the confidence of our patients.

Ultimately a court would take careful account of the opinion of fellow doctors or professional organisations as to whether a decision concerning disclosure was within the reasonable practice of a responsible body of medical practitioners.

References

AG *v.* Guardian [1988] 3 All ER 658.

Beauchamp, T.L. and Childress, J.F. (1989) *Principles of Biomedical Ethics; P335.* Oxford: Oxford University Press.

Bloch, S. and Chodoff, P. (1991) *Psychiatric Ethics.* Oxford: Oxford University Press.

British Medical Association (1988) *Philosophy and Practice of Medical Ethics.* London: BMA.

Department of Health (1996) *The Protection and Use of Patient Information.* London: Department of Health. HSG (96) 18.

Duncan *v.* Medical Practitioners' Disciplinary Committee [1986] 1 NZLR 513, NZ High Court.

General Medical Council (GMC) (2000) *Council Report CR85. Confidentiality: Protecting and Providing Information.* London: GMC.

General Medical Council (GMC) (1995) *HIV and AIDS: The Ethical Considerations. Guidance from the General Medical Council.* London: GMC.

McClelland, R. (1996) 'The basic problem of informed consent in Informed Consent in Psychiatry.' In H.G. Koch, S. Rerter-Theil and H. Helmchen (eds) *European Perspectives of Ethics Law and Clinical Practice.* Baden-Baden: Verlagsgeselschaft.

Palmer *v.* Tees Health Authority Court of Appeal. Times Law Review 1 July, 1999.

Regina *v.* Derby Magistrates' Court, ex parte B (1996) 1 Cr App R 385 HL.

Royal College of Psychiatrists (2000) *Good Practice Guidance on Confidentiality.* London: Royal College of Psychiatrists.

Scottish Home and Health Department (1995) *Confidentiality of Personal Health Information. Code of Practice.* Edinburgh: Scottish Home and Health Department.

W *v.* Egdell [1990] All ER 835.

3

Confidentiality in Community Psychiatry

George Szmukler and Frank Holloway

Today's practice in community psychiatry has evolved to the extent that traditional guidance on confidentiality, such as that from the General Medical Council (GMC), begins to look unrealistic. In this chapter we examine why this is so, and suggest a number of principles that may lead us to practical solutions. The structure of the chapter is as follows: (1) the changes in practice in the community are described; (2) we outline how these changes challenge our traditional notions of confidentiality; (3) ethical principles relating to confidentiality are considered as well as circumstances when it might be justifiably breached; (4) we discuss practical approaches to meeting the challenges.

Introduction

Take the following examples from the GMC guidelines on confidentiality (1991) and bear them in mind when reading the next section describing the current tensions in community-based care (emphases added):

> You must respect requests by patients that information should not be disclosed to third parties, save in *exceptional circumstances* (for example, where the health or safety of others would otherwise be at serious risk).

In respect of disclosure in teams:

> Where the disclosure of relevant information between health care professionals is clearly required *for treatment to which a patient has agreed*, the patient's explicit consent may not be required. For example ... where a physician makes relevant information available to a radiologist when requesting an X-ray.

> If a patient does not wish you to share particular information with other members of the team, you must respect those wishes.

Disclosure may be made in the patient's 'medical interests' if:

> you consider that a patient is incapable of giving consent to treatment...and you have tried unsuccessfully to persuade the patient to allow an appropriate person to be

involved in the consultation. If you are convinced that it is *essential in the patient's medical interests*, you may disclose relevant information to an appropriate person or authority.

Disclosure may be made in the interests of others:

where a failure to disclose information may expose the patient, or others, to *risk of death or serious harm.*

Arguably, if clinicians were to observe these guidelines strictly, basic aspects of patient care would be compromised, and expectations from carers, other agencies, and the community, seriously disappointed.[1]

Contemporary community psychiatry

Psychiatric practice in England and Wales has changed radically since 1954, when mental hospital beds were at their peak (154,000). The locus of care has moved from the mental hospital, via a service based on the district general hospital inpatient, outpatient and day patient unit towards a comprehensive spectrum of care spanning inpatient and community services. Within this system the 'health' and 'social' aspects of care are increasingly brought together in multi-agency community mental health teams (CMHTs) that have responsibility to a defined catchment area. Hospital bed numbers have reduced steadily (to less than 40,000 in 1996), in part replaced by a range of supported housing and residential and nursing home provision that lies outside the National Health Service. By 1998 only 40 of the original 130 mental hospitals were still open. Over this period one entirely new profession has emerged – the community mental health nurse – while other professions, notably social work, have experienced repeated radical changes in role and function. Psychiatrists have perceived a steady weakening of their authority as their institutional base has been eroded and the paradigm of care has moved increasingly towards multi-agency and multidisciplinary teamwork.

Although inpatient admission and outpatient contacts remain numerically important within mental health services, the core function has now become community-based work with the subgroup of the mentally ill who have severe and enduring mental illnesses (DoH 1998). The primary–secondary care interface has taken on increasing significance, moving beyond the traditional gate-keeping role for primary care into an era of referral protocols, rapid access to specialist opinion, joint case registers and shared care.

For the core work of the CMHTs more patient contacts are taking place in people's homes, on the street and in other non-clinical settings, with the responsible consultant psychiatrist being directly involved in only a small proportion of these contacts. The CMHTs will be working to a 'care plan' that will seek to address the dimensions of need which the person presents. The areas of need typically assessed go beyond the simple

1   The General Medical Council published revised guidelines in 2000: *Confidentiality: Protecting and Providing Information.* While similar to those of 1991, the grounds for disclosure have been slightly broadened. The terms 'risk of death or serious harm' are retained. However, the scope may be widened by reference to disclosure in the 'public interest, *usually* (emphasis added) where disclosure is essential to protect the patient, or someone else from risk of death or serious harm (para 14). Or 'where third parties are exposed to a risk so serious that it outweighs the patient's privacy interest.' (para 36).

management of symptomatology into every aspect of the patient's life and will include their social context. See, for example, the Camberwell Assessment of Need (Phelan *et al.* 1995), a tool which assesses 22 domains of need. Figure 3.1 presents a list of people or agencies who might legitimately be involved in a fairly typical, if complex, community care plan of a patient leaving hospital.

- Patient
- Responsible medical officer
- Nearest relative (under the Mental Health Act)
- Carer(s) and friends
- Advocate(s) (including lay and legal advocates)
- Ward nursing team
- Community mental health nurse
- Community psychiatrist
- Social worker(s) (including child care social work team)
- Social services authority care manager
- Housing officer
- Residential care worker(s)
- Day care worker(s)
- Community care worker(s)
- Welfare officer
- Department of Social Security
- Housing Benefit department
- Home Office (for restricted patient)
- Probation officer
- General practitioner
- Police (for certain categories of offender)
- Neighbour(s)
- Employer

Figure 3.1 Potential participants in a complex community care plan for a patient being discharged following an inpatient stay

Services have been encouraged to develop outreach teams that employ the principles of Assertive Community Treatment (ACT) (Stein and Santos 1998) for the management of patients with severe levels of disability or a tendency to disengage with mental health services (with subsequent relapse and readmission). ACT includes as key elements: multidisciplinarity; a shared caseload with all members knowing about all clients on the caseload; explicitly non-medical management (with the psychiatrist as a member of the team but not usually the leader); intensive work with families, carers and community contacts; active dialogue with people in the patient's neighbourhood who may be distressed by aberrant behaviours; work in the clients' own settings focusing on the acquisition of practical living skills; and assertive outreach approaches (Sainsbury Centre for Mental Health 1998, Appendix 6). Another feature of the model is engagement with the local police, partly to ensure that publicly inappropriate behaviour receives its usual social sanction, notwithstanding the presence of a mental illness (Stein and Test 1980).

Not only has the locus of care shifted from the regulated 'private' setting of the hospital to the necessarily more fluid public setting of the community, but the content of mental healthcare is changing. There is increasing emphasis on psychosocial interventions, particularly work with the patient's family, which require more openness to carers and sufferers about the nature of the illness and the available treatment options (Holloway 1998). CMHTs will be in regular dialogue with the patient and their social group and, as their presence becomes known to the local community, are increasingly identified as a resource to complain to when someone behaves in a disturbing fashion in the locality. CMHTs are now regularly asked to respond to requests for information about clients on their caseload. Neighbours may use the NHS complaints procedure to seek information about the return to the community of a patient who has previously caused distress, and not infrequently they may involve their local councillor or member of parliament as their advocate.

Current government policy

Contemporary mental health policy has both shaped and been shaped by the practice of community psychiatry. By the late 1980s it was clear that services were poorly co-ordinated and not in general well targeted towards those most in need (Holloway 1996). A striking feature of policy in the 1990s has been emphasis on the co-ordination of care, with the introduction in 1991 of a Care Programme Approach that mandated a process of assessment, care and review organised by a community keyworker. Patients were to be registered and protocols for the transfer of care between catchment areas were required. Following two well-publicised 'community care' tragedies (the murder of Jonathan Zito by Christopher Clunis and the foray into the lion's den at London Zoo by Ben Silcock) the emphasis began to shift from co-ordination towards the assessment and management of risk, particularly at the point of discharge from hospital. Subsequently a Supervision Register was introduced, requiring the close monitoring of patients deemed to be vulnerable to dangerous acts to themselves or others or to self-neglect. It was intended that Supervision Register status would act as a warning signal to services about a patient's vulnerability or dangerousness: to be effective this would, of course, require such status to be readily known to the wide range of agencies with which patients interact. The Supervision Register was complemented by an amendment to the Mental Health Act allowing 'supervised discharge', although this involved minimal powers over the patient and much responsibility for the keyworker ('supervisor') and 'Community Responsible Medical Officer'. At the time of writing the Department of Health has commissioned a review of the Mental Health Act with a ministerial brief that is widely seen to be a steer towards the introduction of compulsory treatment in the community. Home Office legislation, notably in the field of sex offenders and the compulsory aftercare of sentenced prisoners by the Probation Service, is beginning to impact on community psychiatric practice.

One element of policy has been the mandatory independent inquiry that occurs when a person in contact with mental health services commits a homicide. There is now a large volume of published inquiry reports and, at the time of writing, a further 32 are outstanding. The literature has been well summarised by Petch and Bradley (1997) and represents a formidable, if inchoate, body of considered opinion about best practice in psychiatry. Of particular relevance to issues of confidentiality is the emphasis on the sharing of information between members of the multidisciplinary team, external agencies and carers; the requirement for co-operation between agencies in carrying out risk assessments and developing a risk management plan; and the importance given to effective discharge planning involving all interested parties. Specifically in relation to housing: 'If an application is made for ordinary housing for mentally disordered offenders the forensic history and risk assessment must be disclosed, ideally with the patient's consent, but where there is a risk to others, disclosure may be necessary without such consent' (Petch and Bradley 1997, p.177).

Users of psychiatric services rightly expect confidentiality, but an increasing range of 'stakeholders' in the mental healthcare system have been identified as having a legitimate right to know about the most intimate details of an individual's life. Within this policy regime it is increasingly difficult for professionals to promote the autonomy of their patients/clients and their privacy in the face of the therapeutic gaze of the state.

New challenges to confidentiality

These changing models of psychiatric care and the evolving social policy towards people identified as dangerous present challenges to the traditional medical ethical perspective on patient confidentiality. We give some examples.

Information sharing within the multidisciplinary team and other agencies

In contrast to the hospital, the community is a complex environment in which to provide care, where in addition, distinctions between 'healthcare' and 'social care' become blurred. Patients with severe mental disorders have diverse and complex needs that can only be met by a range of expertise within the CMHTs and often in other services and agencies. Care Programme Approach guidelines recommend that interested parties are invited to meetings which develop and review the patient's care plan: such meetings can push the bounds of confidentiality well beyond traditional limits.

Access to appropriate community support requires a substantial flow of information concerning the patient between service providers. Disclosure 'essential to the patient's medical interests' in this context may be difficult to define or unrealistically narrow. The pressure to reveal information appears inexorable. We have recently been approached by a local authority housing department for a list of all our vulnerable clients with a view to flagging their computerised housing records that they are in contact with mental health service. The intention is benign: to ensure that accruing rent arrears or community charge debts do not result in precipitate action to seek eviction, a frequent and serious hazard for our patients. The effect of complying with this apparently quite reasonable request would be to divulge to another agency information that would traditionally be regarded as entirely confidential.

Furthermore, the key worker or other members of the multidisciplinary team tend to develop a special kind of relationship with the patient, more intimate than previously. As well as medication and conventional psychological interventions, they work with the patient in their ordinary community settings to rehabilitate basic living skills. They may help with budgeting, shopping and cooking, attend appointments with the patient to see other professionals, advocate for services, and work closely with carers, housing officers and other figures in the patient's social network. They may well be contacted should the patient/client become involved with the criminal justice system, perhaps being asked to advise about the appropriate response to offending behaviour. Thus in the course of their 'professional' duties they may acquire much more knowledge about the patient and their world than would have occurred in the clinic, much of which may not be strictly or obviously related to healthcare.

At the same time, recipients of information about the patient, especially from other agencies, perhaps non-statutory, may sometimes have ill-defined obligations concerning its secondary use. If they have protocols governing the use of confidential information, their principles may differ substantially from those of the originating mental healthcare team.

Carers

Informal carers, usually family, play an often unacknowledged but central role in community care. Substantial evidence points to the benefits of involving relatives (or other informal carers) in treating patients suffering from psychotic disorders. Psycho-educational approaches, for instance, are associated with a reduced relapse rate in schizophrenia and offer potential for better family coping and a diminution in their distress. Furthermore, the family commonly provides useful information about the patient and their illness, greatly enhancing care planning. Informal carers can play a prominent role in helping to supervise medication, encouraging participation in treatment programmes, and generally providing an environment conducive to progress.

However, achieving collaboration with carers is often beset with problems over the issue of confidentiality, especially when the patient rejects their involvement. Carer dissatisfaction and even anger may result; while possibly central to the patient's care, they may become sidelined.

A specially taxing problem concerns the justification for involving the family despite a patient's refusal to provide consent. The need may arise when a patient is relapsing and family involvement might prevent further, by now predictable, deterioration. The psychiatrist may judge that the patient's family would be able to help by, for example, providing information, offering support, supervising medication or ensuring a safe environment.

Another set of questions concerns the extent to which carers' own needs should be met by the services. Where there is a danger of serious physical harm to the carer, the clinician's responsibility is usually straightforward. Far more common are less serious threats to their well-being which nonetheless cause suffering. Difficulties in knowing how to cope with burdensome behaviours, a lack of basic knowledge about the illness, and not knowing to whom to turn for help are common. If the patient prohibits contact with the family, it is unclear to what extent the community mental health team nonetheless owes a duty of care to the family.

Working in public places

Active community care will frequently require interventions in the patient's home, hostel or boarding house. If the patient is regarded as being at risk of relapse, even uninvited visits may be made by the team. Indeed visits may continue despite the patient's explicit wishes that they cease. Since much treatment occurs in the community, there is also an increased likelihood that it becomes public. The curiosity of neighbours may be aroused, particularly with repeated visits, and especially if attempts to gain entry are noisily rebuffed by the patient. Neighbours and other members of the public may come in time to recognise CMHT members, and thus that those visited are likely to be patients.

Furthermore, as treatment becomes more visible to the public, new expectations may be generated that a CMHT can be called to deal with a disturbed or difficult person suspected to be a patient. Even if a public assessment is not carried out, an acknowledgement by the mental health team that they may have a role may reveal to bystanders that the difficult person is a mental patient (if already so) or label them as one (if not).

The risk assessment and risk management agenda

Government statements place an increasing emphasis on an obligation of mental health services to preserve the 'safety of others' – for example, family, other carers such as housing workers or support workers, staff in other agencies, and the public at large (DoH 1998). This has been paralleled by increasing expectations from stakeholders that they will be informed directly of risk, or that information will be shared between all potentially relevant parties in a position to reduce that risk.

Clinicians increasingly seek information to assess the level of risk posed by a patient. Information will often be sought from other agencies or individuals, which inevitably provides evidence of the status of the patient and the fact that they may be 'dangerous' (even if subsequently the risk is found to be low). The act of carrying out a risk assessment may itself become a significant intervention in terms of the patient's privacy.

The public interest test for disclosure without the patient's consent has for doctors traditionally been along the lines stated in the GMC guidelines, where failure to disclose may expose others to 'the risk of death or serious harm'. However, there are now major pressures acting to lower the threshold for disclosure. In addition to a general climate demanding measures to enhance safety, guidance accompanying recent legislation sets different tests for disclosure with, as yet, an uncertain relevance for mental health services. NHS Executive guidance on the Sex Offenders Act 1997 (DoH 1997) requires the consultant to advise the hospital managers whether it is in the 'public interest' to inform the police about a patient's discharge from detention under a section of the Mental Health Act (even though the Sex Offenders Act itself only places obligations on the offender). Perhaps ominously, the guidance states: 'While it is essential for each case to be considered in the light of its own facts and no automatic decision made to notify, it is anticipated that the need to protect the public means the balance will generally come down in favour of notification' (Part A, 8). The presumption is thus that notification will occur, and if not there will need to be reasons why not (rather than for). This expectation by the Department of Health appears to contradict GMC guidelines on when confidentiality can be appropriately breached, potentially putting psychiatrists in an untenable position. Section 115 of the Crime and Disorder Act 1998 ensures that any person or organisation has powers to disclose information, for purposes of the Act, to the police, local authorities, probation service or health authority (Home Office 1998). The Act covers a wide range of measures, many not relating to 'serious' crime. A duty to disclose is not imposed; but its lawfulness is established, perhaps with an associated expectation.

We have recently been invited to participate in local police Risk Management Panels established following Home Office guidance accompanying the Sex Offenders Act 1997 (see also Chapter 6). These panels have been set up to assess and manage the risk posed by sex offenders on the Register created by the legislation, but possibly extending to others not registered. The guidance encourages agencies to work together and to establish protocols, including those for sharing information. Mental health services are seen as a potential partner. The information which the panel seeks includes whether the individual is known to the agency, the nature of the involvement, and the name of the key worker and their contact details. Being such a self-evidently good thing from a police point of view, they have had difficulties understanding why we could not participate in the manner requested.

Increasing attention is also being given to 'clinical risk management' in psychiatry, aimed at improving quality or avoiding serious adverse events that may result in litigation, independent inquiries, or damaging publicity. Lipsedge (1995) has summarised the factors contributing to the clinical risk in psychiatry. These include:

professional arrogance combined with a reckless tolerance of deviance leading to a failure by mental health professionals to heed reports by carers and members of the public about disturbed behaviour;

undue emphasis on the civil liberties of psychiatric patients at the expense of tolerating grave suicidal risk and the danger of violent behaviour;

failure to pass on information about potential dangers to other professionals, such as hostel staff, for reasons ranging from inertia, inefficiency, or over-work to a misguided over-protective view of the patient at the expense of the safety of potential victims. (Lipsedge 1995)

The pressure to be ever more free with information about patients' past history and current problems seems to be growing inexorably.

Ethical framework

In this section we examine some ethical principles which help us to understand the meaning of confidentiality.

Meaning of confidentiality and its boundaries

While accounts of the basis for confidentiality vary, two underlying principles are usually invoked (Beauchamp and Childress 1994; BMA 1993). The first is founded on 'privacy' which in turn is related to 'respect for the person'; people have a right to decide how information about themselves should be shared with others. The second is a 'public interest' basis: effective medical care requires patients to be frank about themselves to facilitate diagnosis and treatment; if patients could not trust clinicians to keep their secrets, frank disclosures would cease and medical care would thus be undermined.

However, the boundary surrounding what is properly to be kept confidential is not absolutely clear (Cain 1998 and Chapter 9, this volume). Some ethical codes, following the Hippocratic Oath, cover 'all that the doctor knows about the patient', from whatever source. But more commonly accepted is 'all that the doctor learns about the patient *in the course of his professional practice*'. But the latter, when so much care occurs in the patient's home, or where patient and key worker spend much time together in joint activities relating to daily living skills, may be extensive. Can anything learnt be shared with others as non-confidential? For example, two patients may share a hobby and the clinician may feel that each might welcome the knowledge of the other's interest as a means of enlisting a mutually beneficial source of social support. Is the patient's consent necessary?

Cain (1998) further defines two forms of confidentiality in healthcare. The first or 'strong' form involves a disclosure specifically entrusted to the clinician accompanied by an explicit undertaking to preserve its secrecy. The second, 'weak' form involves an implicit undertaking to preserve confidentiality based on the patient entrusting his 'care', rather than specific secrets, to the clinician. In this case, Cain argues that the limit of confidentiality should be set by 'what the client would have wished'. This, in the absence of further directions, becomes what the 'reasonable' client would wish, and translates into: 'the limit of confidentiality is set by reference to those whose need and right to know relate [exclusively] to [serving] the health care needs of the client'. On this criterion, information relevant to the patient's 'health care needs' may be passed on to other members of the healthcare team who need to know without a breach of confidentiality.

Cain's analysis may go beyond GMC guidelines, but is more easily applicable to team working in community psychiatry. There is still the blurred distinction between 'healthcare' needs and 'social care' needs to contend with. Presumably patients should be given the opportunity to elect the 'strong' form of confidentiality by being informed, perhaps by a leaflet, what 'confidentiality' is taken to mean by the service. All members of the team should also know what is expected of them in keeping information confidential.

Breaching confidentiality

Most authorities agree that the principle of respect for the person does not mean that information will not be passed on but that, if it is to be, it will be done responsibly and for good reasons. Two sets of reasons, apart from disclosure with the patient's consent or disclosures required by law, are accepted:

1. Other people would be put at risk by non-disclosure. The GMC requires the risk to be very serious: 'a risk of death or serious harm'. Society now appears to have other views about the level of potential harm required before disclosure is warranted (see, for example, the discussion in Glancy, Regehr and Bryant 1998, in relation to fitness to drive in Canada and the USA).

2. The patient lacks the capacity to consent, but disclosure is in the interests of the patient's healthcare. The GMC stipulates that disclosure must be 'essential to the patient's medical interests'. This is a 'paternalistic' justification.

Capacity

'Mental incapacity' is assuming an increasing emphasis in justifying interventions against a patient's will (Eastman and Peay 1998; Law Commission 1995; Szmukler and Holloway 1998). We believe it may also be important in relation to confidentiality since it would be hard to argue that it would be proper to disclose information against that patient's wishes, if he or she had full mental capacity to make treatment decisions (or perhaps more specifically, to decide about whether a disclosure should be made to another who might significantly aid treatment).

Definitions of capacity vary, but common elements are the ability to understand and retain information relevant to the decision (including the consequences of deciding one way or the other), and the ability to use that information to make a decision. The latter includes the ability to appreciate that the information applies to the patient's predicament, the ability to reason with that information, and the ability to exercise a choice.

Only if the patient fails on capacity would disclosure be considered; but a further test must then be passed – that disclosure is in the patient's 'best interests'. Definitions of 'best interests' are difficult, but the Law Commission (1995) has proposed guidance for deciding on the matter. Regard should be given to the following:

- the ascertainable past and present wishes and feelings of the person concerned, and the factors that person would consider if able to do so;

- the need to permit and encourage the person to participate or improve his or her ability to participate as fully as possible in anything done for and any decision affecting him or her;

- the views of other persons whom it is appropriate and practical to consult about the person's wishes and feelings and what would be in his or her best interests;

- whether the purpose for which any action or decision is required can be as effectively achieved in a manner less restrictive of the person's freedom of action.

Of interest in our consideration of confidentiality is the third – consulting with others to help establish what is in the patient's 'best interests'. This would suggest that the absence of capacity itself might sometimes justify some disclosure in order to decide on whether non-consensual treatment is warranted.

Paternalism

There are other approaches to justifying paternalistic interventions, although agreement between clinicians may sometimes be difficult to achieve. Beauchamp and Childress (1994) have put it thus: 'Developing a position on issues of paternalism is a matter of appreciating the limits of principles and the need to give them additional content, while attempting to render one's consequent rules and judgements as coherent with other commitments as possible.' It is these 'other commitments' which seem to be changing.

We find the approach to 'paternalistic' actions of Culver and Gert (1982) helpful. A person is acting paternalistically toward another if his action benefits the other; his action involves violating a moral rule with regard to the other; and his action does not have the other's past, present, or immediately forthcoming consent. In justifying a paternalistic act, a series of questions can be asked:

1. What are the moral rules which would be violated if the clinician were to act against the patient's wishes (e.g. limiting freedom of choice, causing psychological pain)? What thus are the evils to be perpetrated on the patient and for how long will they last?

2. What is the seriousness of the evils to be avoided through the paternalistic intervention (e.g. death, disability, worsening of the psychiatric disorder), and what is their likelihood?

3. How does the clinician rank the two sets of evils compared to the patient?

4. Is the patient's preference when comparing the evils to be avoided with the evils to be incurred, irrational – that is, does the patient have a *rational* reason to prefer an outcome with apparently greater evils?

5. Can the clinician advocate publicly for his ranking of the evils to be perpetrated compared to those to be avoided? This might become: would all or most rational people agree that this kind of moral violation should in such circumstances be universally allowed?

These questions address capacity and 'best interests' in a different manner, more philo-sophically and less clinically, but they make clearer the role of conflicting values and where judgements of 'rationality' enter.

DISCLOSURE FOR THE PROTECTION OF OTHERS

It is important to note that justifications for disclosure for the protection of others are not based on capacity or 'best interests' considerations. The patient's well-being is not primary. Questions of 'voluntariness' of behaviour are more appropriate, but these present even more difficulties in definition (Culver and Gert 1982).

There are some generally accepted principles relating to disclosure when others are put at risk or the patient lacks capacity. The information should be the minimum on a 'need to know' basis. The purpose of the disclosure should be clear, and the provider should have a good idea of what they expect the recipient to do with the information received. Potential secondary uses of the information must be clarified.

'Crisis cards'

The strongest justification for the disclosure of confidential information is the patient's consent. However, during illness this consent may not be forthcoming. One way of dealing with this is by an anticipatory 'crisis card' (or advance statement).

'Crisis cards' originated as a voluntary sector initiative to facilitate access to an advocate and to state a patient's preferences for treatment in an emergency when he or she might be too unwell to express their wishes coherently. They are designed to be carried by the patient and have the potential to record a range of useful information about the patient's treatment plan as well as advance statements. 'Crisis cards' have in the past been drawn up without discussion with the treatment team. There is scope for this idea to be developed into what we have termed 'joint crisis plans'. Here the content of the card, while still ultimately determined by the patient, is negotiated with the treatment team. The aim is to reach agreement on the care plan. This occurs when the patient is well enough to make competent judgements about what is in his or her best interests (Sutherby and Szmukler 1998; Sutherby et al. 1999).

Who to contact at times of emergency and the circumstances defining when they should be contacted can be recorded. Lessons learnt from past relapses can assist in drawing up these instructions. Reference to when a patient might become dangerous to others can also be recorded, including statements about who should be notified and how they would be expected to act on the information.

The development of a 'relapse plan' can form part of a sophisticated psychological intervention in the management of a psychotic illness and is certainly consistent with the aim of empowering the service user (Holloway 1998).

Sharing information within the multidisciplinary team and other agencies

We have already discussed where the boundaries of confidentiality might be drawn in relation to the 'care team'. Consent should be obtained before sharing information with another agency. We recommend that before sharing information with another agency, without the patient's consent, one should ask whether the tests for breaching consent, as set out above, have been passed.

Information sharing protocols

When information is regularly exchanged between agencies it may be advisable to draw up protocols specifying principles, rules or expectations. The Data Protection Registrar has prepared a checklist of issues to be addressed when setting up such arrangements. These include:

1. What is the purpose of the information sharing arrangement?

2. Will it be necessary to share personal information in order to fulfil that purpose?

3. Do the parties to the arrangement have the power to disclose personal information for that purpose?

4. How much personal information will need to be shared to achieve the objectives of the arrangement?

5. What if consent of the individual is not sought, or is sought but withheld?

6. How will compliance with other data protection principles be ensured (e.g. how will accuracy of the information be ensured? For how long will it be retained? How will individuals be given access to information held about them? How will the information be stored?).

It will be important for all agencies to develop clear and robust policies in relation to confidentiality: their presence will help to reduce the secondary use of information that is being shared between agencies.

Sharing information with carers

Szmukler and Bloch (1997) have argued for clarification of the ethical basis for working with families of psychotic patients. Much can be achieved in avoiding later dilemmas by an ethically sensitive approach to family engagement at the outset since in practice problems of engagement with families will usually derive from an early failure by the service to seek assertively their involvement in treatment planning. This essentially involves a structured approach by services, spelling out through the process of obtaining informed consent from patient and family, the basis on which care will proceed. The clinician's position in respecting the relative interests of family members and on confidentiality within the family is made explicit although subject to renegotiation with the family as treatment proceeds (Bloch *et al.* 1994).

Once a pattern of family involvement is set, future management of crises becomes much easier. It is surprising that the statutory duty under the 1983 Mental Health Act on the Approved Social Worker to consult the nearest relative when considering an application for admission under Section 3 has not led to improved communication between services and carers for these patients: an opportunity is clearly being regularly missed. Involvement of carers *against the patient's wishes* may be considered in one of two contexts:

- when it would be in the patient's interests;

- when it is aimed at reducing risks to the well-being of the family.

When it would be in the patient's interests

The dilemma concerning confidentiality posed by a relapsing or ill patient who refuses contact with the family turns on whether disclosure in the patient's best interests is sufficient to override confidentiality. A further consideration is the potential negative impact on the future doctor–patient relationship if confidentiality is breached. Many psychiatrists hold that without grounds for compulsory admission, respect for the patient's self-determination is paramount. This may be a considered position, but may well arise out of uncertainties regarding the justifications for alternative actions.

Szmukler and Bloch (1997) suggest a set of factors that could be weighed in the balance in deciding to act against the patient's wishes. One of these is the patient's capacity to make treatment choices, as discussed above. If such a test were to be applied, we could ask whether the patient could be deemed to have capacity to decide on the treatment as a whole, or on the value of carer involvement specifically. We suggest that incapacity should be the first test in deciding to act against a patient's wishes in the interests of his health. If a patient has capacity to make treatment decisions, including family involvement, it would be difficult to override a refusal.

Other commonly encountered factors proposed by Szmukler and Bloch (1997) that might then be considered include:

- The nature and magnitude of the harms to be avoided, and the probability of their occurrence.

- The availability of alternatives which might reduce the likelihood of harm. Other people or helping agencies more attractive to the patient may be able to alleviate the harms.

- The values of patient and family might suggest how family contact will be received. A family typified by good relationships and mutual support, but which the patient as a result of his psychosis sees as rejecting, might be regarded differently to a long-standing dysfunctional one. Cultural norms concerning the role of the family may also be relevant. Following recovery, would the patient be likely to see family involvement as having been desirable? Has previous discussion with patient or family revealed that contact would be acceptable, given the current circumstances?

- The principle of 'the least restrictive' option could apply when family involvement will reduce the likelihood of a greater restriction on the patient's freedom, especially involuntary hospitalisation. This principle is explicit in some mental health statutes, but not in others. But even in the latter case, it is implicit in certain circumstances, as in the requirement to consult the nearest relative before compelling admission under Section 3 of the Mental Health Act 1983 for England and Wales.

These factors share elements with Culver and Gert's justifications for paternalistic interventions described above and could be considered within their framework.

When it is aimed at reducing risks to the well-being of the family

At present, few psychiatrists would probably involve the family against the patient's wishes out of concern about the family's well-being (short of serious, physical danger). Yet we regularly encounter families who struggle with enormous difficulties and even intimidation as a result of their relative's illness. Some may approach the clinician for help; others may wish to do so but feel it is wrong, or are too frightened. If they do, it comes as a harsh blow if they are told that information cannot be given because of 'patient confidentiality'.

Does the clinician have a duty of care towards such carers, over and above that to the patient? The question has been largely ignored. Szmukler and Bloch (1997) argue that with increased family participation in treatment, ambiguities around the care of the family require urgent attention. They point out that a trend towards the recognition of carers' interests has now emerged, and is likely to grow in parallel with the expanding role of informal carers as members of the 'care team' in the community. Examples are a designated formal status for carers in recent legislation (Mental Health (Patients in the Community) Act 1995 for England and Wales; Section 120A of the Victorian (Australia) Mental Health Act 1986), and NHS guidance, albeit inconsistent, concerning the sharing of information within the care team, carers at one point being recognised as potential members (Department of Health 1996). The Carers (Recognition and Services) Act 1995 gives carers (defined as people who provide or intend to provide a substantial amount of care on a regular basis) the right to have their needs assessed by the local social services authority in England and Wales and the right of access to services in relation to those needs.

Szmukler and Bloch (1997) present possible arguments for involving relatives, primarily for their own benefit, but against the patient's wishes. The first views the family as the 'unit' of treatment because the illness is so pervasive, but this probably represents too radical a departure from traditional practice to gain widespread acceptance at present. The second argument invokes the principle of justice or 'fairness', entailing the identification of 'material principles', for example, 'needs' or 'equity', on the basis of which allocation of resources should be determined. In this context, the needs of the family may merit distinctive attention. If these can be met outside the treatment team (for example, by a self-help organisation) then the dilemma is possibly alleviated. Alternatively, if resources capable of meeting the family's needs reside in major part within the treatment team, a set of duties to the family would seem to follow. The third argument, and probably the strongest, reframes relatives' relationships to the patient as not only familial but also as 'carer'. This view is consistent with the trend in legislation which views 'carers' as having special status. As such they may enjoy rights intrinsically attached to all carers, whether relatives or not. These might cover at least an account of the illness and guidance about how to deal with the ill person's problems insofar as they impinge on the carer's life. This might include details about other agencies that offer help.

Thus justifications can be advanced for providing family carers with information aimed at meeting their interests. Several factors might be weighed up in judging when this is appropriate, some resembling those considered earlier: the patient's capacity to recognise actual and potential harms, the seriousness of risk to the family's well-being, available alternatives, and pre-existing family values. If information is to be disclosed non-consensually, it should be confined to a 'need to know' level, that is the minimum necessary for the carer to cope with the situation.

Disclosure in such circumstances is an extremely difficult issue. We believe it is now urgent that professional organisations address the thorny questions surrounding confidentiality and family involvement and, if possible, establish guidelines for their members.

Working in public places and development of care network in community

The public nature of some interventions in community psychiatry and the associated threats to privacy are a significant drawback to current models of care. Before instigating such interventions, the potential for breaches of privacy should be considered. Justifications for an assertive home-based intervention need to be articulated which outweigh the possible harms to the patient arising from breaches of privacy or confidentiality. Such justification will be either in terms of the interests of the patient (capacity is important here) or because of risks to others, as discussed above. Difficulties may arise when the potential benefits relate to 'social' rather than 'health' care. For example, tenure in a community placement may be at risk if an intervention which may need to involve those supporting the patient in that placement is not made. On the other hand, on some occasions community tenure may be jeopardised by drawing the attention of neighbours or others to problems suffered by a service user.

The development of a 'package of care', worked out in a meeting attended by key stakeholders at the time of discharge is now common practice under the Care Programme Approach. If the patient is actively involved in preparation for this meeting and subsequent review meetings, including drawing up the list of invitees, and participates fully in the care planning process, many of the difficulties over confidentiality may be obviated. The patient, when well, may agree to information being exchanged with a number of non-professionals, perhaps in specific circumstances. This may be recorded in the form of a 'crisis card'.

Risk assessment and management agenda

Arguably the most intractable problem faced by community psychiatrists in relation to patient confidentiality is presented by the increasing demands on professionals to assess and 'manage' risk. One clear implication of duties to disclose and inform is that it might not be in the patient's interests to be open and frank with those involved in their treatment. This problem has reached an extreme degree in Canada, where 'it is clear that any treatment records of a patient who is charged with a criminal offence may end up in the hands of the police and subsequently in open court' and the medical records of litigants can be accessed by the defence (Glancy et al. 1998).

There are no easy answers in this situation, and there is no obvious recourse to traditional ethical guidelines such as the patient's 'best interests' (unless such interests are interpreted with extreme elasticity). Honesty with the patient about dilemmas presented by a given situation and careful weighing of the circumstances by the clinician may provide some protection in difficult circumstances (as may a discussion with one's medical defence organisation).

Clinicians should be aware of current best practice in the assessment and management of risk and sensitive to their rather poor ability to predict dangerousness. Poor prediction is due to the rarity of serious violent acts. In a study of all of a community mental health team's patients we calculated that the 'positive predictive value' of an assessment that a patient rated as 'high risk' was likely to be violent to person over the next six months was, at best, one in five; that is, the team would be wrong five times for every time it was right. Indeed more violent acts, in absolute numbers, may come from the 'low risk' patients since, although the risk is lower, there are many more patients in this group (Shergill and Szmukler 1998). For even rarer acts, such as homicide (at a rate of 1 per 8000 psychosis years) the positive predictive value is likely to be negligible, about 1 in 900. A caveat here is that prediction of violence in the immediate future, say the next few hours or days, may be better, but there is little research on the question.

In more general terms it is vital that mental health professionals advocate as powerfully as possible for the traditional values of confidentiality since a world in which patients lost all rights to privacy would significantly undermine the possibilities of effective therapeutic engagement with difficult patients.

Conclusions

We have shown that new models of care in the community have engendered new problems relating to maintaining confidentiality and that traditional guidelines need revision. Interpretations of patients' 'best interests' and 'danger to others' have become more problematic, especially in a climate preoccupied with risk reduction. Ways of enhancing patient involvement in decision making, such as 'crisis cards' or advance statements, thus assume greater importance. Community mental health teams need to become more conversant with ethical principles relating to confidentiality and justifications for breaching it, either in the patient's 'best interests' or because of danger to others. Unless ethical principles are respected, community psychiatry risks eventually finding itself discredited.

References

Bloch, S., Hafner, H., Harari, E. and Szmukler, G. (1994) *The Family in Clinical Psychiatry.* Oxford: Oxford University Press.

British Medical Association (BMA) (1993) *Medical Ethics Today: Its Practice and Philosophy.* London: BMJ Publishing Group.

Cain, P. (1998) 'The limits of confidentiality.' *Nursing Ethics* 5, 158–166.

Culver, C.N. and Gert, B. (1982) *Philosophy in Medicine: Conceptual and Ethical Issues in Medicine and Psychiatry.* Oxford: Oxford University Press.

Department of Health (DoH) (1996) *The Protection and Use of Patient Information.* London: HMSO.

Department of Health (DoH) (1997) *NHS Executive Guidance to Hospital Managers and Local Authority Social Services Departments on the Sex Offenders Act 1997.* London: DHSG(97)37.

Department of Health (DoH) (1998) *Modernising Mental Health Services. Safe, Sound and Supportive.* London: DoH.

Eastman, N. and Peay, J. (1998) 'Bournewood: an indefensible gap in mental health law.' *British Medical Journal* 317, 94–95.

General Medical Council (GMC) (1991) *Confidentiality: Guidance from the General Medical Council.* London: GMC.

Glancy, G.D., Regehr, C. and Bryant, A.G. (1998) 'Confidentiality in crisis. Part I – The duty to inform.' *Canadian Journal of Psychiatry* 43, 1001–1005.

Holloway, F. (1996) 'Community psychiatric care: from libertarianism to coercion: moral panic and mental health policy in Britain.' *Health Care Analysis* 4, 235–244.

Holloway, F. (1998) 'Psychological and social approaches to the management of schizophrenia.' In G. Stein and G. Wilkinson *General Psychiatry. College Seminars in Psychiatry.* London: Gaskell.

Home Office (1998) *Crime and Disorder Act 1998: Guidance on Information Exchange.* London: Home Office.

Law Commission (1995) *Report No. 231. Mental Incapacity.* London: HMSO.

Lipsedge, M. (1995) 'Clinical risk management in psychiatry.' In C. Vincent (ed) *Clinical Risk Management.* London: BMJ Publishing Group.

Lord Chancellor's Office. (1997) *Who Decides? Making Decisions on Behalf of Mentally Incapacitated Adults.* London: HMSO.

Petch, E. and Bradley, C. (1997) 'Learning the lessons from homicide inquiries: adding insult to injury?' *Journal of Forensic Psychiatry* 8, 161–184.

Phelan, M., Slade, M., Thornicroft, G., Dunn, G., Holloway, F., Wykes, T., Strathdee, G., Loftus, L., McCrone, P. and Hayward, P. (1995) 'The Camberwell Assessment of Need (CAN): the validity and reliability of an instrument to assess the needs of the seriously mentally ill.' *British Journal of Psychiatry* 167, 589–595.

Sainsbury Centre for Mental Health (1998) *Keys to Engagement. Review of Care for People with Severe Mental Illness who are Hard to Engage with Services.* London: Sainsbury Centre for Mental Health.

Shergill, S.S. and Szmukler, G. (1998) 'How predictable is violence and suicide in psychiatric practice?' *Journal of Mental Health* 7, 393–401.

Stein, L.I. and Santos, A.B. (1998) *Assertive Community Treatment of Persons with Severe Mental Illness.* New York: Norton.

Stein, L.I. and Test, M.A. (1980) 'Alternatives to mental hospital treatment: I. Conceptual model, treatment program, and clinical evaluation.' *Archives of General Psychiatry* 37, 392–397.

Sutherby, K. and Szmukler, G. (1998) 'Crisis cards and self-help crisis initiatives.' *Psychiatric Bulletin* 22, 4–7.

Sutherby, K., Szmukler, G., Halpern, A., Alexander, M., Thornicroft, G., Johnson, C. and Wright, S. (1999) 'A study of "crisis cards" in a community psychiatric service.' *Acta Psychiatrica Scandinavica, 100,* 56–61.

Szmukler, G. and Bloch, S. (1997) 'Family involvement in the care of people with psychoses: an ethical argument.' *British Journal of Psychiatry* 171, 401–405.

Szmukler, G. and Holloway, F. (1998) 'Mental health legislation is now a harmful anachronism.' *Psychiatric Bulletin* 22, 662–665.

4

Confidentiality and Young People
Myths and Realities
Sue Bailey

Perceived wisdom

The Mental Health Act 1983 Code of Practice 1999 states that 'Children's rights to confidentiality should be strictly observed' (DoH 1999a). It is important that all professionals have a clear understanding of their obligations of confidentiality to children and that any limits to such an obligation are made clear to a child who has the capacity to understand them (DoH 1996).

Children should enjoy the same rights to confidentiality as do adults. Equally, the same limits to confidentiality which apply to adults also apply to children: for example, constraints conferred by terrorism, where serious crimes are likely to have been committed; disclosure in the public interest where serious crime or child abuse is suspected.

If children and young people have the capacity to understand the issue of confidentiality, they can act autonomously, as do adults. Clinicians use the term competent, whereas the law uses the word capacity. In a legal sense capacity refers to a person's ability to perform specific acts such as the giving or refusing of consent for medical treatment. Clinicians, by contrast, may be asked to comment or to formally assess a patient's capacity (competence) to perform such acts. The legal approach to the assessment of capacity is not covered by statute law but is developed through test cases and lies within common law. The clinical assessment of competence by medical and healthcare practitioners which is in accordance with these principles involves the following stages:

1. Deciding whose competence it is necessary to assess.

2. Making an analysis of what is the focus of the competency assessment.

3. Assessing the individual patient in relation to (1) and (2).

The practitioner has to decide if the child or young person is of a sufficient age and understanding and developmental maturity to appreciate the basic tenet of confidentiality, or alternatively the need to impart information to another person. If the child or young person is not capable or competent to make this decision, they may be capable of a lesser level of involvement in the decision, in keeping with their developmental maturity. Other children will be too young even for this level of involvement. Doctors therefore should be prepared to do everything possible to protect the child's right to confidentiality, on their behalf. In this they will enlist the support of the person or persons who hold parental responsibility for the child.

In certain circumstances, confidential information about the child can be disclosed to others, on the authority of the person/persons with parental responsibility. As with adults, situations may arise where, not withstanding the views of the person with parental responsibility, the doctor considers the confidential information about the child will need to be shared with others. In the main therefore the dilemmas are raised by the interplay between developmental immaturity, parental responsibility, the child's competence and the relative right to confidentiality.

Contextual issues

'High risk' children and young people

In a summary for practitioners of their main messages from their review of the research into antisocial behaviour in children and young people, Rutter, Giller and Hagell (1998) stressed both the heterogeneous nature of antisocial behaviour (ASB) and the pervasiveness, persistence, severity and pattern of such behaviour. Important themes drawn out included the overlap with hyperactivity; early onset ASB; and ASB that is violent and associated with later psychopathy, with serious mental disorder, sexual offences, juvenile homicide; drug use and abuse; medically caused crime; and crime associated with emotional disorder. These conclusions sit alongside the needs and risk surveys of young people and emerging findings from the long-term follow-up studies of young people in secure care. (Bullock, Little and Milham 1998). For the latter, five career routes emerged: young people in long-stay care; those in prolonged special education; those whose behaviours suddenly deteriorated in adolescence; one-off grave offenders; and serious persistent offenders. Young people with mental health needs and who offend have broad but often overlapping sets of problems with associated recurrent co-morbidity. The young person and crisis that surrounds them is often accompanied by a mass of information collected from many different agencies in different forms. How, when and where this information is shared and used strikes at the very heart of the issue of confidentiality and high risk young people.

Young people most at risk of having intimate details of their own lives revealed to others are: those with early onset antisocial behaviours; those with the established criminal behaviours of interpersonal violence, arson and, in particular, sexual offences; those older children and adolescents presenting with serious suicide attempts and self-mutilation interspersed with externalising destructive behaviours. All such behaviours give rise to great anxieties within existing service provision for the present and fear, for both girls and boys alike, of the consequences of the development of personality disorder in adult life.

Substance misuse among young people has increased rapidly over the last ten years. The Standing Conference on Drug Abuse (SCODA) 1998 recognised that very specialised and intensive forms of intervention for young drug users with complex care needs would involve specialist residential services and mental health teams including child and adolescent forensic psychiatrists. If services for such young people were to include any secure provision this would raise difficult ethical and moral issues about the sharing of information surrounding substance misuse and risk to physical health.

A further high risk group are those adolescents with early onset psychosis typified by prodromal non-psychotic behavioural disturbance. At greatest risk within this particular group are those who find themselves homeless or in penal remand and detention. Potentially most vulnerable within the adolescent forensic population are those young people who have learning disability. The interconnections between homelessness, mental disorders, substance misuse and offending are complex and remain poorly understood. It is apparent that if a professional wishes to have such a young person placed in a specialist facility then detailed information would need to be shared about each and every aspect of this young person's life.

Services

Although UK health and social services have a long history of working together, the prospect of a comprehensive service for children and adolescents with health and social needs remains elusive. For many we know that health needs exacerbate social needs and vice versa. (Bullock and Little 1999). Current political and professional pressures are for increased joint working which would seem both the logical and effective way forward, especially for certain vulnerable groups of children, i.e. those 'looked after', young offenders in custody and those with mental health problems. However, in the process of undertaking joint working, barriers do arise that encompass the very core of the theoretical structures of both health and social services, that encompass users' responses and lack of confidence about inter-agency preventative strategies (BMJ 1998).

National health service managers can be asked to work with over thirty different professions. It is inevitable therefore that issues of status, rivalry and power arise when experts gather together. Exponentially the gathering together of experts is also accompanied by incremental amounts of information being discussed, revealed and disclosed within the professional groups about the intimate personal details of the life of the child or young person.

Nowhere is this more prominent than in the child protection arena where health and social concerns arise from the context of potential danger to the child (Birchall and Hallet 1995). The ethical questions raised for professionals dealing with child abuse victims continue to attract interest. The potential conflict between the duty to report disclosures for the sake of safeguarding other children and the need to respect clients', in this case usually adult clients', confidentiality causes clear concerns, but resolutions can be found. (Cullen 1998; Harrington 1998). The ideal preferred strategy is to fulfil social duties without distressing patients or leaving them bereft of support and therapy.

Children and young people within social and healthcare systems include some chaotic families where parents and carers still strive to promote their children's welfare.

However, there are still some families who fall short of this ideal. Many factors can contribute to this situation including the unpredictability of antisocial neglectful parents, family size and in some cases substance misuse and acute episodes of mental illness within parents. Class and ethnic attitudes to welfare services are still too often matched by poor understanding by services of cultural and ethnic beliefs and overall a difficulty in accessing relevant and appropriate services at the time they are most needed to reduce risk.

Where children and young people are seen as high risk to self and others, each young person embarks on their care career as an education/mental health, social services or a juvenile justice case – divisions that suggest clear professional territories and boundaries. As 'cases' are seen as increasingly difficult high risk and complex, Bullock and Little (1999) describe a dissolving of boundaries with much toing and froing between agencies. These findings raise questions about the balance between legal and professional criteria for making decisions, which agency takes responsibility, what happens following screening and assessment, who offers a treatment service and how this is delivered. Usually lost deep within the fear and anxiety that often accompanies increasingly complicated legal processes is the issue of the right of the 'child' to confidentiality. They conclude that closing gaps to provide needs-led, well-targeted and effective services requires an intellectual shift towards common understandings, language and a shared conceptual framework. I would argue strongly that part of this framework should include a more honest, open explanation to children of the right, at one end of the continuum, to the increasingly rare phenomenon of absolute confidentiality; while at the other end to the benign paternalistic approach where, in order to find the right placement, care and treatment for a young person, more and more confidential information about the child is shared with increasing numbers of professionals. Confidentiality thus risks becoming a myth.

Developmental issues

An important starting point to an open honest dialogue about confidentiality would be a more informed developmental approach to a child's ability and right to be involved in decisions about their own treatment. Part of this should include a clear explanation of what information could, should and may be shared with other professionals, families and at times, from the 'child's' perspective, with 'strangers' in the pursuit of meeting the child's needs.

What do we really know therefore about how children and young people think and how do we apply this when dealing with the issue of confidentiality, particularly with regard to adolescents who give rise to anxiety and fear in adults leading to resultant tensions between professional groups. Within high-risk young people and families, professionals live under the constant cloud of 'damned if you do and damned if you don't' when exercising their judgement over what intervention, when, and what public outcry if they get the decision wrong. Trial of professionals occurs through newspaper headlines whether a child dies from non-accidental injury or an adolescent goes out and rapes or murders another child.

What empirical research findings do exist on children's cognitive capacities, and how such capacities link into their understanding of issues of consent and confidentiality, have over time been largely ignored by policy makers with an inevitable arbitrariness in legislation. English law is still driven by test cases relating to extreme situations and dilemmas, with respect to adolescents and their right to refuse treatment. However, there is a body of research evidence that suggests important developmental changes continue through the teenage years (Bailey 1996; Brazier and Bridges 1999, personal communication; Justice 1996; Keighting 1990; Rutter and Rutter 1993).

During early adolescence young people's thinking tends to become more abstract, multidimensional, self-reflective and self-aware, with a better understanding of relative concepts. They are better able to hold in mind several different dimensions of a topic at the same time and so generate more alternatives in their decision making. They become better able to monitor their own thinking and that of significant others for inconsistency, for its gaps in information and for the accuracy of its logic. The greater intellectual sophistication which comes during teenage years is accompanied by related developments in the way young people think about themselves. During adolescence, there is a marked increase in emotional introspection, together with a greater tendency to look back with regret and look ahead with apprehension. Not only do young people become increasingly able to consider the long-term consequences of their actions, but they also tend to think about such consequences more in terms of their own sense of responsibility and with increased awareness of the effect of their actions on other people and of the potential actions of others upon themselves.

There are parallel developments in children's capacity to remember events, to recall the timing of happenings, to understand interrogation and to be resistant to the influence of adult suggestions. It is not just that there is a gradual increase in children's mental capacity as such, there are also parallel decreases in children's suggestibility and susceptibility to being swayed in their views by adults who question them.

There are important developmental changes in children's ability to feel guilt and shame. Guilt involves the appreciation of responsibility for negative outcomes, resulting from acts of either commission or omission. Shame is associated with negative feelings about oneself on the basis of a self-perception of being unworthy or bad. The emergence of guilt and shame experienced by adolescents is connected to a growing awareness of when one has caused another person's misfortune; the capacity for self-evaluation and recognition that one has choice and control over one's behaviour. There is evidence that children's ability to express guilt increases with age. Young children are aware that they have done wrong but the way in which they think about this alters as they grow older. Older children are able to use internal justice principles and have concern for victims or wrong acts, whereas younger children tend to be more governed by fear of punishment after detection.

The teenage years also constitute the age period when there are marked changes in emotional disorders. Depressive disorders become much more frequent at this age; rates of suicide and attempted suicide increase dramatically. The reasons for the increase are likely to be complex or in any case poorly understood. However, part of the explanation is likely to lie in age-related changes in young people's ability to experience guilt and self-blame and their propensity to think about the long-term consequences of their actions and life situations. This situation becomes vividly clear to them during the process of court appearances, especially in pursuance of a secure accommodation order, to incarcerate the young person for the very purpose of their self-protection; the process itself making them more vulnerable as intimate details of their lives and their families are laid out before the court. These developments in both intellectual capacity and emotions derive in part from continuing brain development which extends well into the teenage years, and in part from the totality of life experience. During adolescence there is also the important biological transition of puberty, together with the marked hormonal changes involved and the implications for the behaviour and feelings of the young person at any one point in time.

Therefore, there is no single age at which it can be said that physical and mental development has reached maturity. Moreover, there is marked individual variation in timing. This variation is most obvious with respect to the major differences in the age at which young people reach puberty, but it is characteristic of all aspects of development and therefore impinges on a child's need to understand and have explained to them with due care and attention the nature of confidentiality. Accordingly, therefore, any decisions on how young people should be dealt with must take into account this marked individual variation and its impact on issues that may affect a young person for life. Included within this is the understanding of the boundaries of confidentiality, particularly within the patient–doctor/therapist dyad.

Article 8 of the Human Rights Act 1998 establishes the right to respect for private and family life. Underlying the tensions between the welfare of young people and their developmental capacities and a child's right to their say in their own lives is a constant shifting in the relationship between different arenas of social control. The changes are considerable between the pre-school and late adolescent years and between and through cultures. The main arenas of control appear to be the family and peers, the school, the welfare aspects of state provision and, where a child is perceived to have 'gone wrong', the criminal justice system. Younger children would be expected to be provided for and controlled by the first three primarily; young adults by the fourth. The age at which people move out of the first three spheres and into the last provides a focus for sociological and developmental discussion, including a child's capacity/competence to be involved in the issue of confidentiality and disclosure about details of their own life.

Confidentiality in practice

Thus confidentiality should be looked at in the context of the changing attitudes of society reflected in legal judgments with respect to 'older children', and with regard to consent and the concept of adolescent autonomy. The developmental task of adolescence remains autonomy and connection with others, personal development of independence, identity and distinction from and continuity with childhood. Overall legal developments during the last two decades have recognised that children of significant age and understanding are to be attended relatively more autonomy to make their own decisions than was the case in the past (Gillick 1986). Hence the wishes and feelings of children and young people are accorded more weight now in both statute and common law, notwithstanding the relative moderation of statute through Court of Appeal decisions (Court of Appeal in Re R 1992; Devereux, Jones and Dickinson 1993), subsequent to the 1989 Children Act. In Re R (1992), the Court of Appeal stated that 'Gillick-competence' is a developmental concept and will not be lost or acquired on a day-to-day or week-to-week basis.

Professionals and decision makers need to satisfy themselves that where young people are asked to make difficult choices, the choices are truly maximally autonomous. Part of this process is being open with them about the 'absolute' boundaries of confidentiality and the doctor–patient relationship, e.g. breaking confidence. One reason which may lead to the breaking of the confidence of an adolescent is when he or she discloses to a therapist that they are contemplating self-harm. The clinician is then faced with a breaking of confidence to the parents and/or responsible adult. The patient at the time may not necessarily fall within the provision of the Mental Health Act 1983. Nevertheless the same issues of responsibility arise within the Children Act 1989 – the *Children Act Guidance*, in particular volumes 1, 4, 6 and 7 of the guidance – available to all those responsible for the care of children.

Particular issues may arise when working with the child mental healthcare team when members of the team come from clinical and non-clinical backgrounds (e.g. teaching staff). The young people in the care of such teams may have mental disorders, with different levels of and changes in degrees of capacity. This makes a careful and ongoing explanation of the boundaries of confidentiality especially important, explaining and re-explaining to the young person. The right of confidentiality is not state dependent. Explaining and re-explaining at different times to the young person is very important because their mental state may fluctuate greatly during the course of hours or days.

While functioning in relation to several possible legal contexts such as the Children Act 1989 and Mental Health Act 1983, the child psychiatrist may be dealing with a young person who is mentally ill and/or emotionally disturbed, but who is also a perpetrator in their own right. Over a third of adult sexual perpetrators start to offend in adolescence. They may come within the remit of the criminal justice legislation and can now be subject to sex offender registers and schedules. Any and all information about them contained within the breadth of the 'clinical' team may come into the domain of criminal court proceedings.

Examples in practice

Case study 1

A young person (age 15) with severe mental illness and learning difficulties was charged with a serious offence. For some months he was felt to be too ill to attend court and a request by his solicitor for the court to delay proceedings was supported by the proceedings of case conferences concerning the patient. Some of the professionals who contributed documents to the case conference had (understandable) professional positivism where they concentrated on the achievements rather than the disabilities of the young person. Eventually the young person came before the court for trial. The prosecution in this instance was able to mount a strong case in relation to the young person's capacity, based on the positive statements of professionals who had prepared reports for an entirely different purpose. This was appropriately and energetically resisted by the young person's defence counsel, but the process took several days, during which the young person had to sit in court and listen to increasingly devastating details about his own life and past history of his family.

When a young person is involved in criminal proceedings, case notes and medical documents can be used out of context to establish a case which could prove disadvantageous for the young person. When a young person appears in court and they are currently the subject of psychiatric care, clinical information that the defence might use on their behalf would also be accessed by the prosecution, who may use other relatively unguarded statements appearing in clinical notes to the disadvantage of the young person, not only in terms of their own legal case but also the more long-lasting and damaging effects of the emotional impact of such information. The young person's legal representative should be alert to the consequences of providing information to the court which may subsequently be used to their client's disadvantage.

Thus, all professional groups within psychiatric services for young people should be made aware that young people are increasingly the focus of a criminal prosecution. Information recorded by professionals should at all times be objective and, where possible, staff should be alerted that inferences may be drawn from unguarded statements made in clinical notes. Documents relating to the care of patients should not be provided to the courts unless they have been prepared specifically for that purpose, or the court has directly requested disclosure of clinical records. In particular it cannot always be assumed that a young person's legal representative will be aware of the consequences of providing clinical information to the court because their thinking is focused on the distinct and discrete arena of presenting the best legal case for the child. Therefore he will not always be thinking of the wider emotional impact on the child of hearing more and more information disclosed about themselves in the court arena. It may be necessary to recommend a report to be commissioned to draw together a range of assessments for the specific circumstance of a report for court.

Case study 2

Being a child under the Children Act 1989 does not on occasion preclude the need for 'duty to warn' principle (confidential information to be discussed without the child's consent) to apply if the child is presenting serious risk to others. As with adults, assessment of dangerousness needs to be an open dialogue with the patient, in this instance 'a child'. Duty to warn and public interest do not always lie easily together.

A 16-year-old adolescent under Section 3 of the Mental Health Act 1983 is receiving treatment for chronic paranoid schizophrenia. He also has an atypical developmental disorder. The manifestations of his psychotic disorder include paranoid persecutory delusions and second person auditory command hallucinations telling him to harm himself and others. He has a history of threats to kill and observations in the ward reveal an extensive knowledge of pharmacology. It transpired that he had in the past attempted to carry himself off as a doctor by wearing a white coat and he had shown excessive interest while on the ward in the medication given to other patients.

Further observations also demonstrated that he was capable of coercing vulnerable patients into taking overdoses – an act for which he showed no apparent remorse. He started to seek contact with an elderly relative, even though he had previously already rejected contact with his family.

Because of the above, his consent was sought to share details of his history with the relatives in question but he refused to consent. His past high-risk behaviours meant that there was a risk to the relative. The 'duty to warn' principle was applied and the patient's refusal was overridden. When the relative was interviewed, there was a further disclosure of past history of trying to poison other relatives and secretion of other relatives' medication. In the long term it was possible to work through with this patient, as he responded to treatment for his illness, the reasons why his consent was overridden. In active rehabilitation he has been able to work through the feelings of anger, resentment, rejection, abandonment and betrayal he experienced at the time about and towards the clinical team.

The observation of patients' behaviour within a hospital setting requires multiple observations by different people at different times. The opinion derived from these observations needs to be reached on a multi-professional basis; only then can one hope for an objective assessment. The assessment of dangerousness needs to be an open, honest dialogue with patients, always exploring the reasons why they make particular choices when confronted with the evidence of their own behaviour. However, notwithstanding the fact that he was probably competent to withhold his consent for the doctor to warn the relatives, the clinician considered that the duty to warn (consideration of public interest, in this case safety of the relative) had overridden the duty to keep the patient's confidence.

Accurate recording of observation should be kept separate from the process of forming an opinion. It is important to record the basis of the decision to override confidentiality (disclosure without the patient's consent). 'Duty to warn' requires subsequent support for both parties concerned, i.e. the person to whom the disclosure has been made and the patient.

Issues where family (Children Act 1989) proceedings are in process

The proven abuse of children is almost always a criminal offence as well as a reason for intervention of the professionals concerned with the child, the family and the perpetrator. The criminal proceedings, if instituted, are likely to take priority over the long-term arrangements for the child and the prospect of prosecution has inevitably a marked effect upon the alleged abuser, particularly upon his/her willingness to admit what has happened. There is therefore a recognised tension in the interface between the criminal law with its focus upon the accused and his rights and the needs of the child said to be the victim – whose welfare is one of a number of considerations. This should be absent in the civil court where in Children Act proceedings the welfare of the child is paramount. Even here, however, confidentiality cannot be guaranteed when a history of abuse is revealed to the court.

Although family (Children Act 1989) proceedings are held in camera, those participating are specifically prohibited from giving details to third parties. The Guardian ad

Litem is there to rigorously represent the best interests of the child. Professionals should be aware that however apparently uncontroversial or otherwise the individual case, a point of law may arise which may lead to the publication of case details in law reports. (Law reports are frequently anonomysed on the direction of the judge to protect identities of parties being known.) However, when these are later translated into the tabloid press, the details of the case may be so particular that identification is de facto made.

Experts should think carefully about what information is provided in medical reports and consider whether the court needs to know certain details in relation to the child in order to come to an informed and safe decision. Is the information of relevance to the proceedings in question? If in doubt it is always possible to seek further directions from the court. This should be safer than withholding information, even for the best of motives, which may in the event turn out to be relevant to the proceedings and therefore potentially relevant to risk to that child or other children. Doctors cannot withhold information which is relevant, but the making of the decision about what is relevant information is difficult.

Documents which are prepared for the court can be marked with a sentence which emphasises their confidentiality; that this is prepared only for the court and responsible officers thereof and is not for duplication without explicit permission from either the court or the author. In fact such a report can only be released with permission of the court and thus specific permission from the court is needed before releasing a court report to general practitioners and others who might well need it and for it to be of benefit for clinical purposes to the child themselves. Although this may seem restrictive it is a helpful constraint, reducing the chances of reports being unnecessarily distributed. The courts are usually helpful in this regard with the distribution of reports for reasonable clinical purposes.

Sometimes documents which are not prepared as court reports, but for social services departments and other professionals, are presented for court (used in Children Act proceedings with the leave of court). Doctors cannot prevent this happening so it does require clinicians to adopt proper caution in documents which may be circulated to other agencies because they have no absolute right to control the subsequent use of these documents in family proceedings in particular. Increasingly, social services have a policy of open access to files with a limited time frame in which doctors and other health professionals may respond if they do not wish such information to be revealed. The overall implication in all these practices for the doctor is that all information needs to be objective and focused on the child's welfare without any extraneous information in the knowledge that it may form part of family (Children Act) proceedings, in due course.

Confidentiality in child protection

Whatever the starting point of the doctor–patient interaction in matters of child protection, the boundaries and limitations of confidentiality have to be clearly understood. In dealing with the protection of children, for example, courts will require evidence of the abuse, whether non-accidental injury, sexual or emotional. Without some evidence of past abuse or risk for the future they are powerless to act. In order for abuse to be dealt with in an effective manner for the benefit of all, including the community, the disciplines responsible for dealing with any aspect of it have to learn to understand each other and to work together – which will include an understanding of respected agreed approaches and responsibilities with regard to confidentiality. Although problems relating to confidentiality are faced by all professional groups, guidance prepared by members of a joint working party recognise and address with clarity the ethical and practical dilemmas faced, in particular by the medical profession in participating fully in child protection work (Home Office 1991).

The child protection process

In the context of child protection, the following issues should be considered. The Area Child Protection Committee (ACPC) has overall responsibility for developing inter-agency policies and procedures in each locality. However, professionals are major contributors to inter-agency care of children, which includes prevention of harm, whether at the stage of initial referral and assessment, child protection conference, planning, therapeutic intervention or ongoing support of child and family. Close co-operation with other agencies is essential, including other involved health professionals. Health professionals are again urged to keep meticulous records with due regard to confidentiality. They should be prepared to share the information contained in them with others who 'need to know', including the primary carers of children. A health authority per se has a duty to comply with the request for help from a local authority, providing a request is compatible with its own statutory or other duties and does not unduly prejudice the discharge of any of its functions (Section 27 of the Children Act 1989). At present, despite there being no statutory obligation to disclose evidence of abuse, the guidance accompanying the Children Act 1989 is clear about the obligations of all agencies to report concerns about child protection. Specifically, in relation to children, in addition to the qualifications of 'public interests' and 'need to know', a justification for disclosure of confidential material is that it is in the best interest of the child. In child protection cases the overriding principle is to secure the welfare of the child above all other considerations: the paramountcy principle.

All 'working together' documents underline that there is a positive duty on doctors to disclose information to a third party where child abuse is suspected, which is also the position adopted by the General Medical Council (1993). Where a doctor believes that a patient may be the victim of abuse or neglect, the patient's interests are paramount and will usually require a doctor to disclose information to an appropriate responsible person or officer of a statutory agency. This advice will guide doctors' decisions on whether to disclose confidential information relating to abuse and neglect, both to medical colleagues and staff of the statutory agencies. The statutory agencies are social services, NSPCC and the police.

Therefore, disclosure of confidential information in relation to children (adopting the Children Act definition of a child as anybody under the age of 18) is justified in a much more general way than the confidentiality qualifications considered in relation to adults. Given there is this wide scope for disclosure in the case of children, disclosure must nonetheless be tempered by the expectation that the information to be disclosed is relevant. In this regard psychiatrists caring for adults should be aware that many of their patients are parents, some of them caring for young children. They have a duty of care (responsibility) to consider the well-being of these children and to act appropriately if they believe they are being harmed (Oakes 1997).

Medical participation is important in all aspects of child protection work, as is co-operation and openness between professionals. The principles of co-operation and openness have been extended to include the active involvement of parents and children. *Working Together* (Home Office 1991) makes it clear that parents and, where appropriate, children should be given the opportunity to be involved in all aspects of the process. Sometimes, however, participation may be dangerous or the scale of parental participation may need to be carefully considered in the light of the individual case (Jones and Lynch 1998). *Child Protection Messages from Research* (DoH 1995) provides a useful framework from within which practitioners can assess when threshold criteria for abuse are reached. It outlines the way in which abuse is variously defined. Thresholds which legitimise action including sharing of confidential information on the part of child protection agencies are the most important components of any definition of abuse. It summarises research projects which have explored effects of child protection on children and families who experience it, including the side effects of intervention by child protection agencies. Currently the government's *Working Together* guidance is being revised in order to incorporate these changes in practice, as well as the messages that have emerged from research projects. However, the fundamental emphasis of both law and guidance upon improved inter-agency co-operation, focused on maintaining the welfare of the child as a paramount consideration, will be maintained and is likely to be strengthened in the new guidance. Given this climate, clarity concerning confidentiality will be essential for psychiatrists who, as I hope I have illustrated, have to operate within a wide and increasingly complex range of legal ethical contexts in their day-to-day practice. The identified child protection liaison person within an NHS trust, nurse or doctor, can be a valuable source of support in discussing when thresholds to disclose have been reached, but are still often only referred to when a 'crisis' has already been reached.

Epilogue
The 'user's' voice

'Users' current and past should have their voices heard. In listening to young people who have been through child care proceedings, secure accommodation order proceedings (Section 25 Children Act 1989), detention under the Mental Health Act 1983 and/or criminal proceedings can tell us much about the myths and realities of 'in confidence'.

Young offenders

The 1990s saw an escalating tendency within the media to take a voyeuristic interest in young children who offend. In high profile cases, despite the best and absolute determination of carers and therapists, the most intimate details of these young people's lives, their families, their current detention and indeed details of their therapeutic interaction with clinicians can and do appear verbatim in the media – thus making therapeutic engagement and the establishment of a trusting relationship on which to build understanding of themselves, their crime, impact on the victim and safe resolution a sometimes near-impossible task.

Young people at risk

In meeting for the first time a young woman in prison, a useful part of engagement proved to be a shared journey along her road to 'confidentiality'. Witnessing violence as a toddler, multiply physically and sexually abused by family and 'strangers', trust is a lost concept. Fear, anxiety, helplessness, hopelessness and despair are communicated to professionals through the outlets of harm to self and explosive outbursts against others. The young person was rescued from 'abuse' only to catapult through multiple placements – taking out her anger on adults who each attempted to offer consistent non-abusive care. Therapists stepped in and out, past traumas were visited and high-risk behaviour escalated. To contain the fears of professionals and keep safe her 'physical frame', application to court was made to detain her in local authority secure care.

The young person longed for a safe, confiding relationship with just one of the ever-growing procession of professionals there to represent her rights, thoughts, wishes and feelings. Each stepped in, questioned, stepped out and went on to discuss her life with other professionals. Her anger and despair escalated. She fought the system and opposed her secure care order when her life was played out in intimate detail in the theatre of court. Who and where could meet her needs? How many potential placements needed to hear her story in order to find the 'right' placement that could remove her traumas and restore her life? Aged 17, and 28 placements later, 'in confidence' our shared best guess in the sanctum of a doctor–patient dyad is that no less than 1000 professionals have 'legitimately' been made privy to her 'life'. In the isolation of an adult female prison cell, she had found privacy; but also in the context of a placement with few rights, the right as an adult to determine her own destiny and in particular with whom she would share details of her life. In the 'anti-therapeutic' environment of prison she was able safely to engage in therapy and, more importantly, two years' later chose to share her experiences with others and to ask that 'children's rights to confidentiality' are strictly observed while understanding the need to protect and care for a young person.

The year of 1999 brought with it more guidance on how to provide integrated services to young people and how to protect young people from abuse (DoH, 1999b, 1999c). Hopefully, as we follow new consultation guidance we can hold on to the experience of the 'child' within the system, and more especially to their voice in the proceedings and their 'right' to confidentiality. (Bailey and Harbour 1999).

References

Bailey, S. (1996) 'Adolescents who murder.' *Journal of Adolescence 19*, 19–39.

Bailey, S. and Harbour, A. (1999) 'The law and a child's consent to treatment (England and Wales).' *Child Psychology and Psychiatry Review 4*,1, 30–35.

Birchall, E. and Hallett, C. (1995) *Working Together in Child Protection.* London: HMSO.

Brazier, M. and Bridges, C. (1999) Personal communication.

British Medical Journal (BMJ) (1998) 'Editorial comments.' *British Medical Journal*, 7 February.

Bullock, R. and Little, M. (1999) 'The interface between social and health services for children and adolescent persons.' *Current Opinion in Psychiatry 12*, 421–424.

Bullock, R., Little, M. and Milham, S. (1998) *Secure Treatment Outcomes. The Care Career of very Difficult Adolescents*. Dartington: Ashgate.

Court of Appeal in Re R (1992) 1 FLR190.

Cullen, P. (1998) 'Disclosure of child sexual abuse: doctor has duty to warn others.' *British Medical Journal 317*, 208–209.

Department of Health (DoH) (1995) *Child Protection: Messages from Research*. Dartington: Ashgate.

Department of Health (DoH) (1996) *The Protection and Use of Patient Information*. London: HMSO. HSG(96)(18).

Department of Health and Welsh Office (1999a) *Mental Health Act Code of Practice 1999*. London: Department of Health.

Department of Health, Home Office, Department for Education and Employment, National Assembly for Wales (1999b) *Working Together to Safeguard Children – A Guide to Inter-agency Working to Safeguard and Promote the Welfare of Children. Consultation Draft – Quality Protects*. London: Department of Health.

Department of Health (DoH) (1999c) *Framework for the Assessment of Children in Need and their Families, Consultation Draft – Quality Protects*. London: Department of Health.

Devereux, J., Jones, D.P.H. and Dickinson, D. (1993) 'Can children withhold consent to treatment?'

General Medical Council (GMC) (1993) *Current advice on Working Together*. London: GMC.

General Medical Council (GMC) (2000) *Confidentiality: Protecting and Providing Information*. London: GMC.

Gillick *v.* West Norfolk and Wisbeck Health Authority and Another [1986] AC 112.

Harrington, B. (1998) 'Disclosure of sexual abuse: maintaining confidentiality is not in the best interest of women or others' (letter). *British Medical Journal 317*, 208.

Home Office (1991) Department of Health, Department of Education and Science and Welsh Office. *Working Together under the Children Act 1989: A Guide to Arrangements for Interagency Co-operation for the Protection of Children from Abuse*. London: HMSO.

Jones, D.P.H. and Lynch, M. (1998) 'Diagnosing and responding to serious child abuse and factitious illness by proxy.' *British Medical Journal 317*, 484–485.

Justice (1996) *Children and Homicide: Appropriate Procedures for Juveniles in Murder and Manslaughter Cases*. London: Justice.

Keighting, D.P. (1990) 'Adolescent thinking.' In S.S. Feldman and G.R. Elliott (eds) *At the Threshold: The Developing Adolescent*. Cambridge MA: Harvard University Press, pp.54–89.

Oakes, M. (1997) 'Patients as parents.' *British Journal of Psychiatry 170*, 32.

Rutter, M. and Rutter, M. (1993) *Developing Minds: Challenge and Continuity across the Lifespan*. Harmondsworth: Penguin.

Rutter, M., Giller, H. and Hagel, A. (1998) *Antisocial Behaviour by Young People. The Main Messages from a Major New Review of the Research*. Manchester: Social Information Systems.

5

Confidentiality and Child Protection
Judith Trowell

Introduction

The Children Act 1989 came into effect in October 1991 (Home Office 1991a). It transformed the way children were viewed in both civil and private law. The child's best interest was to be paramount and this was to be considered both in private law cases, such as matrimonial disputes, and public law, which involved predominantly concerns about the child's physical and mental health and well being, that is, the area of child protection.

In December 1991, the UK government ratified the UN Convention on the Rights of the Child (UN 1989). This too included a statement that in public and private domains the best interests of the child shall be paramount (Article 3). As did the Children Act, it also included a statement that children have a right in all matters affecting the child to express their views freely, the age and maturity of the child being taken into consideration (Article 12). The Children Act specifies that the child's ascertainable wishes and feelings must be elicited and given due weight in the light of their age and understanding.

It is very clear then that the climate changed, and children and young people were seen as individuals with views which they were entitled to express, experiences they were thought capable of remembering and recounting, and that they were considered capable of having some involvement in any decision-making process that involved or impacted on their lives. *Working Together under the Children Act* also came out in 1991, and this spelt out the roles and responsibilities of the agencies in each geographical area (Home Office 1991b). Area child protection committees (ACPCs) were established to oversee and co-ordinate the inter-agency policy, procedures and practice in each locality. The ACPC was also responsible for ensuring training of all staff, from receptionists, cleaners, professional staff, managers, chief executives and councillors, or trust boards. The ACPC covers education, health (hospital, community and general practitioners), social services, police, probation and the voluntary sector and frequently includes housing. When cases go wrong, and particularly when there is a child death, the ACPC is expected to undertake a review. (Formerly there were inquiries but they were phenomenally expensive and did not justify the time and expense.) These are known as Part 8 Reviews.

Following this, the DoH (1995) has issued guidelines for health authorities and trusts, *Child Protection: Medical Responsibilities*. The importance of child protection is reaffirmed and the role of health service staff. A designated doctor for each health authority has to be appointed (usually a paediatrician) and a designated nurse (usually a senior health visitor). This has improved the recognition of child protection issues among health service staff but, currently, across the UK there are major concerns about the boundary and interface between child protection work and mental health problems; this is across and within agencies. Within social services, children and families staff and adult mental health staff have rarely spoken to each other. In the health services, adult mental health, that is, psychiatrists and community psychiatric nurses, rarely speak to paediatricians. Health visitors, child health nurses and general practitioners have a variable position; some work closely with and are aware of child protection issues, others have little awareness or interest.

In a recent pilot project in the London Borough of Brent and now being repeated elsewhere, few adult psychiatric in or out patients were found to have been asked if they had a partner or, even more rarely, if they had children. This meant the need to liaise with or inquire about the involvement of other agencies in the family did not arise and so child protection considerations were ignored.

In my own practice, cases I see frequently are involved with adult psychiatric services, learning difficulties services, drug treatment services and adult psychotherapy services, in addition to physicians, neurologists, surgeons and their general practitioner (GP). When do we inform each other of worries or concerns? When is it easier to hide behind the statement that we are protecting our patient's confidentiality? It is less trouble to keep quiet, not rock the boat. Perhaps we imagined or misheard what is going on; surely it will all go away. Of course, except in extreme cases, there always is uncertainty. Very often not knowing, but remaining alert to the possibility that something seriously damaging may be occurring and that confidentiality may need to be broken, is an essential aspect of medical responsibility.

The issues

A problem for all concerned and committed doctors is who is my patient: is it the person in front of me, child or adult, or is it the child with parents, or the adult as parent, or is it the family with perhaps several children and maybe grandparents or other extended family members? Of course all patients must be treated with respect and their confidentiality is vital, but we are also expected to exercise our duty and be responsible, when sufficiently concerned, and to inform statutory agencies (the social services or the police) if we consider a child is at risk. This is so even when we consider the adult/parent to be the patient.

This has been made more complex recently. The current thinking is that children in need is a more useful way of referring to vulnerable children, but it has the adverse effect of blurring the boundary in child protection. The children may be in need of services (physically disabled, learning difficulties); they may be asylum seekers or they may be in need of protection (at risk of some form of abuse). Confronted by an adult or young person who may be expressing or behaving in a worrying manner, when do we consider that children in their household or in the community may be in need, or may be in need of protection? Undertaking assessments and recording care plans take time. If, in addition, other agencies or services need to be contacted to discuss if they were also concerned, more time is needed and would 'my patient' complain or become aggressive or cease to co-operate? Judging when to break confidentiality and to discuss with others was never easy. Now it feels more delicate than ever.

Perhaps, most difficult is the situation for GPs, particularly, where the whole family is registered with the one doctor. GPs find it hard to believe that parents or older siblings will harm children and young people. GPs deserve support, supervision and training, particularly in cases of neglect (Bridge Report 1995). The dirty but happy families, where there are fat files and years and years of work by health visitors, schools and GPs, are an especial problem. Often, the boundary between poverty and social problems, and recognition of the threshold when children are being damaged by neglect, is blurred by familiarity over years. Attempts to support the mother, usually a massive input of services and resources, leave professionals so emotionally invested that they cannot see or allow themselves to be aware that the children are being damaged and nothing is changing. Depressed inadequate parents can leave professionals drained and exhausted.

A particular problem is the many cases where there are personality disordered parents and concomitant domestic violence and/or alcoholism. Recognising the risk and the deprivation to which the children are exposed has only recently been highlighted. When does the GP, the CPN, the psychiatrist then decide enough is enough and break confidentiality, alerting social services. Or, more often, social services may already be involved, but not the children and families team and not with a question raised about the possibility of a child at risk. Then, if the question is raised by others, how often, if our 'patient' is mother, stepfather or older sibling, do we attend or write a report for a case conference? So often, it is easier to stay away, 'forget' or hide behind our confidentiality.

Issues in child and family mental health work

In *Moral Dilemmas in Child Welfare* (King 1998), a colleague and I considered the issues as they affect child and family mental health workers (Trowell and Miles 1992). This section draws from this volume.

Consent and confidentiality in child and family mental health

Parents frequently find it very difficult not to know what is occurring during the work with their child. This is not surprising, but the work is predicated on the child being free to say whatever he or she is thinking or feeling without any judgements being made. Whatever emerges can be thought about and accepted as part of the work. As they struggle with their feelings, children are often worried that their parents will be told. However, there are some basic concerns which need to be shared with parents and the clinician will need to exercise judgement as to what, if anything, to say and how not to betray the child's trust. Recently, parents of a 9-year-old child being seen, after the individual session, demanded to know what the child had said. When themes and issues were explained, the father very firmly said, 'Dr Trowell, when I take my child to the GP I am told your daughter has bronchitis, here is a prescription, her chest is infected. I expect you, in the same way, to tell me about my daughter.'

As concern over child abuse has increased, confidentiality has become an even greater moral dilemma, particularly in cases where abuse was not originally suspected. It may be good for the worker to keep confidentiality, but bad for protection of the child in cases where abuse continues to occur. When children start to share information that raises concerns, clinicians have to record the sessions very carefully, and need to keep a balance between respecting the child's trust and the need to keep the child safe. Frequently, the basis of concern is vague – is the child talking about a dream, or a wish or longing, or is the child hinting at something that has really happened? Each case needs to be considered separately and the level of anxiety monitored. When the information from children is both consistent and of major concern, the child should be informed that confidentiality will be broken and given an explanation as to why this has to happen. Work will then need to take place to preserve the therapeutic alliance.

Work with the parent(s) or carer(s) can also raise child protection concerns directly or indirectly. The work needs to continue while, at the same time, the parent should be encouraged to contact social services. If this does not happen, the workers have to explain why social services will be informed against the wishes of the parent. Making this decision can present the workers with a moral dilemma, since it involves not only the child's best interest, but also the workers' anxiety about whether or not the information should be passed on, and their need to protect themselves professionally.

Reporting abuse has become a dilemma for clinicians because of anxiety about the effect on the 'therapeutic relationship'. It is felt to be a betrayal of trust and yet it is also recognised that even where the child or parent becomes angry or subsequently denies the information, it is important to take these concerns seriously. The clinician's decision is difficult in that it cuts across the rules and boundaries of the therapeutic relationship. It may be tempting for the clinician to avoid the issue and ignore what they have heard or to hope it will go away.

In the UK the issues presented by consent have had to be rethought, after the introduction of the Patient's Charter (DHSS 1991). Can both parents and children give consent to treatment for the child? They can be offered help for their problems and the treatment may be described in advance, but until they experience the therapy, it is difficult for either of them to give fully informed consent.

Many clinicians find managing the need to obtain consent difficult, seeing it as a potential intrusion into the development of the therapeutic process. It is possible to talk about the process of making conflicts conscious and offering help to resolve these conflicts so that choices and decision making become more objective, but such accounts do not convey the pain, struggle and distress of the treatment. Normally, parental consent is required and the children are informed. Even where children do give their express agreement, it is unlikely that they really understand what is involved.

Consent arises again as an issue with children when they wish to stop the therapy or when child protection issues emerge. Some children want to stop because they find therapy is not right for them. They are correct in thinking that they cannot benefit from this type of intervention. But children may also want to stop if they are working with the clinician on particularly painful issues, such as the effect of a parent dying, abuse, the move to another foster placement or the breakdown of a previous fostering. It is difficult to know when it is right to stop therapy. A decision has to be made. Is the child not psychologically ready to work? Should he or she, on the other hand, be brought to a realisation that, despite the protests, the work should continue, because the therapy has reached a critical but very painful point? Occasionally, consent comes from elsewhere – parents, social worker, or sometimes the courts, who ask for or order that work be done. Some clinicians do not feel able to work in such circumstances. Others try to see the longer term benefits for the child and continue to offer therapy and to try to engage the child.

Child protection, the law and child and family mental health

The legal system requires certainty and clinical work, in contrast, is predicated on the ability to live with uncertainty and ambiguity. Child protection decisions, like the law, also require clarity. If during the course of treatment it appears that the child may have been abused, the clinician may need to change his or her therapeutic way of working according to the need to question and seek answers, to try to ascertain the facts, or at least obtain sufficient evidence to decide whether to alert the child protection agencies. It may not be possible subsequently to restore the therapeutic alliance and resume the therapeutic work.

Most families come to the Child and Adolescent Mental Health Service as self-referrals or referred by their GP. Issues about child abuse can emerge during assessment or treatment. But some families are sent to the clinic by the courts or social services and they themselves do not want to be there, see no reason to be there, and do not consider that they need any help. The clinician is obliged to decide whether or not to try to impose work. It may be that, in spite of their reluctance, as the work progresses the parents or children begin to understand and change, and then choose to co-operate. Then again, they may not. Many clinicians refuse to work in this way, but some will offer a trial period. This dilemma reflects the contrasting attitudes of clinical work and the law.

Some families forced to come may decide they have to comply, and so appear to co-operate after initial resistance. Deceit is not always easy to detect and so bad therapy may be carried out because it is based on lies – anti-therapeutic therapy (Furniss 1991). This is when an abused child is brought for treatment and the family appears to be co-operative, but in reality the abuse is continuing and the therapy is based on falsehood. The parents' intention here is not to assist the child's recovery but to divert attention away from what is going on covertly. It is bad therapy in that the therapist has not ensured that those responsible for the child's safety have done what was required. The child is left in a damaging situation believing the therapist is colluding with the abuse by continuing to work alongside it. But many clinicians find it extremely difficult to recognise this situation and use confidentiality as a 'screen'.

Whether there are issues of a child's safety or inadequate parenting, there is a dilemma for workers in facing the break-up of families. Divorce, where the family is split up by the adults, is less of a dilemma, although equally distressing. The real dilemma for the clinician arises when they conclude that they need to initiate an action that could lead to the break-up of a family. When working closely with children and their families, it can become too painful for workers even to consider suggesting the family needs to split up or the child be removed. Attachments are established very early and from then on the key individuals are important in the child's life. Knowing this can lead to endless attempts to work for change, even though the possibility of the adult changing in time to avoid too much damage to the child is virtually impossible.

Balancing the needs of the child, the wishes of the child and the capacities and needs of parents is acutely distressing. More so because a therapist knows that it is not possible for children to be removed, placed in another family and have a fresh start, cutting off awareness of the past. Children's internal object relationship will go with them and influence their ongoing relationships. We now see many children who were fostered or adopted seeking out their family of origin in order to understand themselves, and this phenomenon links closely with this view. So, there is a real dilemma here. Can children have the choice to stay with their parents, or should they be removed against their wishes?

Many clinicians will not attend court, believing again that it breaks and betrays the confidentiality. They feel that to do so destroys the therapeutic relationship. This is right to some extent, and often it is preferable if another member of the team who is not doing the direct work should attend court. The professional who goes to court takes the decision that what has emerged gives rise to a cause for concern about the child's welfare, and leaves the therapist to continue the therapeutic work. The situation is different if the case and the work were a 'court' case from the start. Then the child, the carers/parents and the professionals are aware throughout that there will be a hearing.

Where cases that start as clinical cases become court cases, there can be further dilemmas. The therapist may be called and records and notes may be subpoenaed. Is the clinical discourse appropriate in court? The play, the dreams, the transference and counter-transference are not hard facts. Rather they are a means, a way, to understand what the conflict, the problem, was about, to try to work on it. From this, one might be able to comment on the mental state of the individual and have a view about events, but this form of information is not 'evidence', that is legal fact.

Finding a way to use the clinical perspective, the understanding arrived at in this way is not easy and takes time and skill. There is an innate tension between a legal discourse and a clinical discourse. Evidence, 'the facts', are vital to make decisions in court. Clinical discourse values uncertainty, not knowing, and slow thoughtful exploration, and there are times when attempts to introduce the content of sessions into court discussions can be damaging, distorting the material as well as betraying the child (King and Trowell 1992).

Clinical examples

At what age do we respect the child's views and agree these should be implemented, and when do we overrule or consider the child lacks sufficient understanding?

The child is deemed Gillick-competent below the age of 16 years, where they truly understand the nature, purpose and hazards of any particular treatment. The child is then deemed capable of giving consent to the treatment, even where those with parental responsibility have not been informed or do not consent. (Children under 16 years, however, are not deemed capable of refusing life-saving treatment, such as feeding in anorexia or antipsychotic medication, although the doctor and/or health authority need a court to confirm this.) (Medical Defence Union 1996.)

As part of a clinical project, many girls who had experienced contact sexual abuse were offered treatment. A number of girls declined treatment for sexual abuse, insisting that events since the sexual abuse had been investigated were the cause of their problems. One particular girl was very attached indeed to the abuser and desperately wanted to return to her previous situation with him. Several assessment sessions involved her begging to be returned. The full assessment confirmed there was very serious cause for concern, including allegations by other children and relatives and family interviews, adult assessments, plus reports from school. Regular supervised contact was maintained by this 10-year-old girl, but her distress at the separation was very overwhelming. Treatment enabled her to function better at school and her despair lessened, but the wish to return remained strong.

Several years later the girl instigated contact with the clinic and now, aged 15 years, was able to talk in detail about the years of abuse, her shame and anger, as well as her continuing emotional involvement with the abuser. She was able to describe her terror at the separation, the unbearable loss of active sexual contact and her neediness. She was able to talk about her foster home, her school and friends, and her ongoing contact with her family.

This girl consented to information about her being shared because she felt now that what happened was in her best interest, even though we had overruled her wishes and feelings. This is not to imply that the decision at the time was easy. The confidentiality which was broken was the patient's trust that what she so desperately wanted would happen. Exercising clinical judgement was very difficult and involved much internal debate and considerable anxiety about alternatives for this girl. It is interesting to note that adult learning disability colleagues who assessed the abuser were uncertain, until after the second contact, about the abuse concerns.

When is a child to be seen as an abuser rather than a victim, particularly if their own abuse may be uncertain, and when is sexual activity between children normal sexual exploration?

A delightful cute 6-year-old boy with his single mother, on several occasions when visiting friends was found behind the settee with his penis inside the 2-year-old little girl's anus. Both mothers were shocked and horrified and the boy's mother came to Child and Family Mental Health. With great reluctance, she finally agreed to inform social services after several exploratory interviews raised concerns about babysitters and other inhabitants of the block of flats. The mother and son had parent–child work and both mother and son had some individual help. The mother's own childhood physical abuse was worked on and the implications for her son and his attitude to women and girls was a fruitful piece of work.

It seemed very important to confront this as abuse, despite the mother's extreme reluctance and the major work involved in maintaining contact with her. She was all too eager to explain the behaviour as normal exploration. The distress of the little girl was played down by the mother and her son. Only during the work did the boy's excitement and sense of triumph emerge and also his fear both about what he was doing and what he had witnessed while visiting friends in adjacent flats or when there had been babysitters.

A 13-year-old boy, who was found anally abusing 3- and 4-year-old boys, on many occasions, was reluctantly referred because the small children's mother insisted the neighbour's child needed some help. The boy's parents felt it was normal experimentation and nothing serious. There was great distress when the term abuse was used and the need to inform social services was confronted. Social services took the view that if the boy was in treatment they would take no further action other than a monitoring role. The boy and his parents were initially outraged as they had been very strongly against informing social services. They were told it was essential, and if they could not do it the clinic would. Over the next 18 months, the young man slowly became able to consider the impact of his actions on the little children and to consider his relationships, fantasies, dreams, longings and needs. Initially, his parents effectively disowned him; he had to stay with grandparents as they felt disgraced by the involvement of social services. Confidentiality was broken in whose interest? Certainly hopefully the young man's, the small boys' and the potential other children's but the parents felt betrayed and outraged, although they were finally reconciled with their son. The GP, long associated with the parents, clearly found the whole process painful and problematic.

Munchausen by proxy

In child protection, this is one of the more complex and difficult areas. The parents who present their child with symptoms or disorders which, in reality, are induced by the parents, require very careful, sensitive, yet sceptical professionals. The child who is repeatedly brought to hospital by anxious parents may or may not have a life endangering illness, but may be ill because of the actions of the parent. The diabetic child whose management is very worrying may have brittle diabetes, but may have parents who do not administer insulin or who feed the child too much sweet food. The child with recurrent diarrhoea and vomiting may have intestinal problems, but may also be being given salt water or other dehydrating substances. Even more incomprehensible are the parents who give poisons or suffocate their children so that the child is subjected to invasive investigations and prolonged hospitalisation.

In these cases, the GP and the paediatrician are in the front line and may become concerned about the mental state of the child or the parent. However, the psychiatrist may well be the one who recognises the possibility that this is not chronic unexplained illness but parent-induced illness. Sharing this as a possibility with medical colleagues and then social services is seen as a major breach of confidentiality and can result in serious professional splitting. The parent can be very concerned, anxious and distressed about the child's state so that paediatric colleagues feel supportive and concerned; the child and family mental health service and child and family social services are seen as cruel and unreasonable. These children do die not infrequently and managing the splitting and the breaking of confidentiality, often by involving the courts, is not easy.

Discussion

The clinical examples have focused on the importance of breaking confidentiality, sharing the clinicians' knowledge of the case, their clinical judgement and their own reflections and grasp of the situation in order to safeguard the child. This has been emphasised because, all too often, it can be avoided and the painful situation side-stepped. The dilemma is that early on it can be extremely difficult to judge how to proceed. It is clearly wrong to break confidentiality and share information simply to protect one's own professional reputation. It is appropriate to explore carefully, anonymously to consult colleagues and to admit to uncertainty. The complexity of the work and the need to take time is recognised; in only the rare case does one need to act now. Often, the justification for not breaking confidentiality is that colleagues in other services, particularly social services, will act in a precipitate way, mainly to protect themselves by following the procedures. Another justification is that in the event of a child being removed, then the substitute care likely to be available is often worse than the care at the hands of parents.

Sometimes, of course, this is true, but where colleagues build relationships of mutual respect, time to explore and stay with the uncertainty is understood and valued. What is important is to be as honest and straightforward with colleagues as possible.

But perhaps the more difficult task for physicians is the negotiation that needs to take place with the child, the young person, the parent. Only rarely is confidentiality breached without first informing the patient, child or adult. This can result in outrage, fear or distress, but the possibility of first recognising the nature of the situation and needing to take it seriously and then considering ways forward can be very helpful. Only rarely are children removed from their families, but for a while someone may need to leave the home. Even when a child does need a safe place, a family group conference or mediation involving social services may produce a solution acceptable to all. Work can then proceed with the individuals and the family to restore and rehabilitate the child.

Children in need and children in need of protection mainly grow up in their families. Many of these parents experienced physical, emotional or sexual harm themselves. Confidentiality based on the twin concept of respecting the individuals but being able to recognise and confront what is unacceptable can, in the end, lead to real therapeutic progress and improvement.

References

Brent and NSPCC (1997) *Long-Term Problems...Short-Term Solutions.* London: NSPCC.

Bridge Child Care Consultancy (1995) *Paul – Death through Neglect.* London: Islington ACPC and the Bridge Child Care Consultancy.

Department of Health and Social Services (1991) *Patients' Charter.* London: DHSS.

Department of Health (DoH) (1995) *Child Protection: Medical Responsibilities.* London: HMSO.

Furniss, T. (1991) *The Multi-Professional Handbook of Child Sexual Abuse.* London: Routledge.

Home Office (1991a) *The Children Act 1989.* London: HMSO.

Home Office (1991b) Department of Health, Department of Education and Science and Welsh Office. *Working Together under the Children Act 1989.* London: HMSO.

King, M. (1998) *Moral Dilemmas in Child Welfare.* London: Routledge.

King, M. and Trowell, J. (1992) *Children's Welfare and the Law.* London: Sage.

Medical Defence Union (1996) *Consent to Treatment.* London: Medical Defence Union.

Trowell, J. and Miles, G. (1998) 'Moral dilemmas for psychoanalytic practice for children and families.' In M. King (ed) *Moral Agendas for Child Welfare.* London: Routledge.

United Nations (1989) *UN Convention on the Rights of the Child.* Geneva: UN.

6

Confidentiality in Dual Responsibility Settings

Adarsh Kaul

Psychiatrists, similar to other doctors, have a professional duty of care towards their patients under the civil law which requires them to carry out their duties in accordance with a body of reasonable medical opinion (*Bolam* v. *Friern Hospital Management Committee* [1957]). Confidentiality of patient-related information has always been a very important aspect of this duty of care. Any serious breach of this duty of care can lead to a charge of negligence. In addition, doctors also need to follow specific professional duties as outlined by the General Medical Council (1995) and a failure to do so can lead to disciplinary measures including being barred from practising in the UK.

The primary duty of the psychiatrist has always been considered to be towards his/her patients. While consideration of third party interests such as risk of harm to others by a patient as a result of his/her illness has been one of the criteria for detention in hospital under the 1959 and the 1983 Mental Health Acts, the use of these powers is not mandatory. Apart from the general duties as a citizen, and when a child is considered to be at risk (DoH 1991), psychiatrists have not traditionally considered public protection to be one of their duties. However, during the past decade psychiatrists have increasingly had to become preoccupied with the 'risk agenda'. As a result disclosure, rather than maintaining the confidential nature of patient information, has been seen as good practice in patients who are considered to be at risk of committing serious offences, especially violent offences. This theme has been reinforced by various homicide inquiries (Peay 1996; Ritchie, Dick and Lingham 1994) and government directives and guidelines (DoH 1994a; Home Office, 1995). The conflicting demands of the confidentiality aspect of duty of care, disclosure in public interest and risk of legal and professional sanctions if found negligent in either of the two have left psychiatrists feeling that they are damned if they do and damned if they do not. Such a dilemma is well illustrated by the case of Miss Z.

The case of Miss Z

Dr A was asked to see Miss Z in her capacity as the duty psychiatrist for a court-based diversion scheme in November 1992. Dr A had previous knowledge of Miss Z in that in May 1990 she had been asked, as a senior registrar, to visit Miss Z when she had absconded from hospital, having been admitted the night before in a disturbed state under the influence of large amounts of alcohol. It was at the end of this visit that Miss Z produced a hammer from underneath a coffee table and told Dr A that if she had attempted to persuade her to come back into hospital she would have used the hammer. Miss Z remained under the care of Dr A's consultant colleague and in July 1990 she was admitted to psychiatric hospital where, according to her medical notes, her behaviour was threatening and aggressive. She was transferred to a locked ward where Dr A saw her again in July 1990 in her capacity as the consultant psychiatrist for the unit. During 1990 and 1991 the hospital switchboard received a number of threatening telephone calls by a female caller who did not identify herself and on at least one occasion attempted to obtain Dr A's home telephone number from the switchboard operator on the pretence that she was a friend. Because Miss Z's voice was easily recognisable there was a strong suspicion that this caller was Miss Z. Dr A had also read in Miss Z's medical records that she had been diagnosed by more than one consultant psychiatrist as having a severe personality disorder with alcohol-related problems. There were frequent references to aggressive and threatening behaviour towards staff.

When asked to provide an assessment at the court diversion scheme on Miss Z in November 1992, Dr A declined to interview Miss Z in view of Miss Z's previous behaviour and threats to Dr A. After discussing the allegations against Miss Z with the police sergeant at the magistrates' court, Dr A decided, on the basis of her previous knowledge of Miss Z, her diagnosis of severe personality disorder which had been confirmed by other consultant psychiatrists, her recurrent abuse of alcohol and her well documented history of aggressive behaviour, that there was a significant risk of further aggressive behaviour, particularly if intoxicated.

Dr A had not obtained Miss Z's consent to disclose information to the courts and hence debated whether disclosure of this information to the magistrates' court was in the public interest. Dr A was aware of paragraph 86 of the General Medical Council *Professional Conduct and Discipline: Fitness to Practice* (GMC 1992) which states: 'rarely, cases may arise in which disclosure in the public interest may be justified, for example, a situation in which the failure to disclose appropriate information would expose the patient, or someone else to a risk of death or serious harm'. Dr A had previously received legal opinion on how serious a crime must be for the public interest to prevail and had been advised that one option was to follow Section 116 of the 1984 Police and Criminal Evidence Act which contains the definition of a 'serious arrestable offence'. The offence with which Miss Z was charged was a serious arrestable offence as per these criteria. In view of these considerations Dr A decided that disclosure of information to the magistrates' court regarding Miss Z was in the public interest. Dr A was also concerned that if she did not disclose the history known to her and the defendant had been granted bail and had then attacked a member of the public then she might have found herself facing the charge that she had withheld information which could have prevented the dangerous behaviour.

Dr A's decision to disclose confidential information to the Court regarding Miss Z on the basis of public interest would also have been supported by subsequent guidelines and inquiry reports addressing such issues. For instance Circular 12/1995 on *Mentally Disordered Offenders: Interagency Working* says:

> The full and timely sharing of information (subject to any overriding requirements of confidentiality) by all agencies having contact with Mentally Disordered Offenders – in the Criminal Justice System, in Health Services, in Social Services and in the independent sector – is essential if each agency is to discharge its responsibilities effectively and to take sound decisions where health, liberty and the safety of the public are all at stake. Information about an offender's past and current psychiatric state is necessary to enable the criminal justice agencies and the Courts to take decisions about charging, prosecution, remand and disposal following convictions. (Home Office 1995)

Similarly *Building Bridges* states:

> The use of information is a sensitive issue for mental health services. There have been serious incidents in the past where a failure to pass on information has put a patient, staff or the public at risk. For example, the report of the inquiry into the care and treatment of Christopher Clunis (Ritchie, Dick and Lingham 1994) criticised a number of agencies for failing to pass on information about Mr Clunis' act of violence and stated as a matter of good practice, the sharing of relevant information is vital if multi-disciplinary and interagency care is to function effectively. At the same time, mentally ill people are entitled to the same confidential handling of information about the health or social care as any other patient or client. (DoH 1996 p.19)

It goes on to say:

> There may be particular circumstances in which disclosure of information is required by statute or Court Order or exceptionally, in the absence of consent, can be justified in the public interest (for example, in certain circumstances this may be so if someone has a history of violence).

These recommendations, which may be considered as good practice guidelines, are further backed by legislation in the form of Crime and Disorder Act 1998 (Carol and Ward 1998), Section 115 of which deals with disclosure of information. This section provides a new power, the power that public bodies have to disclose information 'to a relevant authority or to a person acting on behalf of such an authority where disclosure is necessary or expedient for the purposes of any provision of the Act'. 'Relevant authority' is defined by Section 115 in such a way as to authorise disclosure of information to agencies such as police, a district or county council, a probation committee or a health authority. While the power to disclose information is not the same as duty to do so, legal or ethical, it is not difficult to see how this may be interpreted in such a way (Carol and Ward 1998).

In 1993–94 Miss Z complained to the GMC regarding Dr A's conduct in respect to confidentiality. The Preliminary Proceedings Committee (PCC) of the General Medical Council (1994) considered the complaint. The committee were 'not convinced that the need to provide an assessment of a defendant's *current* psychiatric condition necessarily justified disclosure of *previous* psychiatric treatment without consent, details of which were known only by virtue of coincidental contact with the defendant'. They went on to say:

> The committee have determined that it is not necessary on this occasion to refer your case to the Professional Conduct Committee for enquiry into a charge against you. Nevertheless, the information regarding this matter will be retained and might be taken into account if information were to be received of any further behaviour on your part of a similar nature.

In effect Dr A was being issued with the football equivalent of a yellow card. The committee were almost saying that it was permissible in the public interest to disclose the current psychiatric condition, but not the evidence of previous behaviour which had contributed towards the current assessment. This clearly flies in the face of observations of the report of the inquiry into the care and treatment of Christopher Clunis (Ritchie *et al.* 1994), which noted 'important failures' in a number of respects including 'to consider or assess Christopher Clunis' past history of violence and to assess his propensity for violence in the future'. The inquiry noted 'time and again violent incidents were minimised or omitted from records, or referred to in the most general of terms'. It is also difficult to understand as to how the courts can be presented with a diagnosis, for example, of antisocial personality disorder without referring to previous history of antisocial behaviour. The PCC Committee when questioned commented 'disclosure of a patient's medical history may in some cases be necessary and relevant, but doctors must be able to demonstrate that, for example, information they have held for some time gives rise to a risk which had not been apparent earlier'. This view clearly ignores concepts of threshold, the dimensional rather than categorical nature of risk, and that the assessment of the gravity and imminence of risk behaviour may be considered to positively correlate with the number of times similar behaviour has occurred before. Clearly Dr A had exercised her judgement on the issue of confidentiality and disclosure of information in the public interest but her interpretation of these issues seems to have fallen foul of that of the GMC. The legal decision most often quoted to clarify some of these issues of medical confidentiality is that of *W* v. *Egdell and others* [1990].

W v. Egdell

Brief details of this case are as follows: W, who had shot and killed five people and wounded two others, was detained as a patient in a secure hospital without limit of time as a potential threat to public safety. Ten years after he had been detained he applied to a mental health review tribunal to be discharged or to assist in the process of transfer to a regional secure unit. His solicitors instructed Dr Egdell, a consultant psychiatrist, to examine W and report on his mental condition with a view to using the report to support his application to the tribunal. In his report Dr E opposed W's transfer and sent the report to W's solicitors in the belief that it would be placed before the tribunal. The solicitors, in view of the contents of the report, withdrew his application to the tribunal.

When Dr E learnt that the application had been withdrawn and that neither the tribunal nor the hospital where W was being managed had received a copy of his report he contacted the medical director of the hospital. Having discussed the case, the two agreed that the hospital should receive a copy of the report in the interests of W's further treatment. As Dr E had also stressed the importance of sending a copy of his report to the Home Secretary because of its relevance to the exercise of the Home Secretary's discretionary powers to refer W's case to a mental health review tribunal, the hospital forwarded a copy to the Home Office and another copy to the Department of Health and Social Security. The Home Secretary, in turn, forwarded the report to the tribunal when referring W's case to them for consideration as he was required to do every three years. When W discovered that the report had been disclosed he issued writs against Dr E and also against the Secretary of State for Health, the Home Secretary, the hospital board and the mental health tribunal seeking: (a) an injunction to restrain the respective defendants from using or disclosing the report; (b) delivery up of all copies of the report; (c) damages against Dr E, the Home Secretary and the hospital board for breach of the duty of confidence.

The Court held that the duty of confidence owed by a doctor to a patient, detained in a secure hospital in the interests of public safety, who had instructed him to prepare a report for the patient was subordinate to his public duty to disclose the results of his examination to the authorities responsible for the patient if, in his opinion, such disclosure was necessary to ensure that the authorities were fully informed about the patient's condition. Accordingly, the duty of confidence owed by Dr E to W did not bar Dr E from disclosing his report on W's mental condition to the hospital charged with W's clinical care, since it was relevant to his treatment, or to the Home Secretary or the mental health review tribunal, since they needed to be fully informed about W's mental condition when making decisions concerning his future. Hence W's case against Dr E and the other defendants failed and was dismissed. In the Court's view it was clear that Dr E had a duty of confidence towards W. The question was as to the breadth of that duty and did the duty extend so as to bar disclosure. The Court also considered two possibly opposing public interests. First, there was the public interest involved in maintaining confidence of communication between the doctor and a patient. On this issue the Court said: 'In the long run, preservation of confidentiality is the only way of securing public health, otherwise doctors will be discredited as a source of education, for future individual patients "will not come forward if doctors are going to squeal on them". Consequently, confidentiality is vital to secure public as well as private health.' In balancing the public interest involved in maintaining confidentiality and any countervailing public interest which favours disclosure, the Court held that W was 'not an ordinary member of the public' and hence the duty owed by Dr E to W was not his only duty as he also had a duty to the public which required him to place before the proper authorities the results of his examination if, in his opinion, the public interest so required. The Court also considered whether Dr E's opinion was covered by legal professional privilege and formed the view that the 'information acquired from W formed part of the facts on which Dr E's opinion expressed in the report was based. Neither the opinion, nor the facts on which it was based, whether obtained from W or from Dr E's perusal of the records, were, in my judgement, protected by legal professional privilege'.

However, while this judgement is helpful in establishing that confidentiality can be breached in the public interest, the generalisability of this may be questioned on the basis that the Court refers to 'the very special circumstances of this case' and that the Court considered that W was 'not an ordinary member of the public', and that he had been detained in a special hospital under a restriction order having committed very serious offences.

The dilemmas faced by Dr A and Dr Egdell relating to confidentiality, as mentioned above, are frequently encountered by practising psychiatrists in their normal day-to-day work. For instance, an ever-increasing circle of people is now considered to be part of the multidisciplinary team including at times representatives from housing and occasionally the education authority and police. It could be argued that the principle of 'need to know' would suggest that these agencies which contribute towards overall 'care' of a patient need to have relevant information about the patient in order appropriately to carry out their responsibilities towards the patient and others. However, many psychiatrists have struggled as to whether confidential information should be given to those members of the team who do not belong to a profession with a strictly enforced professional code and who may not preserve records under the same circumstances of confidentiality and yet may have a legitimate interest. Moreover, it is often unclear and not in any obvious way determined as to what it is that these other agencies need to know. The need to know must be genuine, not merely curiosity (*Birmingham CC* v. *O* [1983] 1 All ER 497).

The patient's consent to sharing confidential information may have been obtained on the basis that it is in their interest of being able to acquire appropriate housing and attendance at rehabilitative facilities such as further education that such information is shared. Indeed agencies such as housing and colleges of education are now getting into the habit of asking for a 'risk assessment' before considering patients for their facilities and it is often less than clear as to what use they make of this information and indeed whether they always have the ability objectively to consider the information that they are being given. It is not uncommon to see agencies that do not have a history of working closely with mental health professionals getting increasingly anxious about the risk information they are provided with, rather than being contained by the risk management message that is often given as a safeguard against risk behaviours. As a result sharing information may at times go against the interests of the patient in that he/she is disenfranchised from receiving services without any definite public interest being served. Such dilemmas about confidentiality and duty of care towards the patient and responsibilities towards the public are even more pronounced for mental health professionals who work in dual settings, for example, those who in addition to their hospital and community-based practice also work in court diversion schemes and prisons and attend risk conferences and public protection panels.

Court diversion schemes

Court diversion schemes were first introduced towards the late 1980s and they mushroomed following the encouragement and funding that followed in the wake of Home Office Circular 66/90 (Home Office 1990). These court diversion schemes were intended to facilitate psychiatric hospitalisation and/or psychiatric care for mentally disordered offenders appearing before magistrates' courts and to cut down the waiting time for such care to be obtained. Given the name of such schemes and their actual or implied objectives, it is not difficult to see why diversion from custody started to be used as an outcome indicator of these schemes. This was irrespective of the fact that diversion depended upon activities and decisions of other agencies such as the courts for whom mental health needs were only one of the considerations when making such decisions.

Lack of easily accessible resources, and the fact that increasingly diversion schemes are dealing with the personality disordered and/or substance abusers rather than the severely mentally ill, has put additional pressures on such schemes that consider diversion from custody as a positive outcome. These schemes work under immense time pressures which are not particularly conducive to the judgements that need to be made while balancing the issues of confidentiality and public interest. The environment in which these schemes work is one where public interest rather than the offender's needs is the major preoccupation. Referrals are accepted from a variety of agencies such as probation, courts, solicitors, police, etc. which historically have not seriously considered the issue of confidentiality and hence more often than not the offender's consent has not been sought by the referrer. Indeed the courts and some of the other agencies are quite surprised and bewildered that confidentiality is even an issue for those who are before the courts and who have allegedly committed some offence, irrespective of the severity of the offence. Even when consent is sought and given, it is less than clear if the consent given is a fully informed one. The court diversion team is often portrayed as professionals who are there to help the offender. However, there is often a mismatch between the assessors and the assessed as to the 'help' that is being sought or given. The priority of the offender and his/her solicitor is often to get bail or at least not to be remanded in custody. As mentioned above, for the diversion scheme, diversion from custody is seen as a positive outcome. Hence there is almost an unspoken collusion between the offender, his legal representatives and the court diversion team in terms of outcome of such an assessment.

This whole exercise begins to become even more difficult when there is a conflict between what the offender and his/her solicitor is expecting from such an assessment, which is diversion from custody, and the assessment that might indicate that in the interests of public safety the person should not be diverted from custody. In the past probation bail information officers have had significant difficulties with this issue as they had instructions only to provide 'positive information' to the courts, implying that they could withhold information that could lead to a 'negative' outcome such as remand into custody. However, over the past decade with probation moving towards becoming a risk management agency this is no longer an issue for them. Unfortunately this has also meant that there has been a further progressive attrition of consideration of client confidentiality.

Mental health and risk assessments carried out by the court diversion schemes once done cannot be undone and this process carries the burden/responsibility of judgements having to be made as to what one does with the information. Relaying appropriate information to prison medical officers, in the case of those remanded into custody and to GPs for those who are given bail from court may be appropriate on the basis of need to know. Indeed the 'need to know' principle can, according to *W* v. *Egdell*, justify disclosure against the express prohibition of the patient. However, whether such information should be provided to the courts when consent is being denied and in what circumstances this could be done is less than straightforward. The GMC guidelines suggest that such information can be disclosed in the public interest if risk of serious harm is significant. Unfortunately, this task is not so easy when one considers the accuracy, or lack, of risk prediction as well as the lack of definition of 'serious harm' as well as 'significant'. Magistrates and clerks to the court on the other hand expect, and even demand, that they are routinely provided with the assessment of court diversion teams irrespective of the nature and severity of offence or whether consent has been given. However, if such information is not directly and routinely provided by the court diversion teams to the courts then there is a risk to the credibility of these teams as assessments provided to solicitors in general or in specific terms can be used and occasionally abused by the legal profession in the 'interests' of their clients. Moreover there is a reluctance to appear to be 'awkward' in the prevailing climate of inter-agency working and sharing information being seen as good practice.

Psychiatrists in prisons

Psychiatrists usually visit prisons either when instructed by a solicitor or when contracted by the prison directly or indirectly through their employers, to contribute towards the mental healthcare of prisoners.

A solicitor is committed to acting for his client and act on his/her client's instructions. Solicitors feel compelled to act on them even when they may be aware that the instructions which they are being given are not necessarily in the best interests of their client. Often the solicitors' view of what is in the best interests of his or her client may be from the perspective of length of stay in a prison/hospital rather than (a) what disposal might best meet the mental health needs of the client; and (b) that hospitalisation and psychiatric care may prevent further offending and imprisonment. Faced with the dilemma of his or her client receiving a sentence of hospital order with unlimited restrictions as opposed to a determinate sentence, it is not difficult to see how some solicitors might choose the latter when advising their clients. The report prepared by the psychiatrist when working as an agent for the patient's solicitor is the property of the solicitor and his/her client who may decide how to use the report. There is no obligation on the part of the defence solicitor to disclose the report to the court or the Crown Prosecution Service. There may even be a reluctance to share the information with prison healthcare officers due to the fear that the report, or its contents, may become available to the court. The issues here for the psychiatrist are that of duty of confidence vs public interest and *W* v. *Egdell* would suggest that disclosure in the public interest is appropriate. The fact that there is a duty of care towards a patient even when the assessment has been carried out under the instruction of the solicitor for the preparation of a medico/legal report is not in dispute. However it is less than clear as to the length to which the practitioner, in such a situation, should go in order to fulfil his duty of care, especially if it is against the patient's expressed wishes.

Some of the dilemmas faced by a psychiatrist who is contracted to provide sessional work to prisons are not dissimilar to those of the prison doctors. Gunn and Taylor (1993) have described the conflict faced by prison doctors, especially when there is a conflict of interest between the patient's health requirements and that of the institution to maintain good order and discipline. Such visiting professionals can occasionally be asked to advise a prison doctor as to whether the offender is fit for punishment which may be seen as collusion on the part of the doctor. Visiting psychiatrists usually document their notes in the inmate medical record and it is good practice that the prison medical officer with the responsibility of providing care to the patient has access to all information whether the patient consents or not. However, the prison inmate medical record is the property of the prison and hence prison managers such as governors can have access to it and to the information contained within it.

Such dilemmas are well illustrated by an offender/patient of the author who is serving a life sentence for homicide. For a number of years he has had sadistic fantasies and the index offence was as a consequence of him acting on them. In the prison some of the staff have become incorporated in his fantasies of violence. Psychological work that is required necessitates disclosure, assessment and monitoring of these fantasies. However, the prison system feels impelled to take action in response to the presence of these fantasies by putting him in segregation as a protective measure against the prison staff who are subjects of his sadistic fantasies. Hence any psychological work results in a punitive response. This not only further curtails the patient's motivation to work on these issues but also further escalates the dangerous nature of these fantasies as he finds himself in a position where he has no control over his own circumstances and such fantasies are used to obtain a sense of mastery over his environment.

Risk conferences

Risk conferences are multi-agency meetings which are usually arranged at the request of non-health agencies such as probation and are often attended by agencies such as housing and police. Psychiatrists involved with the care and treatment of the person being conferenced are usually invited to these meetings. These meetings are not dissimilar to a care programme approach (CPA) review meeting, but the content is more dominated by 'risk' rather than 'care' issues. With risk to others being very central to the Supervision Register (DoH 1994b) and to the determination of CPA level and response, in theory, there should be no need for these risk conferences. In practice the Supervision Register has failed to deliver its intended objective or is not used and the principal risk management agencies such as police and probation are by and large seldom invited to CPA meetings. This may be a reflection of the resistance, despite increasing pressures, that mental health professionals have to being asked to contribute towards public protection. Such risk conferences are often held when principles of multi-agency working, and protocols set up for the same, are unclear or non-existent and where the knowledge of other agencies as to the workings of the health providers is somewhat inadequate. The principles of duty of care, confidentiality and disclosure on the basis of need to know and public interest are similar to that described earlier. However one is repeatedly struck by the low priority given to confidentiality by non-health agencies.

Even where confidentiality protocols exist, they do so in response to the Data Protection Act (Data Protection Register 1994) and these protocols are at best referred to in passing rather than being used in a meaningful way.

The fact that a patient has offended, whatever the seriousness of the offence, and that someone/anyone considers him or her to be a risk, irrespective of the accuracy of this assessment, seems to be a licence to disclose all information known about a patient. Given the difficulties in determining dangerousness, it is often unclear as to how dangerous the patient must be for public interest to override confidentiality. These difficulties in assessing dangerousness and consequent disclosure become further pronounced when no dangerous act has actually been committed but the patient has a number of dangerous thoughts, beliefs and plans which may be based in fantasy or psychoses. Moreover, there is a risk that patients who by and large freely share dangerous thoughts and fantasies with their doctors would not do so if they felt that this information would not remain confidential. It is not improbable that in the long run if patients do not feel assured of confidentiality they would stop sharing such information with their psychiatrists, with the paradoxical consequence of an increase in risk behaviour rather than a decrease which is being sought by disclosure of risk information. Nevertheless, doctors are seen as being obstructive when any concerns about disclosure are raised. This may be partly because professionals from other agencies, which do not have a professional body such as the GMC and do not have a professional duty of care, are not aware of the legal and professional sanctions that a psychiatrist who cannot justify breach of confidentiality can attract.

Public protection panels

Public protection panels, or other structures with similar remit but different names, are formal multi-agency panels that are increasingly being set up by statutory agencies which have some responsibility for or come into contact with dangerous offenders. These panels were set up partly in response to the frequent findings of homicide and similar inquiries that risk information was being poorly communicated across agencies (Peay 1996). These panels were also supposed to serve the purpose of doing something/anything to manage risky individuals. However it could be argued, with some justification, that these panels came into being as the statutory bodies had to be seen to be providing an appropriate response to the perceived 'problem' of increasing violent crimes. The probation service usually takes a lead in managing these panels which have senior representatives from agencies such as police, social services, prison, housing and psychiatrists/psychologists from the local provider trust serving as core panel members. The individual panels are usually attended by professionals who either have some involvement with or some relevant information about the individual being discussed. A confidentiality 'caution' is invariably given stressing principles such as 'need to know', etc. Consent is seldom obtained based on two assumptions: first, that if a potentially dangerous individual is informed about such a panel being held then the risks are likely to increase; second, if an individual is considered dangerous enough to be referred to the public protection panel then public interest must automatically override confidentiality rights. Unfortunately the second assumption has the risk that in any individual case whether public interest necessarily trumps the individual's right to confidentiality is not rigorously tested; especially so as the gatekeepers to the panels are often agencies that do not necessarily have a tradition of giving confidentiality the degree of primacy that doctors and allied mental health professionals do.

These issues are even more pertinent when a dangerous offence has not actually been committed but the potential of such an offence being committed is considered to be high with the associated problems of prediction of dangerousness mentioned earlier. The proposals being currently considered in the consultation document on dangerous people with severe personality disorder (Home Office and DoH 1999), whereby public protection panels may be the gateway to 'preventative detention', further raises the importance of the relevant issues being scrupulously considered by these panels.

The public protection panels produce a risk management plan and consider registration on a public protection register. Registration can be for periods averaging around three years and there is no appeal mechanism. Indeed if the panel believes that this information may further increase the risk the registered individual may not even be made aware of having been placed on such a register. This is of concern as the benefit of registration is often as unclear as was the case with Supervision Register (DoH 1994b). The risk management plans are high on supervision, monitoring and external controls and low on treatment aimed at the offender developing internal controls. This skew is less so where mental health professionals are actively involved in the management of a potentially dangerous individual. With the police's ability to provide additional targeted surveillance there is a risk that the risk management plan may boil down to 'get the person into custody' plan.

Psychiatrists usually attend public protection panels either (a) as the psychiatrist involved in the management of a particular patient who is considered dangerous; or (b) as an 'expert' core panel member. The psychiatrist attending the panel meeting in his/her role of contributing towards the management of a potentially dangerous patient may find the risk management plan useful as it may open doors to certain resources such as supervised probation hostels, etc. They may also find it useful that the burden of management is not predominantly theirs. Moreover in the event of a mishap they can feel assured that they did everything possible to manage the risks and would be seen as having done so. However, issues that cause conflict are not dissimilar to those that arise in risk conferences as mentioned earlier in the chapter. Unfortunately the psychiatrist cannot, at times, escape feeling that he/she is part of a 'conspiratorial network' of agencies and professionals concerned with protection of the public and preventative detention of the potentially dangerous individual without any particular treatment benefits to the individual.

The psychiatrist who is part of the public protection panel as an 'expert' does not have the duty of care or confidence as he/she may never have seen or assessed the patient whose case is before the panel. However, the burden is no less of finding her/himself as the only person on the panel defending the principles of confidentiality and the potential offender's right to the same, especially if the referral threshold is not high enough or is adjusted downwards for expedience to cover deficits in resources and inadequate inter-agency policies and procedures. Any attempts to advise a higher threshold and to err on the side of not being registered increasingly begin to wilt under the pressure of the mythical assumptions about the benefit of registration that the public, politicians and even other statutory agencies have. Little attention is paid to the almost non-existent benefits of registration, in the absence of a national database, if the registered individual decides to leave the area where he is registered.

Conclusions

Psychiatrists generally, and especially those working in dual responsibility settings, have come under increasing pressure to disclose information about their patients in the interest of public protection. This has come about through recommendations and guidance in homicide inquiry reports and government circulars rather than having a basis in law. Even where case laws exist they are limited in their scope and cannot always be generalised to all situations. Neither the General Medical Council nor the Royal College of Psychiatrists has provided appropriate and specific code of practice in response to the shift in this balance towards disclosure, thus further increasing the prac-titioner's concerns about being sued for negligence and/or disciplinary action by the GMC. Many psychiatrists in the UK see the demand for disclosure of information in those with a potential for violence as the thin end of the wedge. The concern is that for those with a history of contact with mental health services the concept of 'public interest' may progressively get widened to other antisocial behaviours, not necessarily just those involving risk of serious violence. Hence the implications of the implementa-tion of European directive on privacy in UK in October 2000, which will supersede existing case laws and government directives, would be interesting. Mental health laws in other European countries place the emphasis on the protection of the individual patient's rights and the duty of the psychiatrist to the individual (Adshead 1999) and this may influence the balance that the European directive strikes.

References

Adshead, G. (1999) 'Duties of psychiatrists: treat the patient or protect the public?' *Advances in Psychiatric Treatment 5*, 5, 321–328.

Birmingham CC *v.* O [1983] 1 All ER 497,

Bolam *v.* Friern Hospital Management Committee [1957] 1 WLR 582.

Carol, R. and Ward, R. (1998) *Crime and Disorder Act 1998*. Bristol: Jordans Publishing.

Data Protection Register (1994) *Data Protection Act 1984: The Guidelines – 3rd series*. London: Office of the Data Protection Registrar.

Department of Health and Department of Education (1991) *Working Together: Under the Children's Act 1989*. London: HMSO.

Department of Health (DoH) (1994a) *Guidelines on the Discharge of Mentally Disordered People and Their Continuing Care in the Community HSG (94) 27/LASSL (94) 4*. London: DoH.

Department of Health (DoH) (1994b) *Introduction of Supervision Registers for Mentally Ill People from 1 April 1994 HSG (94) 5*. London: DoH.

Department of Health (DoH) (1996) *Building Bridges, A Guide to Arrangements for Inter-Agency Working for the Care and Protection of Severely Mentally Ill People*. London: DoH.

General Medical Council (GMC) (1992) *Professional Conduct and Discipline: Fitness to Practice*. London: GMC.

General Medical Council (1995) *Guidance to Doctors.* London: GMC.

General Medical Council (1994) from a letter from the Preliminary Proceedings Committee to the recipient. (Available on request from the author.) London: GMC.

Gunn, J. and Taylor, P. (1993) *Forensic Psychiatry: Clinical, Legal and Ethical Issues.* London: Butterworth Heinemann, pp.870–871.

Home Office (1990) *Provision for Mentally Disordered Offenders (Home Office Circular 66/90).* London: Home Office.

Home Office (1995) *Mentally Disordered Offenders: Inter-agency Working (Home Office Circular 12/95).* London: Home Office.

Home Office and Department of Health (1999) *Managing Dangerous People with Severe Personality Disorder, Proposals for Policy Development.* London: Home Office and DoH.

Peay, J. (ed) (1996) *Inquiries after Homicide.* London: Duckworth.

Ritchie, J., Dick, D. and Lingham, R. (1994) *The Report of the Inquiry into the Care and Treatment of Christopher Clunis.* London: HMSO.

W v. Egdell [1990] 1 All ER 835.

7

The Misapplication
of 'Reasonable Mindedness'

Is Psychoanalysis Possible with the Present
Reporting Laws in the USA and UK?

Christopher Bollas

Assessing how legislative, regulatory, commercial, and judicial invasions of the confidential relation between a patient and his psychoanalyst have affected the therapeutic efficacy of psychoanalysis requires at least a basic reminder of how the process works. Freud's technique is based on the relation between two essential factors: the patient's free association of ideas and the analyst's 'evenly suspended attentiveness', a frame of mind intended to be free of 'conscious expectation', 'memory', and 'reflection'. 'And by these means' the analyst according to Freud intended 'to catch the drift of the patient's unconscious life with his own unconscious' (p.239).[1]

By creating a form of neutrality, free of pre-judgement or prejudice, the psychoanalyst established a 'blank screen' upon which the patient could speak his ideas, report feelings, collect memories, and become disturbed in his customary form of relating to the other, otherwise known as the transference. This unusual relationship constituted a new type of human space, one in which a person was free to become a patient, revealing his or her inner world in ways never before accomplished.

Both participants came to take part in a process intrinsically free of moral judgement. Indeed disclosure of deeply embarrassing thoughts or behaviours was not met with a censorial attitude by the psychoanalyst, but with a type of respect established through psychoanalytical listening and the work of the patient's further associations. The method recognised the complex unconscious nature of all human conflict and psychology – individual psychology – fashioned a localised privilege; it suspended theological judgement and judicial consequence in the interests of freedom of speech.

---

1   See Sigmund Freud, 'The two encyclopadeia articles' (1923) in *The Standard Edition of the Complete Psychological Works of Sigmund Freud*, vol. 18, pp.235–259.

One need not be a psychoanalyst to know that a 'limited confidentiality' deters some people from seeking help.[2] The closure of treatment centres for sexual deviants is only one example of this obvious effect. For all kinds of violently prone individuals – from husbands who beat their wives or smack their children, to men who stalk women and think of killing them, to young mothers who shake their babies when angered, to women who are planning to kill their violent husbands – who would have sought help from psychotherapy services now often do not do so for the obvious reason that they rightfully fear that disclosure of their situations will not be kept in confidence. They will not be able to think through their conflicts and come to their own decision. In certain countries, the USA for example, where there is widespread interpretive latitude over when the therapist can presume confidence and when he is required by law, by regulatory license requirement, by professional code of ethics, or by fear of civil litigation to breach confidence, there is an epidemic contamination of the presumed state of confidentiality. Indeed the US President, William Clinton, who might have benefited from some form of psychotherapy or family counselling, was wise not to do so as the Independent Prosecutor could have subpoenaed the therapist to appear in court, as he did with the psychologist who treated Monica Lewinsky. Clinton was left to use the only remaining privileges in the USA, attorney–client, clerical and spousal. Meanwhile, Lewinsky's therapy sessions, given to the grand jury and then passed on to Congress, were disseminated over the internet for anyone in the world to read.

One may have to be a psychoanalyst or at least to have had a psychoanalysis to comprehend the more devastating effect of reporting requirements on this truly remarkable human invention. As all of us are criminal in our unconscious life, the unwitting effect of compromised confidentiality is to hinder the psychoanalytical process for both participants. Were it simply a matter of the conscious influence of both participants there would be no problem, as a patient could say to himself that as he was not criminal and had no serious intent to be so, then any potential reporting could be simply put out of mind. That is not, however, how the mind works. The progressive realisation on the part of the clinical population that reporting does take place has been unconsciously perceived as a 'policing of the mind', and this element has become a dynamic factor in the therapeutic process.

Let me give an example which I hope illuminates the difference between the conscious effects of reporting laws and the unconscious effects of mandatory disclosure.

---

2   A questionnaire formed by David Nowell in 1991 was used to assess the range of subjects' willingness to self-disclose information, i.e. whether they had been depressed, taken drugs, had thought of suicide, etc., following receipt of a Psychology Clinic Client Awareness Form. Two groups of undergraduates were given the same form, except in the passage pertaining to confidentiality. One group was given absolute confidentiality; the other group was informed that they could expect confidentiality unless in the opinion of the clinic they were of potential harm to themselves or to others. The results proved that the subjects promised absolute confidentiality were more self-disclosing than the group offered comparatively limited confidentiality. See D.D. Nowell (1991) 'The effects of varying information regarding limits of confidentiality on willingness to self-disclose.' Unpublished master's thesis, University of Alabama, Tuscaloosa, discussed in 'If it's not absolutely confidential, will information be disclosed?' by David Nowell and Jean Spruill in *Ethical Conflicts in Psychology*, Donald N. Bersoff (ed). American Psychological Association (1995) pp.185–188.

A patient is troubled by a weekend visit to a family because one of the children has asked him if all fathers ask to see their children's penis. As he thinks about the respective father he reconstructs certain memories of past visits and wonders if this father's spontaneity is inappropriately impulsive, perhaps a sign of sexual deviance with his children. Yet he knows that if he tells his therapist he may be asked for further details and the therapist may very likely report the matter to the police as he has been informed of possible child molestation. This does not mean that the father in question will be prosecuted. It means that the child concerned may be temporarily removed from the home, given psychological interview and tests, and that the father and other family members may also be interviewed. Whether the patient tells his therapist or not, he is fully conscious of the conflict he faces.

Let us re-imagine this as an unconscious conflict. The patient begins the session drifting in thought and has yet to say anything. He thinks of a book he read the day before, he finds himself musing about something he said on the phone to a friend which seems typical of certain faults of his character, he thinks of the visit on the weekend and the expressions of the child, he thinks of a film he has read about in the newspaper, he thinks about a political party conference and the fate of a particular political party. Some three minutes have passed and he feels he is on the verge of speech, without quite knowing what he will say. He finds himself talking about the book as his ideas spring rather freely from this mental object. Were we to have the kind of access to his inner processes of thought that we shall never have, we might observe a moment's consideration of discussing the uncomfortable visit to the family on the weekend, only to note that the patient discarded it in favour of something freer of mind, less constricting. If so, we might be observing an act of repression, as the patient unconsciously turned from an uncomfortable idea to less conflicted mental contents.

The signs of repression, however, are usually revealed paradoxically enough because the elimination of mental contents leaves traces in the sands of consciousness and often enough in time the analyst will detect this. Unless of course there is equal reason for the psychoanalyst to avoid the issue. I supervised Polish clinicians – inside and outside that country – for some years during the Iron Curtain era and I was able to observe an unwritten agreement between patient and analyst not only not to bring up ideas critical of state power, but more importantly there was an avoidance of expressions of aggression of any kind. This contract was not conscious and it was exceedingly difficult to help these psychotherapists facilitate the flow of ideas that both participants felt endangered them.

Supervising clinicians in many of the United States most of which have adopted mandatory reporting laws for child sexual abuse and intent to commit violent harm against the other, it is not difficult to see how clinicians and patients avoid issues surrounding sexuality and aggression. In some cases this is a conscious aversion, but there is also an unconscious elimination of sexual and aggressive mental contents.[3] The laws,

---

3   T.P.Wise conducted a survey in 1978 following the adoption of the Tarasoff rule. He sent a questionnaire to 1272 psychologists in California and discovered that 16 per cent of the therapists were more reluctant to investigate topics of potential danger. He also found that therapists were

codes, regulatory requirements and commercial pressures to report from patients' sessions have had a chilling effect on those psychotherapists who wish to practise psychoanalytically. In a single week in New York, for example, the front page of *The New York Times* read 'Killer blames his therapist, and jury agrees'. It is an account of how a jury held a psychiatrist liable for the killing spree of a former patient – who killed eight months after he left treatment – which the *Times* argues 'send[s] a destructive message: that the legal system is willing to let people hold someone else accountable for their actions'[4] and adds that 'psychiatrists here [North Carolina] and around the country say the verdict may discourage therapists from treating psychotic patients'.[5] On the previous day, the *Times* followed up on a previous front page story, now bannered 'Jury Finds Psychiatrist Was Negligent in Pedophile Case'. It is the story of a prominent psychoanalyst who did not report his analysand – a psychiatric resident undertaking analytical training – and who then went on to sexually abuse a child. The analyst was sued by the victim of the abuse.

These accounts are not unusual. They are ordinary. And as the *Times* reported, clinicians avoid cases they believe may prove litigiously dangerous – so those specialising in child therapy, in the treatment of psychosis, and in work with the sexually deviant find their work compromised not simply by the possibility of finding themselves in the real world, but more to the point, affected by a mentality that has reconstructed the function of psychotherapy according to the needs of the state.

Indeed, this new mentality – which understands psychotherapy to have two clients, the patient and the state – is proving exceedingly attractive to new generations of psychotherapists who have trained in the last fifteen years. Rather than finding the disclosure of sessional material to the state a breach of confidentiality, these new informants[6] have embraced the spirit of these laws and codes and now see themselves as fulfilling a broader therapeutic task: they are looking after society. Again, examples help to bring the problem down to earth.

At a large conference sponsored by a prestigious university a psychologist in her early thirties presents work with a man who had 'problems controlling his violence'. For some three years a man in the construction industry sought treatment for marital problems, and one day informed his therapist that he had been so angry with his 7-year-old son that he had 'hit him'. How had he hit him, asked the therapist? He had smacked him with the back of his hand on his shoulder. Had this happened before, she asked. Now and then, he said. He had spanked the child a few times. He had a temper, he knew that, and now and then he lost it and he felt badly about it. The therapist made the decision that she was obliged to inform the authorities of possible injury to the child and

lowering the threshold for warning, obviously an expression of their anxiety. For a discussion of this study and others, see 'The impact of *Tarasoff* on clinical practice' by Kathleen M. Quinn in *Ethical Conflicts in Psychology*, Donald N. Bersoff (ed). American Psychological Association (1995) pp.182–184.

4   *New York Times*, 10 October 1998, front page.
5   Ibid. p.12.
6   The effect of the reporting laws in the USA has been to turn psychotherapists into 'new informants'. See *The New Informants Betrayal of Confidentiality in Psychoanalysis and Psychotherapy*, by Christopher Bollas and David Sundelson. London: Karnac (1995).

she informed social services, who in turn informed the police, and that afternoon the child was removed from his school and placed in foster care.

Thus began a very long saga, as the child was removed from the parents for many months, before finally being returned to the family. The patient, interestingly enough, remained in treatment with his psychologist who – now reporting her work after the eighth year of psychotherapy – presented the case as an example of how an intervention of this type was effective. What was noticeable to the visiting supervisor, to whom she was presenting the case in a public forum, however, was how deeply fearful of her was her patient and how he had continued with her because she had installed herself in his mind as a kind of psychic-auditor who praised him for his obedience to her notion of appropriate behaviour and without any hesitation warned him of the consequences of his acting on any of his angry feelings which he continued to disclose to her. She was unaware of the formation of a type of sado-masochistic police–patient therapeutic alliance in which the patient could not remove himself from a type of torment, which was over-determined by the strange form of 'tough love' applied by his psychologist.

This psychologist's case presentation had an immediate and palpable effect. No one in the room knew what to say, except for the visiting supervisor. The group of some eighty people seemed too frightened to speak. This young psychologist was very proud of her local reputation and gave seminars on how to abide by the reporting laws. She was understood to be an expert in dealing with child and domestic abuse. Furthermore, she did comply with the law as it was written. No one was publicly prepared to question her judgement, to ask questions about how she might otherwise have approached the clinical situation, and so forth. Indeed, as these new informants graduate from schools of social work, psychology and psychiatric residency they generate a mentality that instils fear in those clinicians who have grave concerns about the abandonment of confidentiality.

In themselves, however, they are promoting a new kind of psychotherapy, often in the name of psychoanalysis. Many therapists are forming complex transferences of their own to the state, and some patients, rather than finding this intrusive or worrying, actually put this new alliance to cynical use. For example, knowing that a 'memory' of a sexual abuse could lead to charges against a parent, with the psychotherapist testifying in court, more than a few patients have 'discovered' such memories and sought to punish their elders in court.

It might be argued, especially in Europe, that these are extreme cases and further-more this is an American phenomenon. Yet I submit that each time we examine a case of confidence disclosed to the state, we shall not escape the feeling that 'this is an extreme example', or 'no one would ordinarily be put in that position', or 'that can't happen here'. The urgent sense of 'no', this is 'too extreme', even odious, and 'not here', 'not of our way of doing things' is human and understandable. It does register true shock over what indeed is a traumatic situation. But is it shocking because these are extreme cases, or is it shocking because each violation of a patient's right to confidentiality is deeply wrong? If so, arguing that the shock lies in the choice of example or in the country that applies it projects into the other the self's own sense of shock, guilt and responsibility over what it knows to be deeply wrong.

Close on the heels of the 'this is an extreme example' is another frame of mind that 'it is reasonable for psychotherapists to report to the state in highly select and well guarded circumstances'. It is unrealistic, the argument goes, for therapists to expect themselves to enjoy a total privilege, which anyway has never been secured in common law, and which certainly is not to be found in the history of legislation. This argument calls for psychotherapists to be 'reasonable minded', not to be overcome by the few overly dramatic exceptional misapplications of the laws, and to find ways to work with the inevitable social requirement that more effective means are found to place certain people in custodial care. 'Reasonable mindedness' is a very attractive position, which operates best if it can find a middle ground between two nominated extremes. In our discussion, reasonable mindedness would proclaim a middle way between the 'purist position' of no reporting at all – or strict confidentiality – and 'no privilege at all' which would be its opposite. It seems reasonable to propose, then, 'qualified confidentiality' or 'confidentiality within the law'.

But the ideology of reasonable mindedness which might wish to go unexamined by virtue of its attractiveness (the virtue of virtue) must always be examined within its applied context. Between the purist notion that the police should never torture prisoners on remand, accused of terrorist activities, and its opposite that the police should collect information by systematically torturing prisoners, a reasonable minded argument would be that the police should not ordinarily torture prisoners except in very special circumstances. Reasonable mindedness blithely asks that we 'balance the interests' of those concerned, a comforting end-in-itself phrase with which we must all agree. The request that psychotherapists report child molesters and people apparently on the verge of violence against someone else seems reasonable enough. We could also add other very reasonable exceptions to strict confidence in which we 'balance the interests' of all the parties: the patient, the analyst, the process, any outsider who might be harmed, the needs of the state to prevent crime, and so forth. But this attractive frame of mind avoids the fact that it operates under the unstated assumption that psychoanalytic psychotherapy and psychoanalysis need not function.

Something so admirable – the reasonable minded point of view – has itself become an insidious instrument in the corruption of confidentiality. The effect of the call to reasonable mindedness has the effect of automatically casting the concept of strict confidence into the extreme post. To believe in strict confidence is either to seek unrealistic – if not outlandish claims for one's profession – or to be extremist in one's thinking (hardly the place of social comfort for the psychoanalyst). Wittingly or not, the psychoanalyst is encouraged to be reasonable and to adopt such reasonable mindedness into his practice and whenever it seems necessary to indicate so to the patient.

In practice this takes the form of clinicians letting prospective patients know in the initial interview of the existence of reporting requirements, but at the same time assuring the patient that this is a reasonable request which of course would be highly unlikely to affect either of them in their work together.

Sounds reasonable, doesn't it?

That this attractive argument has by sleight of application removed the right of confidentiality might go unnoticed. That is certainly what has happened in many of the states in the USA when this reasonable position was proposed by the authorities. Under the aegis of reasonableness it seems foolish, risky, anti-social, and worst of all supportive of the sexual deviants and violent criminals walking the streets to oppose this 'middle way'; one presumed to provide the service of psychotherapy on the one hand and yet protect the vulnerable from harm. The adoption of this assumption into the analytical relationship – where it operates in the name of reason, considerate thought and social responsibility – introduces 'law abidance' as one of the aims of psychoanalytic work. In the back of their minds each knows that were the patient to disclose a sexually offensive act – and I mean not without irony an act that would make him an offender – or if he tells of another person committing sexually offensive acts that the analyst would then have to consider reporting; but, according to reasonable mindedness this is so highly unlikely that it is put to rest and out of mind.

What is avoided by this new structure is once again the unconscious effects of state presence in the consulting room. A misapplication of the ideology of reasonable mindedness has imposed a type of tyranny upon the unconscious so effectively that the self is disarmed of verbal protest. '"Therapists always have to live with that dual responsibility and so does the law," says Phyllis Coleman, a family law specialist at Nova Southeastern University in Fort Lauderdale' Florida, reports USA TODAY[7] referring to the two responsibilities: the one to the patient, the other to the state. 'It's a delicate balance that can be subject to re-adjustment,' she concludes. Phrasings such as this – 'a delicate balance', or 'subject to re-adjustment' – launder the violent reality of reporting requirements by cleaning it in the prose of reasonable mindedness. This normalisation of the invasive does not remove the remarkably changed reality for the patient and his therapist. For it is not simply as we have stated that the therapist knows now that his other client is the state, so too does the patient. As discussed, even if this fact does not bear upon any of the patient's personal inclinations – sexual, aggressive or otherwise – it is clear that the psychotherapeutic space enjoys no confidentiality at all. This is no longer a relation where one person can assume that what he discusses with his psychotherapist is in confidence. Like it or not, and whether he knows it or not, he is also addressing the state.

Matters would be less complicated if we abandoned pretence to confidentiality. As it does not effectively exist any longer in many Western countries, why fool patients by saying that it does, and that only in very special select circumstances does it cease to exist? I think the answer lies in the fact that psychoanalysts cannot actually bring themselves to acknowledge just what they have conceded to the state. The reasons for this are beyond the scope of this chapter as my brief is to discuss the effect on practice of reporting laws. In this respect, however, the analytical community brings to its consulting room and to its practice a form of denial, both of the deleterious effect of these laws and of their own complicity in abandoning their patients to the state. Much of the professional failure to fight for the necessity of confidentiality falls to the therapeutic communities long-standing lack of a meaningful professional organisation, as the psychotherapy and psychoanalytic organisations are really postgraduate scientific societies that occasionally sponsor conferences and may publish a journal. They have never 'professed' their expertise, and they have failed to establish clear codes of ethics, appeal procedures for complainants, guidelines for finding a colleague guilty of malpractice and so forth. These professional responsibilities have been left to the customary disciplines of origin, to psychiatry, psychology, or social work which are much stronger professions.

How does this affect practice?

As individuals cultured within disciplines of origin – psychiatry, social work, psychology – that have for the most part developed their professions to a higher standard, the comparative neglect of the discipline of contemporary practice – psychotherapy or psychoanalysis – amount to forms of self-diminishment or, as a psychoanalyst might put it, to forms of auto-castration. At the very least, psychoanalysts know they have failed to adequately protect their patients in a basic sense, in that they have failed to construct a profession that among other things would provide professional cover for the patient. This was to be left to others, manifestly to the discipline of origin, but more aptly: left to others.

Leaving the profession to others filters down in the unconscious to an attitude toward psychoanalytic practice itself: leaving the definition of the analytic process to others to define. Wittingly or not, psychoanalysts having failed to profess themselves have more than left the door open for anyone who would assume the authority they have failed to establish. Reading the decisions of certain appellate judges in cases in the USA it is more than ironic to find eloquent arguments on behalf of strict confidentiality alongside undisguised bewilderment over the failure of the psychotherapist to defend his practice more vigorously.

We find then that the effect of the mentality arising out of the new informants is to further disarm the psychoanalyst in his place of practice, which now serves as ironic objective correlative of his failures. It is hardly surprising if in some respects this factor is unwelcome and met with an understandable negative hallucination that would wish to make these factors disappear. If the analyst is already reporting to insurance companies which have long since abandoned the more closely guarded clinical information of twenty years ago, then he is contributing to the corruption of his own standards before the patient's eye. Once again, both participants might seek to assert reasonable mindedness as a cure, but this simply perverts the intent of middle ground thinking, now used as a balm for a progressively degrading destruction of clinical confidentiality. On the visible margins of practice is a problem deriving from its very heart, a problem having to do with a failure of courage in the clinician, failures of vision, failures of professional organisation, and failure to talk frankly with the patient about the imposing dilemma the practice faces. The generative passivity of analytical listening is now attached to the malignant passivity of a profession that will not defend itself.

All these factors considered, is psychoanalysis possible within the present reporting laws in the USA and UK? It is certainly possible in name, but the very reliance of the psychoanalytical process on the potential for unhindered freedom of thought and speech, itself dependent on the patient's understanding that self-expression is strictly confidential, means that the process itself will be affected. Some areas of analytical practice will suffer more than others, clearly in cities where there is a more draconian application of reporting requirements, and in forms of practice – with children, psychotics and deviants – where reporting laws are more operative. Although legislation might seek to restrict the degree of invasiveness and responsible magistrates might cast out inappropriate demands for clinical information, the last ten years reveal a much wider degree of exposure than was likely to have been contemplated in the first place. Civil actions alone against psychotherapists, compelled to disclose sessional material in courts of law, have contributed to the new mentality of disclosure. But in the USA, of equal effect are the state licensing regulations which have widened the obligation to report. It is one thing for a psychoanalyst to consider being held in contempt of court. It is another matter to face the loss of his licence to practise. Although clinicians are not yet licensed in the UK the development of the BCP and the UKCP are almost certainly transitions toward forms of licensing. One day in the not too distant future, the European Union – engaged now in the common standardisation of services and commodities – will no doubt regulate the world of psychotherapy.

I have argued that the call to psychoanalysts to 'balance interests of self and state' and to be 'reasonable minded' is a misapplication of these virtuous concepts, which applied in the context described above serves as a sleight of hand to eliminate psychoanalytic functioning. Along with the psychoanalyst's difficulties in vigorously arguing on behalf of his profession this call to reason is false balm to a troubled soul.

Forms of psychotherapy will be possible within the present reporting laws. And psychoanalytical ideas will certainly be of use in the treatment of individuals. But psychoanalysis itself, as analysts are just now beginning to realise, cannot in time survive state intrusion into the consulting room. I am tempted to say 'this should be obvious' or 'it stands to reason', but I know this is not so obvious and people will oppose it with their own seemingly sound reasons.

There is a profound conflict between the individual's rights to privacy and the public's right to know. We live in an era when human privacy is fast becoming a cultural artefact. If the invasion of human privacy continues at its present pace, the psychoanalyst's anguish will seem quaint at best and delusional at worst.

8

The Myth of Confidentiality

A Social Work View

Jacki Pritchard

Introduction

I wonder how many times an individual social worker has said to a client, 'Anything you say to me is confidential.' But what does it mean exactly – certainly not what it immediately implies – total secrecy. Social workers do share information with a variety of people because they usually work in a multidisciplinary way and in many situations the client probably has no idea about the professional boundaries that may be crossed. Confidentiality has always been a contentious issue and professionals in all fields continue to debate what we mean by the term and how we should practice. In this chapter I want to consider what happens in day-to-day social work practice with adults and to discuss some of the professional dilemmas which face social workers[1] and other staff working in a social services department.

What is meant by confidentiality?

When I trained as a social worker 18 years ago, I can remember a lot of attention being given to the issue of confidentiality and professional boundaries. Certain exercises I participated in remain clear in my mind to this day. At that point in time, I felt confident that I knew what *I* meant about keeping confidentiality. However, once I started practising as a qualified social worker, I began to face numerous dilemmas and to question my own values and beliefs. Every professional will have experienced this. You are faced with new or different situations and sometimes it is very difficult to know what to do because of ethical and moral issues. What has also become clear to me over the years is how other professionals may perceive confidentiality differently. We talk about multidisciplinary working every day of our working lives, but very often we do not understand each

---

1   I intend to use the term social worker throughout the chapter, but the term is meant to include all qualified and unqualified workers who may be undertaking assessments and long-term work with adults. This is because I am aware that so many different job titles exist within social services departments in the UK.

other's roles and value systems. Consequently, our actions, decision-making processes and interventions may differ quite considerably.

In layman's terms, keeping a confidence means 'telling no one' and this may be how the client interprets confidentiality. 'Confidential' is defined in the Oxford English Dictionary as: 'spoken or given in confidence; private; entrusted with secrets; confiding'.

Another definition is found in a social work dictionary:

'Confidentiality: the safeguarding of privacy in relation to information about service users' (Thomas and Pierson 1995, p.87).

The client may assume that whatever s/he tells the social worker will be kept between the two of them. However, a social worker should not guarantee absolute confidentiality, because some information must be shared. It is crucial at the beginning of any involvement with a client that the social worker explains what is meant by confidential in social work terms. The client's understanding of the term confidential may be very different to that of the social worker. Most social workers will assure their managers that they do 'explain about confidentiality' whenever they become involved with a new client, but I question how explicit they are about this. When I have interviewed clients for research purposes (Pritchard 1999) it has been clear that few clients have really understood what may happen to some of the information they have disclosed. Social workers should be upfront and honest about the fact that they cannot keep information to themselves. Each worker is accountable to a manager and to the department as a whole. Therefore, they do not have the same role as a priest, that is the social work interview is not a 'confessional'. The client must be made aware that the worker discusses cases with the line manager and that records are kept. The reality is that the line manager may decide that the information acquired should be shared further either within the agency or outside, a point which will be discussed in greater detail later.

When thinking about the implications of sharing information, it makes one realise that confidentiality does not really exist. We all fall into patterns of behaviour which we then take for granted and probably do not question what we are doing. For example, social workers will talk about valuing support from their team members. They talk about their clients and cases to their colleagues – so is this breaking confidentiality? How would the client feel if s/he knew that complete strangers were party to this personal information. The social worker needs to consider how wide are the boundaries – the manager, the team, other sections within the department (e.g. staff in home care, day care/residential settings, finance), or other departments within the local authority? There are other forums where information is exchanged and yet again thought needs to be given to whether the client really understands what happens to information which is supplied freely. For example, does a client with a mental health problem know who is part of a community mental health team? Members of that team (which could include social workers, community psychiatric nurses, outreach workers) may sit in meetings sharing information. Similarly, a multidisciplinary team (including nurses, physiotherapists, speech therapists, dieticians) may meet on a hospital ward when the consultant does his ward round. Does the patient know that these meetings take place? Finally, in a residential unit does a resident know that information is shared in team meetings, handovers and written in logbooks?

As a trainer I spend a lot of time talking about confidentiality and getting workers to participate in exercises in order to find out how they put the theory into practice. When asked to write a definition of confidentiality, most workers find the task extremely difficult. They say they know what they mean in their heads, but find it hard to express in written form. So how do they explain confidentiality to clients? It becomes evident that practices can vary greatly; some workers readily share information, others do not. It is not always clear whether workers regularly get consent from the client about sharing information or contacting other people to obtain information. There seems to be inconsistency in practices and this is something which should be addressed by first line managers as well as at senior management level.

There are also distinct differences between social workers working in the children and families sector and those working in the adult sector. This is because the former group are working within a statutory framework, that is under the Children Act 1989, which states clearly that if a child is thought to be at risk of harm then information must be shared in a multidisciplinary way. This is not the case when working with adults. The law assumes that an adult can make an informed decision and consequently does not need the same protection as a child. Of course we know that the reality is often different. There are adults who have certain disabilities or medical conditions which can affect their mental capacity and therefore may put them at risk of harm. In some of these situations, if information is not shared then the degree of risk can be increased. And who will be blamed if something goes wrong? The social worker.

Need for policy and guidance

Social services departments need to have clear guidance about what they do with information and how to act upon information given. There is guidance regarding written records which are kept. There are specific rights of access to personal information:

1. Computer held records – the Data Protection Act 1984. Access can be restricted if it would result in physical or mental harm befalling either the person or anybody else.

2. Manually held records – access is governed by the Access to Personal Files Act 1987 and Access to Personal Files (Social Services) Regulations 1989 (Mandelstam 1998, p.120).

However, the problems regarding the sharing of information go much wider than who has access to written information. Attention must be given to verbal information which is given freely by the client. We are living in dangerous and scary times, when every worker has 'to cover his/her own back' in case something does go wrong. This has never been more so than now when litigation in the UK is on the increase (Carson 1996). Workers need to be supported by their departments and this has to be done by clear policies and specific guidance. Of course we have broad terms of reference: for example, the NHS and Community Care Act 1990 states that we have 'the duty of care'; but workers need the details spelt out. When should we break confidentiality? It would be helpful if the whole issue of confidentiality and the dilemmas it presents were debated more publicly by organisations such as the Association of Directors of Social Services (ADSS), British Association of Social Work (BASW), Social Services Inspectorate (SSI). A code of practice needs to be provided so that local guidance and policies can be developed by local authorities and other agencies.

Confidentiality may be referred to briefly in other policy documents, e.g. whistle-blowing, adult abuse, risk assessment and risk management. But often workers are not clear about how to assess the risk factors, predict the likelihood of harm, and when to break confidentiality. Other professionals do have access to some specific guidance, for example:

> A solicitor is under a duty to keep confidential to his or her firm the affairs of clients and to ensure that the staff do the same ... the duty to keep a client's confidences can be overridden in certain exceptional circumstances. (Law Society 1993, British Medical Association/Law Society, p.5)

> Doctors are bound by a professional duty to maintain confidentiality of personal health information unless the patient gives valid consent to disclosure or, if the patient is incapable of giving consent, the doctor believes disclosure to be in that person's best interests. (British Medical Association/Law Society 1995, p.6)

So what should happen? Social workers in the adult sector are working under various legislation whether it is to do with mental health, disability or community care. The thrust behind the ways of working is to encourage the multidisciplinary approach. Consequently, the social worker is going to have to share information with other professionals and perhaps workers in the private or voluntary sectors. Information will be shared in the best interest of the client, but sometimes it is not clear exactly what or how much to share. Crucial questions which need to be asked by every worker are:

- What is relevant?
- Who needs to know?

The NHS and Community Care Act 1990 'imposes on local authorities a statutory requirement to co-ordinate arrangements for assessing community care needs on an inter-agency basis' (DoH 1991, p.19). The Department of Health recommended that local authorities, health authorities/boards and other care agencies should adopt common principles for the sharing of information. The principles of confidentiality were stated as:

- information should be used only for the purposes for which it was given;
- information about a user/patient should normally be shared only with the consent of that person;
- information should be shared on a 'need to know' basis;
- users and carers should be advised why and with whom information concerning them has been shared;
- all confidential information should be rigorously safeguarded (DoH 1991, p.34).

Setting up the structures to promote good practice is very necessary but, as was stated above, clearer guidance is needed for the individual worker. The dilemmas about confidentiality occur when the assessment is taking place and future support and care is being planned. Crucial to the assessment of need is the implicit assessment of risk. When undertaking a risk assessment it may be necessary to gather information from other professionals and individuals involved with the client – family members, neighbours, volunteers, advocates. If the client is mentally sound and does not agree to the social worker contacting other people, then a decision has to be made about whether it is in the client's best interest to proceed. Where the client cannot make an informed decision, it is critical that information is gathered to assess the client's capabilities. The risk assessment and risk management processes have been well documented elsewhere (Kemshall and Pritchard 1996, 1997) and need not be repeated here, but the social worker does have to identify risks to be taken, predict the worst possible outcomes and the likelihood of those occurring. In order to do this thoroughly, detailed information must be collected.

Sometimes the worker will struggle with the decision to break confidentiality, not only because of wanting to promote self-determination but also to maintain a trusting relationship with the client. If the social worker is struggling with such a dilemma, then s/he must use the line manager to discuss what should happen. No worker should ever operate in isolation when difficult decisions have to be made. All decision making should be shared. Confidentiality may have to be broken when it is thought that the client, workers or other people may be at risk of harm. The dilemma is often about the fact that a perfectly mentally sound person does not want anyone else to know what has happened or is happening to them. The principle of self-determination is of paramount importance, but the social worker may have to consider several questions:

- Has a crime been committed?
- Is a crime likely to occur in the future?
- Is the client at risk of harm?
- Could other people be at risk of harm?

The following case studies illustrate some common examples of dilemmas faced by social workers.

Case study 1

Miss B is 70 years old and lives with her brother, who has an alcohol problem. Mr B becomes very violent when he is drunk and frequently physically abuses his sister. The injuries are often extensive, but Miss B always refuses to go to hospital or see her GP. She talks openly to her social worker about what her brother does to her but refuses to make a statement to the police and says that if the worker informs the police she will deny everything.

The social worker knows that the frequency of the attacks is increasing and is concerned for Miss B's safety. The dilemma for the social worker is that if she informs the police Miss B may not allow her access in the future, so there would be no one to monitor the situation. It is necessary for the social worker to discuss the situation with her line manager, who must decide whether to implement the vulnerable adults procedure and carry out a formal investigation (with or without the police).

Case study 2

Anthea, who is 45 years old, was in a car crash several years ago and is severely physically disabled. She currently lives alone and manages well with the support of home care staff. Anthea has told her social worker that her brother, Stuart, is soon to be released from prison and will be coming to live with her. He has served a prison sentence for raping and stabbing a young woman. Anthea asks the social worker not to tell anyone else about her brother's past.

In this situation, the social worker cannot keep this information to herself, because other workers are going into the house and could be at risk of violence from Stuart. The prison service will have assessed Stuart and the likelihood of his re-offending. The social worker will want to obtain more information from the prison service and probation service and then a risk planning meeting will be convened. In this case, confidentiality has to be broken because other people may be at risk of violence. The concept of dangerousness has received much attention, especially from practitioners dealing with offenders (Brooks 1984; Butler Committee 1975; Monahan 1981; Scott 1977; Walker 1996). However, it is also an important concept for those working in the social and healthcare fields.

Consideration has to be given to whether someone is dangerous and whether the general public is at risk. In recent years there has been much more emphasis on *public protection* and both social workers and their managers have to take this into their assessment when considering whether to break confidentiality.

Sometimes the situation is not so straightforward, because the social worker is working with both client and family members who may have different wishes and viewpoints as illustrated in Case Study 3.

Case study 3

Mrs H has been confused for about two years, but so far has remained living in her own home with an intensive care package. Home care staff visit her twice a day (morning and evenings) in the week and three times a day at the weekends (additional lunchtime call). She attends an elderly mentally ill (EMI) day centre five days a week and also has regular respite care. It is acknowledged that Mrs H has never got on with her only daughter, Beryl, who only visits every couple of months or so. Mrs H has deteriorated over the winter months and has started leaving on the gas cooker and fire overnight, which she has not previously done. The social worker has become more concerned about the possible dangers (fire, gas explosion), but wishes to respect Mrs H's wish to remain in her own home. Beryl is insisting that her mother should go into residential care. Mrs H is adamant that Beryl should not attend the risk planning meeting.

The main consideration for the social worker is whether Mrs H can make an informed decision. Mrs H is confused but she often has very lucid moments and can make her wishes known. Friends and neighbours know that Mrs H has never wanted to go into a home and does not want her daughter involved in her life.

In some cases workers disagree about what should happen because they have different values and attitudes themselves.

Case study 4

Mrs Edwards is a 65-year-old Afro-Caribbean woman, who attends a day centre in order to give her husband, the main carer, a break. Mrs Edwards has been upset at the day centre when one of the male staff touched her breasts. She lodged a formal complaint and an investigation is underway. She does not want her husband to know what has happened. The manager of the day centre thinks that Mr Edwards should know what has happened to his wife and wants to inform him herself.

Mrs Edwards's social worker and the day centre manager disagree about breaking confidentiality. The social worker argues that it is Mrs Edwards's right to decide whether she tells her husband, whereas the day centre manager believes that, as the husband and main carer, Mr Edwards has the right to know everything about his wife.

Dilemmas regarding family members' 'rights' are common. Family members often think they have the right to information which they do not.

Case study 5

David is 28 years old and has a learning disability. He lives in supported accommodation, can function very well and staff believe he can make informed decisions. David was hit by another service user, which resulted in cuts on his face and a black eye. David refuses to see his mother when she visits, because he knows 'she'll make a fuss'. However, she barges past staff and goes into David's room. He refuses to tell her what has happened, so she demands to know from staff.

The staff supported David in his decision not to tell his mother what had happened to him.

Good practice

David Carson states:

> It is essential to appreciate that the law, at best, provides checklists, procedures and frameworks. It provides a foundation for professionals to work within and to utilize to justify their risks; it rarely provides direct answers. If practitioners want to avoid the risk of liability then they need to organize the law's concepts and procedures to their own ends, and before the harm occurs. (Carson 1996, p.5)

In September 1998 the Crime and Disorder Act was introduced. Section 115 of the Act introduces the 'sharing information principle' which may be helpful to workers when they are struggling with issues around confidentiality:

> [The Section] offers a good deal of support to practice of limited and responsible sharing of information in the joint agency process of detecting and preventing offences to victims, adults in particular ... *anyone* has the power to disclose information to any of the following:

- the police
- the probation service
- a local authority
- a health authority. (Leslie 1998, pp.7–8)

Key issues

1. Who does the social worker share information with?

2. What do they share? How much of the personal information?

3. Concept of the 'need to know' basis.

4. What does multidisciplinary mean? Which professionals?

5. Who has access to records (e.g. team clerk)?

6. Assessing risk properly.

References

British Medical Association/The Law Society (1995) *Assessment of Mental Capacity: Guidance for Doctors and Lawyers.* London: BMA/The Law Society.

Brooks, A.D. (1984) 'Defining the dangerousness of the mentally ill: involuntary commitment.' In M. Craft and A. Craft (eds) *Mentally Abnormal Offenders.* London: Ballière Tindall.

Butler Committee (1975) Home Office and Department of Health and Social Security. *Report of the Committee on Mentally Disordered Offenders.* London: HMSO. Cmnd. 6244.

Carson, D. (1996) 'Risking legal repercussions.' In H. Kemshall and J. Pritchard (eds) *Good Practice in Risk Assessment and Risk Management 1.* London: Jessica Kingsley Publishers.

Department of Health, Social Services Inspectorate (1991) *Care Management and Assessment: Practitioners' Guide.* London: The Stationery Office.

Kemshall, H. and Pritchard, J. (eds) (1996) *Good Practice in Risk Assessment and Risk Management 1.* London: Jessica Kingsley Publishers.

Kemshall, H. and Pritchard, J. (eds) (1997) *Good Practice in Risk Assessment 2.* London: Jessica Kingsley Publishers.

Law Society (1993) *The Guide to the Professional Conduct of Solicitors,* 6th edn. London: Law Society.

Leslie, S. (1998) 'Information sharing between agencies; new legal developments and their impact on protecting vulnerable adults.' *PAVA Newsletter 3,* 7–8.

Mandelstam, M. (1998) *An A–Z of Community Care Law.* London: Jessica Kingsley Publishers.

Monahan, J. (1981) *The Clinical Prediction of Violence.* Beverley Hills: Sage.

Pritchard, J. (1999) 'Good practice victim's perspectives.' In J. Pritchard (ed) *Elder Abuse Work: Best Practice in Britain and Canada.* London: Jessica Kingsley Publishers.

Scott, P. (1977) 'Assessing dangerousness in criminals.' *British Journal of Psychiatry 131,* 127–142.

Thomas, M. and Pierson, J. (1995) *Dictionary of Social Work.* London: Collins.

Walker, N. (ed) (1996) *Dangerous People.* London: Blackstone Press.

9

The Limits of Confidentiality in Healthcare

Paul Cain

The issue of confidentiality is recognised as being of great importance in professional work, and has been extensively addressed in the literature.

In particular, the question of when breaches of confidentiality are justified, i.e. the question of what, morally, is the point at which confidentiality may justifiably be broken, has been widely discussed. However, little attention has been given to the question, what is the point at which confidentiality has, as a matter of fact, been broken? At issue here is the conceptual scope of the obligation of confidentiality. This is the issue addressed in this chapter.

The importance of this question of scope is evident, for any discussion of whether confidentiality should be broken, that is, whether a breach is justifiable, presupposes a view of when it has been broken. The difficulty of the question is perhaps less evident for in some contexts, such as the priestly confessional, the counselling relationship or the sharing of a confidence with a friend, a breach of confidentiality can be said to consist simply in the disclosure of confidential information to a third party. However, in the context of healthcare this straightforward notion of a breach may not apply, for healthcare is typically delivered through teams. It may take place in large institutions such as psychiatric hospitals, in small centres such as a doctor's surgery, or in family homes in the community – in all of which settings more than one individual is involved. Also it is delivered to patients or clients in varying states and conditions (the potential relevance of this for confidentiality is clarified below). Hence, as I shall argue, the question of what are the limits of confidentiality in healthcare does not admit of a simple answer.

What I wish to establish, therefore, is a criterion, or criteria, for the concept of 'breaking confidentiality'. A first step must be to clarify what counts as confidential information and how the obligation of confidentiality arises.

Confidential information and the obligation to keep confidences

To label information as confidential is to designate it as information that ought not to be disclosed. To be under an obligation of confidentiality is to be obliged to keep information to oneself. (This is, incidentally, reflected in the French term for confidentiality, 'le secret professionel'.)What information, in relations between healthcare professionals and their patients or clients, should be confidential, and how is the obligation of confidentiality set up?

As regards the first question, what information should be confidential, there is scope for debate. On one view, not all information about patients or clients is confidential. This is implicit in Clause 10 of the United Kingdom Central Council for Nursing, Midwives and Health Visitors' *Code of Professional Conduct* (UKCC 1992) which, in stating that every nurse shall 'protect all confidential information concerning patients and clients', clearly implies that some information is not confidential.

The view that not all information is confidential is reiterated in the UKCC *Guidelines for Professional Practice* (1996). This singles out 'private and personal information' as what should be confidential ('to trust another person with private and personal information about yourself is a significant matter'), thereby excluding information about a client that is in some sense already in the public domain, or could be said not to be personal. (This view may be implied also in the General Medical Council's booklet Confidentiality: Protecting and Providing Information (2000) which singles out information 'which is private and sensitive' (p.2)). There is authoritative backing, therefore, for the view that not all information about patients or clients is confidential.

On another view, any information whatsoever about patients and clients should be confidential. An earlier document issued by the UKCC in 1987, their advisory paper on confidentiality, reflects this view in a certain ambiguity. Here, although reference is made to 'private and personal information', it is also made, simply, to information 'obtained in the course of professional practice', and to information that has been 'obtained inadvertently' where it is clear from the context that such information is viewed as confidential. This alternative view is apparently envisaged also by the College of Nurses of Ontario: its *Guidelines for Professional Behaviour* (1995) single out as confidential 'all information relating to the physical, psychological and social health of clients', but add that 'any information collected during the course of providing nursing services is confidential'.

Which of these two views should be favoured? In support of the first view it can be argued that part of the point of confidentiality is to protect a client's privacy, that respect for privacy is one underlying principle and that, therefore, it makes sense to single out personal and private information as confidential. This, though, has to contend with the fact that, in practice, it may be difficult to identify what, for any given client, is private and personal. People's conceptions of privacy vary. (This has been highlighted for me in a discussion with nurses where the colour of a person's carpet was picked out as a clear example of what was not private, but where it emerged that some would deeply resent such information being disclosed: for them it was 'private and personal' and should therefore be confidential.)

This view, therefore, leaves the healthcare worker free to share with others the whole range of information about a client that he or she judges to fall outside the category of private and personal; but this is a freedom to get it wrong. Surely this means that a rule of practice that all information about clients is confidential should be favoured: only so can respect for privacy be ensured.

There is room for debate also with regard to the second question: How is the obligation of confidentiality set up? Gillon (1986) says that one of the conditions necessary 'to create a moral duty of confidentiality' is that a person must 'undertake – that is, explicitly or implicitly promise – not to disclose another's secrets'. The GMC appears to reflect this view, in emphasising the importance of giving 'assurances about confidentiality', without which 'patients may be reluctant to give doctors the information they need in order to provide good care'. (The plural 'assurances' suggests an explicit undertaking, contrasted with such implicit 'assurance' as might derive simply from how the profession is viewed.) Likewise, the UKCC *Guidelines* (1996, p.26) assert that the standards of confidentiality should be made known by the health professional 'at the first point of contact'.

This undertaking is the basis for an act of trust: information is imparted 'in confidence'. Joseph and Onek (1991) say that confidentiality 'can be defined as entrusting information to another with the expectation that it will be kept private'. The element of actively entrusting information is implicit in the UKCC claim already cited: 'to trust another person with private and personal information'.

This account of confidentiality is, clearly, applicable in many practice contexts (for example, in the private consultation in a general practitioner's surgery); but it is not at all clear how it can accommodate the full range of contexts and situations that arise in healthcare.

For example, in carrying out home visits, doctors, nurses and health visitors may acquire much information not specifically entrusted to them. They may simply notice things and, further, when meeting a client in such contexts it may not be natural, easy, or indeed typical, to give a clear undertaking regarding confidentiality. Nevertheless, in such contexts arguably there is an obligation of confidentiality that, no doubt, these professionals would acknowledge. Again, in work with clients who are unconscious, severely demented, or who have severe learning disabilities, there is no intentional disclosure; information is not entrusted and no undertaking is given not to disclose information about the client. How could there be where communication is impossible? Yet here too there is an obligation of confidentiality.

An alternative view is therefore needed of how the obligation of confidentiality is set up that can take account of these aspects of professional practice. This alternative view could be that it is set up simply in virtue of the professional role. The UKCC *Guidelines* hint at such a view in noting that, with regard to confidential information, 'you could ... discover the information in the course of your work', and the GMC may imply such a view in referring, simply, to 'information about people which doctors learn in a professional capacity'.

This view could find support in Bayles' argument (1989) that since clients are dependent on the professionals to whom they go for help, the latter must be trustworthy; that this involves the possession of certain virtues; that one of these virtues is discretion;

and that one way of being discreet is to keep confidences. The obligation of confidentiality is thus firmly rooted in the professional role.

Such a view can clearly accommodate that range of contexts in which there is no disclosure of information, no request that information be kept secret, and no explicit promise of non-disclosure on the part of the professional, where nevertheless there is an acknowledged duty of confidentiality. Interestingly, the divergence between the two views as to how to account for the obligation of confidentiality is not great. This can be seen in the light of two arguments.

The first is this. Clients typically have to trust professionals (being, as Bayles points out, in a dependent relationship). In the case of healthcare, they have to entrust themselves to professionals. To entrust oneself is more fundamental than, and therefore embraces, entrusting items of information about oneself. Hence, although in the alternative version considered no particular items of information are specifically entrusted as confidences, the element of trust, extending to trust that information conveyed will be kept safe, is intrinsic to the relationship.

Second, it may be recalled that Gillon (1986) makes reference to *implicit* promising. Although an explicit, verbal undertaking is present in what might be called the paradigm case of promising, there are situations in which one can coherently speak of an implicit promise. Implicit promising may be grounded in the relationship between the persons involved, which justifies a person's expectation and assumption that information will be kept safe. In the professional–client relationship, such expectations and assumptions are grounded in the client's belief that the professional is trustworthy, and in their own need to trust. Hence it can be claimed that in the professional role there is at least an implicit promise of confidentiality. This view is, indeed, enshrined in the College of Nurses of Ontario's *Guidelines* (1995), which lay down that 'nurses make an implicit promise to maintain confidentiality'.

As a necessary preface to discussion of the limits of confidentiality, the discussion so far has focused on two questions: What information is confidential? What sets up the obligation of confidentiality? I have argued that all information acquired about patients and clients should be regarded as confidential, and that the obligation of confidentiality – an obligation not to disclose information – is set up by virtue of the professional role. This suggests that the limits of confidentiality are reached when such information is disclosed to a third party. This conclusion, however, invites exploration and requires, as will be argued, much qualification.

The limits of confidentiality

The UKCC advisory paper (1987) seems to allow that any disclosure of information, even among health professionals, constitutes a breach. Section D, entitled 'Deliberate breach of confidentiality in the public interest or that of the individual patient/client' refers to sharing information 'with other professionals in the health and social work fields' (Section D, para.3), and the context indicates that this sharing is seen as a breach. Acceptance of this would mean that, in practice, confidentiality is impossible, for healthcare is typically delivered through teams, and information relating to clients' health is routinely, and of necessity, shared within teams. Confidentiality as a practical possibility has to accommodate the notion of shared secrets.

This can be done if it is stipulated that such disclosure must be sanctioned by the client. Respect for confidences is grounded, in part, in respect for autonomy. Indeed, Bok (1986) claims this to be the prime underlying principle: 'the first and fundamental premise is that of individual autonomy over personal information'. Hence, where the client has autonomously consented to the sharing of information there cannot be a failure to keep a confidence: by giving his or her permission, the client has extended the boundary to include those persons with whom information is shared. If there is informed consent, there can, logically, be no breach.

The importance of a client's consent is acknowledged in the authoritative sources to which reference has been made. The GMC (2000) states that 'seeking patients' consent to disclosure is part of good communication between doctors and patients, and is an essential part of respect for patients' autonomy and privacy' (p.8) and lays down that 'If you are asked to provide information about patients you should...seek patients' consent to disclosure of information wherever possible' (p.4). UKCC echoes this in referring to the patient's or client's right to believe that information 'will not be released to others without their permission', and lays down that practitioners 'always need to obtain the explicit consent of a patient or client' before disclosing information.

There is, however, an ambivalence in both documents. The UKCC notes that 'it is impractical to obtain the consent of the patient or client every time you need to share information with other health professionals'. The GMC likewise says that 'where patients have consented to treatment, express consent is not usually needed before relevant personal information is shared to enable the treatment to be provided'. If, as has been argued, the limits of confidentiality are set by consent, these concessions – surely realistic – appear to entail the unpalatable conclusion that healthcare practice displays an intrinsic lack of respect for confidences. This conclusion can, however, be avoided if it is accepted that consent can be implicit, and that it is reasonable to assume such implicit consent where treatment clearly involves more than one professional.

Explicit (or implicit) autonomous consent thus marks the limit of confidentiality, so that to act without the patient's consent is to go beyond the limit, to break confidentiality.

What account can be given, though, of situations where consent of either kind is lacking; where, for example, the patient is dementing or psychotic. I will explore this by reviewing various possibilities in turn.

(i) The limit of confidentiality is set by what the client would have wished

What the client would have wished must, clearly, be central to an account of the limit of confidentiality in such cases. This is because of the principle of respect and the obligation to be trustworthy. However, since healthcare staff do not, generally speaking, have an intimate knowledge of their clients, such that they can confidently judge what the client would have wished, for this criterion to be applicable to practice an account is needed of what it would be reasonable to suppose the client would have wished the limit of confidentiality to be, had he or she been in a position to make their wishes known. In other words, 'what the client would have wished' has to be given content.

(ii) The limit of confidentiality is set by reference to who has a need to know

This is initially attractive, as it allows within the boundary those in the healthcare team who may share the task of caring for the client. It is, however, too permissive, as the following example illustrates.

A client confided in the nurse that he was having unprotected sex with his partner. The nurse knew that he was HIV positive. She was aware, therefore, of a dilemma: not to tell the partner would protect confidentiality – and yet this would also risk harm. In this case, the fact that the situation was felt as a dilemma indicates that telling the partner was perceived as a breach of confidentiality – and yet, undoubtedly, the partner had a need to know. This case suggests that (ii) should be replaced by (iii).

(iii) The limit of confidentiality is set by those who have a right to know

However, this is also unsatisfactory, since the fact that her partner was HIV is clearly information to which she had a right. She had a right to know, but the nurse, at least in respect of the principle of confidentiality, judged that she did not have a right to tell. (She might justifiably have told: but in that case, there would have been a breach of confidentiality.) We therefore need to revise (ii) and (iii) to read as (iv).

(iv) The limit of confidentiality is set by reference to those whose need and right to know relate to the healthcare needs of the client

This builds in a necessary restriction, and also clarifies the position of the healthcare team: their right to know derives from their need to know – which in turn derives from the obligation to meet the needs of the client. It also points to a distinction between two kinds of information that may be disclosed, namely, a distinction between what is and what is not relevant to the client's healthcare needs. Only the former, on this criterion, may be passed on to other members of the healthcare team, without a breach of confidentiality.

This last account does, surely, provide a satisfactory way of marking the limit of confidentiality, and so of marking the boundary beyond which we should talk of breaking confidentiality. This is because the only reason that healthcare workers, in their professional role, acquire information about people, is because these people are their clients, who have particular health needs. Given the importance of respect and trust, such information can, therefore, be shared without breach of confidentiality only with those involved in their care.

It is relevant to emphasise that the limit identified in (iv) is proposed as a clarification of (i): it is proposed as a reasoned account of what a client 'would have wished' the limits of confidentiality to be, had his or her wishes been communicated. It may be, however, that the limit identified in (iv) does not apply in all cases – and the following situation may be an example.

A nurse on a psychiatric ward learnt, in the course of conversation with a new admission, that he was a keen golfer. She told a patient in a nearby bed (also a keen golfer), with a view to promoting a welcoming atmosphere. While on the one hand this appears to fall outside the limit identified in (iv) – since patients on a ward are not among those 'whose need and right to know relate to the healthcare needs of the client' – the intuition that this was not a breach of confidentiality is supported by the fact that the overriding criterion is criterion (i), 'what the client would have wished', for it is reasonable to suppose that the nurse's action was in line with what her patient would have wanted her to do. (Golfers have much in common!)

The limits of confidentiality and anonymity

What has not yet been clarified is whether a breach of confidentiality has occurred if a client's case is referred to anonymously. This may occur in a number of ways: nurses on one ward may discuss a case with colleagues on another ward who are not involved in the case; a nurse may discuss a client with her partner, perhaps out of a need to unburden herself; a case may be written up in a medical or nursing journal; a case may be discussed by students, as part of their training. Should this occur, as it most typically may, without the client's consent, or in violation of the limit identified in (iv), the argument so far would place it outside the limit of confidentiality, i.e. there would be a breach.

In discussing this, it is useful to distinguish three cases: one where, anonymity notwithstanding, the client is identified by a third party as the subject of the information; one where the client is identifiable, but is not, as it turns out, identified; and one in which the client cannot be identified.

In the first case, there is unquestionably a breach: sharing of information, although anonymous, was without consent and the client was identified, so both respect for autonomy and respect for privacy were violated.

The second case – the client is identifiable, but is not identified – may also be regarded as a breach, though on somewhat different grounds. Bok (1986) says, correctly I believe, that 'confidentiality refers to the boundaries surrounding shared secrets and to the process of guarding these boundaries', and in this case there has been a failure to maintain intact the protective boundary. The image of a city wall with a gaping hole in it – the wall has been breached – comes to mind.

It may be felt that, in the third case, where there is anonymity and the client cannot be identified, no breach has occurred; but how to give a reasoned account for this view? It could be argued that an account emerges from reflection on the implications of criterion (i), which, as I have made clear, is more fundamental than (iv), since (iv) is simply an attempt to give content to (i). Criterion (i) lays down that 'the limit of confidentiality is set by what the client would have wished', and the question could be put, why would clients wish that their case should not be discussed anonymously if they cannot be identified?

Underlying this question is the assumption that the point of confidentiality is to protect privacy, to erect a barrier against possible embarrassment. Against this it could be argued that there is a sense in which clients own personal information and that professionals, whose access to it is only legitimised by their involvement in the client's care, do not have the right to extend this ownership beyond the limits of those who are directly involved in the client's care. Underlying this argument is the assumption that the point of confidentiality, in addition to protecting privacy and ensuring a barrier against possible embarrassment, is to respect autonomy.

Perhaps here we are up against the limits of what can be established by reasoning alone as to what a reasonable client's wishes might be. My intuition is that the argument supporting the view that no breach has occurred carries more weight, but I am not clear how this intuition can be shown to be correct. What I think can confidently be said is that the more such anonymous disclosure is responsible, i.e. directed to good ends, such as the unburdening of stress or the education of students, the more likely it is to conform to the wishes of the reasonable client, and therefore the less likely it is to constitute a breach of confidentiality.

What if no information is disclosed?

A final reflection on the limits of confidentiality suggests that situations can be envisaged where no information is disclosed, yet where it might nevertheless be appropriate to talk about a breach. The examples that come to mind involve some form of negligence or carelessness. For example, a community mental health nurse by oversight leaves her diary, containing details of patients, in a café; a general practitioner forgets to lock a filing cabinet. If the diary is handed in without being opened, and the cleaning lady does not look in the cabinet and read the files, would these be breaches of confidentiality? To say that they would, would be to embrace a blurring of the distinction between practice that risks a breach of confidentiality and practice that constitutes a breach, and to run counter to the standard view, adopted in this discussion, that going beyond the limit of confidentiality involves, by definition, disclosure of information. On the other hand, clearly in such cases there is a failure to protect the boundary around confidential information which, it was argued, does constitute a breach.

Conclusion

This discussion has been an attempt to clarify the limits of confidentiality, in the sense of the boundary beyond which confidentiality would be broken. I have claimed that the limit is set by the wishes of the client, and that, where these are not known (whether because the client is unable to communicate or because his or her views have not been sought) the limit is set by what the client would have wished. Since the latter is a vague and unworkable notion, demanding too intimate a knowledge of individual clients, I have attempted to give content to the notion of what the reasonable client would wish. This, I argued, would identify the limit by reference to those whose need and right to know relate to the client's own healthcare needs. Sharing information anonymously in such a way that the client cannot be identified, I suggested, falls within the limit of confidentiality.

What in theory emerges as a simple statement may, in practice, turn out to be less straightforward, for where a client is able to make his or her wishes known this may be in (possibly unavoidable) ignorance of the extent to which information disclosed may have to be shared – for what the treatment may require may not be precisely known – and, where the client is not able to make his or her wishes known, the proposed analysis may not match what he or she would have wished, and this (*ex hypothesi*) is not known. Further there is the need for judgement about what the analysis implies: for example, are the surgery receptionist, the hospital porter or the neighbour among those who have 'a need and a right to know'? To note this uncertainty is to draw attention to a common-place fact, that the 'fit' between concepts and practice is not always exact, and that no amount of theoretical 'fine-tuning' can dispense with the need for individual judgement.

Acknowledgements

Some material in this chapter is reprinted from Cain, Paul (1999) 'Respecting and breaking confidences: conceptual, ethical and educational issues.' *Nurse Education Today* *19*, 175–181. By kind permission of Churchill Livingstone. Also from Cain, Paul (1998) 'The limits of confidentiality.' *Nursing Ethics 5*, 2, 158–165. By kind permission of Arnold.

References

Bayles, M. (1989) *Professional Ethics*, 2nd edn. Belmont, CA: Wadsworth.

Bok, S. (1986) *Secrets. On the Ethics of Concealment and Revelation.* Oxford: Oxford University Press.

College of Nurses of Ontario (1995) *Guidelines for Professional Behaviour.* Ontario: College of Nurses of Ontario.

General Medical Council (GMC) (2000) *Confidentiality: Protecting and Providing Information.* London: GMC.

Gillon, R. (1986) *Philosophical Medical Ethics.* Chichester: Wiley.

Joseph, D. and Onek, J. (1991) 'Confidentiality in psychiatry.' In S. Bloch and P. Chodoff (eds) *Psychiatric Ethics.* Oxford: Oxford University Press.

United Kingdom Central Council for Nursing, Midwifery and Health Visitors (UKCC) (1987) *Confidentiality. An Elaboration of Clause 9 of the Second Edition of UKCC's Code of Professional Conduct for the Nurse, Midwife and Health Visitor.* London: UKCC.

United Kingdom Central Council for Nursing, Midwifery and Health Visitors (UKCC) (1992) *Code of Professional Conduct.* London: UKCC.

United Kingdom Central Council for Nursing, Midwifery and Health Visitors (UKCC) (1996) *Guidelines for Professional Practice.* London: UKCC.

10

Confidentiality

A Legal View

Andrew Hall

The accused, X, is charged with the rape and homicide of his former girlfriend who died as a result of an overdose of prescribed drugs. There is uncontested evidence of recent sexual intercourse between the parties and it is common ground that the sedatives taken were prescribed to the defendant. The Crown's case is that the deceased was drugged by X to procure unconsensual intercourse and that, at the very least, he is guilty of her manslaughter. The defence case is that there was no rape, and that the deceased tragically took her own life while in a psychologically vulnerable state. The defence are seeking disclosure of medical and social services records which it is anticipated will contain a history of depression, impulsive behaviour and suicidal ideation. Following his arrest, X was assessed as to his fitness for interview by a doctor called by the police. The interview was conducted in the presence of officers who made notes of damaging admissions made to the doctor during the consultation. After charge, those admissions were repeated to X's solicitors and to a psychiatrist instructed by the defence. New lawyers are now in place. They have been given the psychiatric report but not the earlier proof of evidence. A second psychiatric opinion is now sought.

This fictional, but not wholly unrealistic, scenario highlights a series of technical problems about confidentiality to which the current law of England and Wales provides few straightforward or coherent answers. Such questions are of enormous practical importance in the daily practice of both lawyers and doctors involved in litigation and yet the source of considerable confusion and uncertainty for both. The purpose of this chapter is to examine the roots of that confusion in the development of the current law, and to consider whether incorporation of the European Convention, together with a recognised right to privacy, will provide the guidance arguably now absent.

Confidential relationships

The concept of public interest immunity provides one vehicle for the protection of confidential information. The courts may direct that material may be withheld from disclosure, and not adduced in evidence, whenever the public interest in non-disclosure is held to outweigh the competing interest that, in the administration of justice, the courts should have the fullest possible access to all relevant evidence. Specific examples of matters covered by public interest immunity include information relating to state interests, the prevention and detection of crime, the protection of children, and the judicial process. This list is, however, not exhaustive. In *D* v. *NSPCC*, Lord Hailsham observed: The categories of public interest immunity are not closed, and must alter from time to time whether by restriction or extension as social conditions and social legislation develop.[1]

Legal professional privilege

Conceptually linked to the notion of public interest immunity is the principle of legal professional privilege, the basis of which lies in the confidential relationship which must necessarily exist between lawyer and client. While the legal categories are separate there is a logical unity between the two concepts; sometimes the latter being seen as a species of the former. Communications between a lawyer and his/her client may not be revealed except with the consent of the client. An investigating authority may not seize written communications between solicitor and client which concern the seeking or provision of legal advice, or touch upon anticipated litigation. Moreover, legal privilege may extend to correspondence between a lawyer and potential witnesses, including expert witnesses. Thus, the rights of investigating police officers to search and seize documents from a suspect's lawyers are strictly circumscribed. Materials which may not be seized under the legislation[2] include:

(a) communications between a professional legal adviser and his client or any person representing his client made in connection with the giving of legal advice to the client;

(b) communications between a professional legal adviser and his client or any person representing his client or between such an adviser or his client or any such representative and any other person made in connection with or in contemplation of legal proceedings and for the purposes of such proceedings; and

(c) items enclosed with or referred to in such communications and made –

(i) in connection with the giving of legal advice; or

(ii) in connection with or in contemplation of legal proceedings and for the purposes of such proceedings

when they are in the possession of a person who is entitled to possession of them.

Thus, for example, a copy of a client's proof of evidence or a letter from the client providing information about events to his solicitor, would be covered by paragraph (a). A letter of instruction sent by the solicitor to a consultant forensic psychiatrist, enclosing copies of such documents would be subject to paragraphs (b) and (c). All would be

---

1   [1978] AC 171 at 230 E.
2   Police and Criminal Evidence Act 1984 s10(1).

covered by legal professional privilege and neither lawyer nor expert may be required to divulge the contents of such communications.

Similarly, while there is an important public interest in criminal cases in ensuring that all relevant evidence is made available to the defence, *R v. Derby Magistrates ex. parte B*,[3] makes quite clear that legal professional privilege should be upheld as the predominant public interest. This may apply even where the beneficiary of the privilege no longer has any recognisable interest in preserving confidentiality. The rationale is that the freedom of a client to consult his legal advisors, without fear of his communications being revealed, is a fundamental condition upon which the whole administration of justice rests.

The facts of the Derby case illustrate the weight of that principle even where injustice may arise to a criminal defendant. B, the applicant went for a walk with a 16-year-old girl who was later found murdered. He subsequently made a statement to the police admitting sole responsibility for the murder. Shortly before the trial, however, he retracted that statement and alleged that, although he had been at the scene of the crime, it was his stepfather who had killed the girl. The applicant was acquitted. Thereafter the stepfather was charged with murder and committal proceedings were begun. The applicant gave evidence for the Crown and repeated his allegation. Counsel for the stepfather, in cross-examination, asked about the instructions which the applicant had first given his solicitors. When the applicant refused to answer on the grounds of legal privilege, the defendant's lawyers applied for a witness summons requiring the solicitor to produce the proof of evidence and attendance notes.

Reliance was placed upon the developing law of 'disclosure' in criminal cases which imposes duties upon the prosecution to supply materials to the defence which might undermine the prosecution case or open up a new line of defence. In this area of the law, the application of public interest immunity principles has been substantially reduced as a result of a series of miscarriages arising from failure to disclose (see, for example, *R v. Ward*).[4] Procedures have been developed which enable the judge to examine the relevant materials, hear submissions upon them, and then rule as to disclosure by applying a balance between the confidentiality of the materials and the injustice which might arise in the event of denying access to them.[5] Items subject to legal professional privilege had not, hitherto, been the focus of attention and accordingly the unusual circumstances of *ex parte B* were a fruitful ground for argument.

The decision of the magistrate to order production in this case was the subject of a series of appeals, eventually reaching the House of Lords. The House concluded that if a balancing exercise were called for in evaluating competing public interests:

> it was performed once and for all in the 16th Century, and since then has applied across the board in every case, irrespective of the client's individual merits.[6]

3   [1996] AC 487 HL.
4   (1993) 96 Cr. App. R 77.
5   *R v. Johnson, Rowe and Davies, The Guardian*, 31 July 1993, CA.
6   [1996] AC 487 at 508 E.

The primacy of the principle outweighed all other considerations. As for the risk of injustice:

> There may be cases where the principle will work hardship on a third party seeking to assert his innocence. But in the overall interests of the administration of justice it is better that the principle should be preserved intact.[7]

Other cases, however, have sought to limit the operation of this simple and universal principle. The alternative approach has primarily been developed in the area of child care law where the jurisprudence has been shaped by the unique procedural approach to litigation in the family courts. Here, proceedings under the Children Act 1989 are to some extent inquisitorial and the judge has an overriding duty to consider the welfare of the child who is the subject of proceedings. Thus, a judge may require further evidence to be obtained or tendered, or investigations to be conducted, whether or not the parties to the litigation agree. Special procedural rules operate to ensure that all material relevant to a consideration of the child's welfare should be made available to the court, and the parties themselves are under a duty to make disclosure of all information and material in their possession relevant to the issues in contention.

In this context, it is easy to see how the special procedures and jurisprudence might provide a fertile ground for argument that the hard and fast rule of legal professional privilege crystallised in *ex parte B* ought not to prevail.

In re L[8] (A Minor) [1997] AC 16 (HL)

This case concerned care proceedings arising from the admission of a small child to hospital suffering from methadone poisoning. It was the parents' case that the drug had been taken by the child accidentally. In support, they sought leave to obtain an expert's report to investigate the frequency of ingestion of the drug by the child. In order to do so they had to obtain the court's consent to disclose court papers relating to the proceedings, including the hospital notes which had been filed. As a condition of granting this consent, the parents were required, in the ordinary way in these proceedings, to file a copy of the report with the court. This meant that the local authority inevitably would obtain access. Once this course had been adopted, the police indicated a wish to have a copy of the report in connection with their own investigations into the poisoning of the child. They sought an order from the judge in the family proceedings to secure this and the parents opposed. The order for disclosure made by the judge was the subject of the subsequent appeal made by the mother on the basis of legal professional privilege.

In the House of Lords, there was a remarkable division of opinion. The majority of three Law Lords decided that the order made was a proper one. In a strong dissenting judgement, supported by Lord Mustill, Lord Nicholls of Birkenhead argued that allowing disclosure in these circumstances was in direct contradiction to the decision of the House in *ex parte B.* The 1969 Act was not intended, he argued, to abrogate legal pro-

---

7   op. cit. at 509 H – 510 A.
8   [1997] AC 16 HL.

fessional privilege in family cases and had not done so. The effect of holding that family proceedings were to that extent different from all other litigation was to deprive parents in those proceedings of the normal freedom to consult lawyers and potential witnesses, and to do so confidentially:

> I can see no reason why parties to family proceedings should not be as much entitled to a fair hearing having these features and safeguards as are parties to other court proceedings. Indeed, it must be doubtful whether a parent who is denied the opportunity to obtain legal advice in confidence is accorded a fair hearing to which he is entitled under article 6(1), read in conjunction with article 8, of the European Convention for the Protection of Human Rights and Fundamental Freedoms.[9]

Nevertheless, the majority view prevailed and has subsequently been applied in judgements of the Court of Appeal, for example, *Vernon* v. *Bosley*.[10] A distinction is necessarily drawn between family cases and others. However, the judgement has wider implications and may have an effect in other types of cases.

The way in which *re L* avoided conflict with *ex parte B* was remarkably subtle. That case, it was said, concerned dealings between a solicitor and his client and did not specifically consider the position as to third parties. In other words, direct communications between lawyer and client are inviolable and absolute, but not reports prepared by experts (on the instructions of the client) for the purposes of litigation. These, it would seem, fall into a separate and lower category of legal professional privilege – that of 'litigation privilege'. The former is not subject to any balancing exercise, but the latter is susceptible to this if a countervailing interest requires it. In proceedings in which the judge's overriding duty concerns the welfare of the child, disclosure may be necessary if this, on balance, is necessary to preserve those fundamental interests.

It remains, of course, necessary to see whether the dilution of litigation privilege will be countenanced in cases outside the family court sphere. One can, of course, appreciate the arguments for a special status for such proceedings although, for myself, I prefer the view of Lord Nicholls:

> Legal professional privilege is sometimes classified under two sub-headings; legal advice privilege and litigation privilege. The former, covering communications between a client and his legal adviser, is available whether or not proceedings are in existence or contemplated. The latter embraces a wider class of communications, such as those between the legal adviser and potential witnesses. These are privileged only when proceedings are in existence or contemplated. In the course of the submissions reliance was placed upon this distinction. It was suggested that the (1969) Act has impliedly abrogated litigation privilege, while leaving legal advice privilege untouched. I cannot accept this. The two sub-headings are integral parts of a single privilege. In the context of court proceedings, the purpose of legal advice privilege would be frustrated if the legal adviser could not approach potential witnesses in confidence before advising his client. This is as much true in family proceedings as any other. This remains as true after

9   Per Nicholls LJ op. cit. at page 32 H.
10   Unreported 13 December 1996.

the passing of the Children Act 1989 as before. The public interest reflected in the paramountcy principle does not self-evidently outweigh the public interest reflected in litigation privilege.[11]

Whatever the merits of the argument in family proceedings, it seems unlikely that *re L* will override *ex parte B* in the criminal context. To do so would be in direct conflict with the defining provisions of Police and Criminal Evidence Act 1984[12] and quite contrary to the current practice of the courts. In that sphere, legal confidentiality remains sacrosanct. That, of course, has an effect upon the medical expert whose own correspondence and reports may be covered by general legal professional privilege.

Medical confidentiality

It is of some significance that the inviolability of legal confidentiality is a principle developed by lawyers. Other confidential relationships have fared less well. It is long established in law that no such privilege arises out of the relationship between a patient and doctor, however confidential and rooted in professional trust.[13] Rather, the degree of confidentiality is determined by professional and ethical standards of which the law, to some degree, takes cognisance.

Enforcing medical confidentiality

The modern version of the Hippocratic Oath introduced by the World Medical Association as the Declaration of Geneva includes the statement: 'I will respect the secrets which are confided in me, even after the patient has died.'

There is no doubt that the relationship of doctor and patient carries with it legal obligations of confidence in respect of information obtained by the doctor in a medical capacity. However, guidance provided by the General Medical Council makes clear that there may be occasions where the doctor is entitled to make disclosures without the patient's consent. The principle is not absolute, because it would defeat the object for which it exists if it precluded the doctor from making disclosure in circumstances in which professional judgement indicated it was in the patient's best interests to do so, or where the preservation of confidence could be seriously harmful for other reasons.

The fullest judicial statement of the principles of, and qualifications to, medical confidence is to be found in *Duncan v. Medical Practitioners' Disciplinary Committee.*[14]

Without trust, the doctor/patient relationship would not function so as to allow freedom for the patient to disclose all manner of confidences and secrets in the practical certainty that they would repose with the doctor. There rests with the doctor a strong ethical obligation to observe a strict confidentiality by holding inviolate the confidences and secrets he receives in the course of his professional ministerings ... but it cannot be

11 Op. cit. at 33 C – F.
12 Op. cit. s. 10(1).
13 For example, *Wilson* v. *Rastall* [1792 4 TR 753 and the Duchess of Kingston's Case (1776) 20. St. Tr 355 at 472].
14 [1986] 1 NZLR 513.

left there without identifying the existence of qualifications and modifications ... he may be required by law to disclose ... There may be occasions, they are fortunately rare, when a doctor receives information involving a patient that another's life is immediately endangered and urgent action is required. Then the doctor must exercise his professional judgement based upon the circumstances, and if he fairly and reasonably believes that such a danger exists then he must act unhesitatingly to prevent injury or loss of life even if there is to be a breach of confidentiality.[15]

Applying that 'qualification' to actuality fell to the Court of Appeal in the case of *Egdell*[16] in 1990. The plaintiff, a paranoid schizophrenic, shot and killed five people and injured two others. He pleaded guilty to manslaughter on the ground of diminished responsibility and was ordered to be detained in a secure hospital. For the purpose of an application to a mental health review tribunal, with a view towards his ultimate release, the plaintiff retained Dr Egdell, a consultant psychiatrist, to report on his state of mental health. The doctor formed a more serious view of the plaintiff's condition than had the medical officer responsible for his treatment and his report was adverse to his application which was withdrawn. The plaintiff specifically refused to consent to the report being disclosed. Nevertheless, Dr Egdell decided to send copies to the assistant medical director at the hospital in the knowledge that they would thereafter be disclosed to the Home Office and be likely to feature in any further consideration of his eventual treatment and release. The plaintiff brought an action against Dr Egdell claiming breach of confidence and seeking injunctions to prevent consideration of the report.

In dismissing an appeal against a refusal to grant the plaintiff the relief sought, the Court of Appeal held that although the plaintiff had a personal interest to ensure that the confidence he reposed in the psychiatrist was not breached, the maintenance of the duty of confidence by a doctor to his patient was not a matter of private but of public interest. However, that public interest had to be balanced against the public interest in protecting others against possible violence; that the nature of the crimes committed by the plaintiff made it a matter of public interest that those responsible for treating and managing him had all the relevant information concerning his mental state before releasing him from hospital; that the information in the report was relevant information and the public interest in its restricted disclosure to the proper authorities outweighed the public interest that the plaintiff's confidences should be respected. Since the defendant's disclosure had been in accordance with the GMC's guidelines on professional conduct, the plaintiff's case had properly been dismissed.

Egdell was followed later in the same year by a further example of the court's approval of this 'public duty qualification' in the case of *Crozier.*[17] The appellant pleaded guilty to the attempted murder of his sister. Sentencing was postponed but the defence called no psychiatric evidence and the appellant was sentenced to nine years imprisonment. The defence were, however, in possession of an expert report which had been prepared at their request by Dr McDonald. This was plainly adverse to the defendant

15   [1986] 1 NZLR 513.
16   *W* v. *Egdell* [1990] 1 Ch. 359.
17   *R* v. *Crozier* 8 BMLR 128.

and contrary to an earlier report prepared for the court by Dr Wright which concluded that the appellant was sane. Dr McDonald arrived at court in time to hear sentence being pronounced and was so alarmed by it that he voluntarily disclosed his report to counsel for the prosecution. As a result the Crown applied for a variation of the sentence and Dr McDonald gave evidence at a further hearing which concluded with the making of a hospital order under s37 coupled with a restriction order[18] and the appellant was then committed to Broadmoor Hospital.

On appeal the court held that the disclosure of the report in these circumstances was both appropriate and necessary. A consultant psychiatrist who becomes aware, even in the course of a confidential relationship, of information which leads him to fear that sentencing on the basis of inadequate information may result in a real risk of danger to the public is entitled to communicate the grounds of his concern to the responsible authorities.

Requiring disclosure

There is, in law, no property in a witness. The mere fact that an expert has been instructed by one side in litigation does not prevent him/her being called by the other side. If a witness has relevant and admissible evidence to give s/he will be compellable and required to produce any relevant documentation which may be in his/her possession. Although legal privilege will attach to any instructions or communications between the expert and the lawyers who originally commissioned a report, it does not apply to the expert's opinion, and will not to the items or documents upon which that opinion is based.

In R v. R[19] a handwriting expert was provided with samples of the defendant's handwriting for the purposes of comparison. His report must have been unfavourable since the defence decided against calling him. The Crown then took their opportunity to require him to attend and to produce the samples. The legitimacy of that course was approved by the Court of Appeal.

In R v. King[20] an apparently contrary position was taken in relation to a blood sample, although the case may be distinguished on the basis that the sample was provided specifically for the purposes of the criminal proceedings and thus fell within the category of materials covered by legal privilege.

Breaking confidences

The Police and Criminal Evidence Act 1984 imposes strict restrictions on the extent to which access may be obtained to confidential information for the purposes of a criminal investigation.[21] Nevertheless, with the authority of a circuit judge, even highly confiden-

18   Sections 37 and 41 Mental Health Act 1983.
19   [1995] 1 Cr.App. R 183 CA.
20   77 Cr App. R 1 CA.
21   See, in particular, Sections 8 to 13 and Schedule 1.

tial medical records and files may be the subject of a special procedure warrant to require disclosure.

If access to confidential material has been obtained, or where cross-examination seeks to elicit such material, the court has a discretion to excuse a witness from answering a question when to do so would involve a breach of confidence. In *Hunter* v. *Mann*[22] Lord Widgery CJ said, *obiter*:

> If a doctor, giving evidence...is asked a question which he finds embarrassing because it involves him talking about things which he would normally regard as confidential, he can seek the protection of the judge and ask the judge if it is necessary for him to answer. The judge, by virtue of the overriding discretion to control his court which all English judges have, can, if he thinks fit, tell the doctor that he need not answer the question. Whether or not the judge would take that line, of course, depends largely on the importance of the potential answer to the issues being tried.[23]

Before a court compels disclosure, it should be satisfied that the potential answer is relevant and necessary in the sense that it will serve a useful purpose in relation to the proceedings in hand.[24] If so satisfied, the court, before deciding, will still have to weigh the conflicting interests which so dominate the others as to demand that confidentiality either be overridden or respected. On the one hand is the respect due to confidence; on the other is the ultimate interest of the community in justice being done. In *British Steel Corp.* v. *Granada Television Ltd*, Lord Wilberforce said:

> Courts have an inherent wish to respect this confidence whether it arises between doctor and patient, priest and penitent, banker and customer, between persons giving testimonials to employees, or in other relationships. A relationship of confidence between a journalist and his source is in no different category. But in all these cases the court may have to decide that the interest in preserving this confidence is outweighed by other interests to which the law attaches importance (at pp. 1168–1169).

Failure to comply with a ruling to disclose otherwise confidential material would amount to a contempt of court and could lead to penal sanctions against the recalcitrant witness.

Admissibility of evidence

More recent cases have considered the position in the context of the Police and Criminal Evidence Act provisions which protect the suspect in the police station, and govern the admissibility of confessions and other evidence at trial.

---

22 59 Cr. App. R 37 DC.
23 Ibid, at page 41.
24 *AG* v. *Mulholland and Foster*, supra.

R v. McDonald [25]

M, the accused, took drugs on a regular basis with two others, L with whom he had co-habited for years, and S, the deceased. One day when the three had been consuming drugs M killed S. He struck him on the head with a statuette, rendering him unconscious, then stabbed him repeatedly with two knives (breaking the first), and finally held a dog's choke chain round his neck to strangle him. In a later statement to the police, M said that he had not intended to kill S, but merely to knock him out with the statuette and he had later panicked. Later he wrote to S's parents explaining that he had killed S as a result of S boasting of having sexual relations with L in M's mother's bed. He was seen by a psychiatrist, Dr P, for the issues of fitness to plead, diminished responsibility and general mental state to be considered. At M's trial for murder the issue was provocation. Dr P gave evidence that he had asked M why he had written to S's parents in the terms in which he did. M had told him that he had to make up some reason for his behaviour.

On appeal the defence argued that the trial judge should have used his discretion [26] to exclude the evidence. It was conceded that the disclosure was not covered by privilege but contended that it was unfair to admit a confession obtained in an aura of trust and confidence encouraging frankness which distinguished it from confessions which were sometimes made to fellow prisoners, prison officers and the like. It had been ruled that a doctor's opinion on a medical matter was inadmissible where the accused had been misled as to the doctor's function [27] but the question of adducing evidence on a factual matter had not been considered. The court held that the discretion under s78 had to be exercised on the basis of fairness to both prosecution and defence. In the circumstances of the present case the defence based its claim to provocation solely upon the contents of the letter which had been adduced as part of the Crown's case. In this situation the jury would be misled by being excluded from considering the significance of M's comment to Dr P on the contents of the letter.

R v. Gayle [28]

G was convicted with his cousin of attempted murder. The victim R had been a doorman for a disco at which G had attended in the early hours of 1 January 1992. G was refused admission and an altercation took place during which R hit G with a bottle, cutting his lip. The prosecution case was that G then threatened to kill R, and came back two hours later with his cousin who shot R.

Shortly after G's arrest two weeks later, he was examined by a doctor. He was asked for a written consent to be examined, and told by the doctor not to say anything which he did not wish the police to hear. During the course of the examination G was asked if he had any recent injuries. In reply he said that he had injured his knee on New Year's Eve and had been in a hospital casualty department all night. He also said that he had received a cut to his lip some days before this.

25 [1991] Crim. LR 122 CA.
26 Under S78 Police and Criminal Evidence Act 1984.
27 R v. Payne (1963) 47 Cr. App. R 122, as explained by Lane CJ. in R v. Smith (1979) 69 Cr. App. R 378.
28 (1991) Cr. LR 122 CA.

The defence objected to the admission of these comments. The prosecution argued that they demonstrated an attempt to construct a false alibi for the night in question. In ruling the material admissible, it was held that the judge had properly exercised his discretion, coupled as it was by a warning to the jury as to the proper approach to lies told by the defendant.

Legal privilege and medical confidences

Having examined the roots of these two important areas, it is instructive to compare legal confidentiality with the treatment of medical confidences. The former is a species of private right which is for the client alone to waive. The latter is a public interest, and as such may be balanced against competing public interests. The client/patient appears to have no right of privacy. In many circumstances, his consent to disclosure may not result in the production of relevant medical information about him, and his refusal to consent will not prevent material damaging to his interests from being divulged.

The lack of a rationale which is consistent results in uncertainty and may very well lead to injustice. It is certainly unsatisfactory that the protection of medical confidentiality – in the context of litigation – depends upon receiving a 'piggy-back' from legal professional privilege. Moreover, lack of consistency has been exacerbated because the courts have made a special case of family court litigation which is likely to cause substantial difficulty in rationalising the law in the future.

In these circumstances, the absence of a coherent approach by the medical profession, and widespread confusion among lawyers, is perhaps understandable. For my own part, I would favour the establishment of a legally enforceable right of confidentiality for patients involved in litigation. This would, whatever one's perspective, have the benefits of consistency and clarity. At Common Law, the procedures by which issues of confidentiality are decided are disparate and jurisprudentially unsatisfactory. Cases are determined upon an ad hoc basis in accordance with the court's view of the public interest considerations relevant to the particular type of litigation. Different principles appear to apply in the family and criminal courts. In the latter, whether confidentiality is protected will depend upon who has possession of the material and who asserts a right to it or to have access. The current hotchpotch of case law, statutory provisions and regulations make proper legal analysis of the principles virtually impossible.

Incorporation of the European Convention on Human Rights

It will be apparent from the above analysis that no general right of privacy is recognised by the English Common Law. Judicial pronouncements to that effect are commonplace, for example in *R* v. *Khan*[29] a case concerning covert surveillance techniques employed by the police. However, by virtue of Article 8 of the European Convention on Human Rights:

29   (1996) 2 Cr. App. R 440 HL.

1. Everyone has the right to respect for his private and family life, his home and his correspondence.

2. There shall be no interference by a public authority with the exercise of this right except such as is in accordance with the law and is necessary in a democratic society in the interests of national security, public safety or the economic well being of the country, for the prevention of disorder or crime, for the protection of health or morals, or for the protection of the rights and freedoms of others.

By virtue of section 6(1) of the Human Rights Act 1998, it will be unlawful, upon implementation, for a public authority, including a court or tribunal, to act in a way which is incompatible with that right. It follows that health authorities and individual health professionals may no longer be able to rely upon existing General Medical Council guidance as to the limits of medical confidence. Doing so might result in an injunction or render them liable in an action for damages under the provisions of Section 8 of the Act. Moreover, in considering issues of disclosure and admissibility, the courts may be forced to abandon long-established Common Law principles if they are found to be inconsistent with the right to privacy, or out of step with the developing European jurisprudence on the subject. It is a salient reminder of the root and branch reappraisal of current practices and procedures which implementation makes necessary.

The protection of medical confidences under convention rights

In the European Court, the issue whether courts may require the disclosure of medical confidences has already been addressed in the case of Z v. Finland [1997].[30] Here, a defendant had been tried for a series of offences of manslaughter upon the basis that he had engaged in sexual intercourse with a number of women in the knowledge that he was HIV positive and likely to infect them with a fatal disease. In order to secure a conviction, it was necessary for the prosecution to establish the date when his own medical condition would have been apparent to him. In order to do so, the authorities seized the medical files of the wife of the accused who was herself infected with the disease. They also required her medical adviser to give evidence at the trial. In giving judgment, convicting the accused, the court both identified the wife and made reference to her medical condition, although it simultaneously banned any publication of these details for a period of ten years. Upon appeal, the appeal court upheld the judgment and the publicity order, but published in its own judgment the name of the unfortunate woman and details of her condition, and compounded matters by faxing these details to the press.

It was accepted by the European Court that the complainant's right to privacy under Article 8 had been interfered with. Moreover, unlike the current position in England and Wales, in Finland specific statutory provisions existed to permit the seizure of medical records, and compel testimony from the doctor in such circumstances. The actions of the

30   (1997) 25 EHRR 371.

prosecuting authorities were therefore 'accordingly to law', in compliance with Article 8. The Finnish government argued successfully that the aim of such provisions was to prevent crime and to protect the health and well being of others. In the context of this case, it is difficult to see how such an argument might be defeated. Accordingly, the central issue for the court to determine was whether such measures, and their use in this case, could be justified as being 'necessary in a democratic society'.

While the ultimate conclusion of the court was that, in the particular circumstances of the case, the public interest in the investigation and prosecution of crime here outweighed medical confidentiality, it was not a decision reached lightly. The circumstances in which a patient's record might be seized, and her medical advisers required to testify as to her health, were extremely limited and the most careful scrutiny of such matters was necessary by local courts. Even in such circumstances, the material would only be available where sufficient safeguards existed to protect the interests of the patient.

It was of significance, in considering the position under Finnish law, that such draconian measures were only available in serious criminal cases punishable with six years imprisonment or longer. Moreover, while the complainant had no right to argue her own case before the trial court, her views had been made known to that tribunal and were specifically and carefully considered in the balancing exercise which had been called for. Thereafter, steps had been taken to ensure that the relevant medical evidence was tendered in a private session of the court, and orders as to non-publication extended for a period of years following the trial. Finally, all those involved in the proceedings were bound by a duty to treat the material disclosed in the utmost confidence, and under penalty of criminal or civil proceedings should this be disregarded. In the event, the court found no violation in relation to the conduct of the trial court in these circumstances save that the bar upon publication, for ten years, was inadequate and should have been longer. A violation was found, however, in relation to the conduct of the appeal court and its decision to publish its own judgment naming the complainant. Such action, in essence, had defeated the steps taken at first instance to mitigate the injury suffered by the defendant's wife.

Conclusions

British practitioners and judges have been alerted to the likely impact upon their practice arising from incorporation. While in many areas familiar principles will apply in balancing interests in the litigation process, the intellectual process required for reaching a determination may differ considerably. It will be necessary, in some cases, to re-evaluate long cherished legal principles such as legal professional privilege. In some cases, the requirement for interferences with the right to privacy to be 'sanctioned by law' will require legislation. Importantly, the doctor who breaches medical confidences in reliance upon a professional code of practice may not in future be protected against legal action by an aggrieved patient in the absence of statutory provision. However, benefits may include a measure of consistency in evaluating aspects of confidentiality when placing them in the scales against competing social interests.

11

The Limits of Confidentiality

A Legal View

Anthony Harbour

Introduction

This chapter looks at how the notion of absolute confidentiality is modified, and qualified in practice.

General principles

A duty of confidence arises when confidential information comes to the knowledge of a person (the confidant) in circumstances where he has notice, or is held to have agreed, that the information is confidential, with the effect that it would be just in all the circumstances that he should be precluded from disclosing the information to others.[1]

It is legally well established that the relationship between doctor and patient constitutes such a circumstance. Therefore in the event of breach of this legal duty legal action may follow including injunction and damages. The nature of the confidential relationship needs to be delineated. The relationship between doctor and patient creates an obligation of confidence. However the patient can, by consenting to the disclosure of information, waive that obligation. Although information is described as being confidential, in reality the person to whom the duty of confidentiality is owed can, in general terms, do what he/she chooses with the information.

Children's rights

How is a child defined? The Children Act definition of a child as 'anybody under the age of eighteen'[2] is used throughout this chapter.

Young people aged 16 or 17 are regarded as adults for purposes of consent to treatment and are therefore entitled to the same duty of confidence as adults. Children

---

1   *A-G* v. *Guardian* (No 2) (1988) 3 All England Law Reports 545.
2   Children Act 1989 section 105(1).

under 16 who have the capacity and understanding to take decisions about their own treatment are entitled also to decide whether personal information may be passed on and generally to have their confidence respected.[3]

The limits of confidentiality

Confidentiality is not absolute. There are a number of qualifications to the obligations of confidence: most obviously where a patient consents to disclosure of confidential information and where a court requires confidential information to be provided. Qualifications are also contained in statute. Two often used, and imprecisely defined, concepts are also used to qualify confidentiality – the public interest and 'need to know'.

Statute

Various statutory provisions affect, and modify, the obligation of confidence.

1. *Disclosure is required:*

   - The Road Traffic Act 1988 requires that persons, including health professionals, must provide the police on request with any information that might identify a driver who is alleged to have committed a traffic offence.

   - The Public Health (Control of Diseases) Act 1984 requires a doctor to notify actual or suspected cases of patients suffering from various forms of infectious diseases to the local authority.

   - Various statutory instruments relate to the notification of industrial accidents and diseases, notification of births and deaths, and registration of addicts.

2. *Disclosure may be compelled:*

   - Under the Supreme Court Act 1981 court orders may be made for disclosure of medical records in certain categories of litigation.

   - The Police and Criminal Evidence Act 1984 allows the police to gain access to medical records for the purpose of a criminal investigation on the order of a judge.

3. *Confidentiality may be qualified:*

   - The Mental Health Act 1983 qualifies the obligation of confidence by requiring that a patient's nearest relative must be consulted before an application for admission under the Act is made.

   - Under the Mental Health (Patients in the Community) Act 1995 the RMO (responsible medical officer) is required to consult a patient's nearest relative before making a supervision application. The patient is entitled to object to

---

3   *Protection and Use of Patient Information* (1996) Department of Health, para.4.10 and Mental Health Act Code of Practice (1999) para.31.21.

this consultation proceeding. The RMO can consult regardless of the patient's expressed wish if the 'patient has a propensity to violent or dangerous behaviour towards other'.

4. *Protection of confidentiality of third parties by statute.*

- The Access to Medical Reports Act 1988 allows access to be refused in order to maintain the confidentiality of the doctor's informants. The Access to Health Records Act 1990 allows a health record to be withheld for a similar, and other, reasons.

Public interest

Rarely, disclosure may be justified on the ground that it is in the public interest which, in certain circumstances such as, for example, investigation by the police of a grave or very serious crime, might override the doctor's duty to maintain his patient's confidence.[4]

In the Egdell case Dr Egdell was instructed by solicitors representing a patient detained in a special hospital in the context of the patient's application to a mental health review tribunal. Dr Egdell's appraisal of the patient was at variance with the patient's RMO – Dr Egdell decided that the patient represented a much greater risk to the public than was recognised by his RMO. Once Dr Egdell's views became known to the patient's lawyers they withdrew his application to the tribunal, with the effect that the report was not disclosed. Because Dr Egdell was concerned about the patient's potential dangerousness he made the report available to the hospital authority responsible for the patient's detention, without the patient's consent. The Home Office was also provided with the report. The patient's lawyers attempted to restrain the distribution of the report. They were unsuccessful. The judge decided that the public interest in disclosure overrode the patient's right to confidentiality.

Guidance provided by the General Medical Council[5] refers to public interest disclosure as being necessary to protect the patient, or others, from risk of death or serious harm. The UKCC provides the following guidance:

The public interest means the interests of an individual, or groups of individuals or of society as a whole, and would, for example, cover matters such as serious crime, child abuse, drug trafficking or other activities which place others at serious risk.[6]

The concept of public interest in justifying disclosure of confidential information tends to be used in practice in much the same way as the practitioners of emergency medicine use the notion of the 'common law', that is to justify any action which feels right. However, the concept has been quite narrowly and precisely defined by the courts. The judge in the Egdell case referred to the 'very special circumstances' of the case in not preventing unauthorised disclosure. If the concept is going to have any utility, beyond a

---

4 *W v. Egdell* [1990] 1 All England Law Reports.
5 *Confidentiality. Duties of a Doctor* (GMC 1995, para.18)
6 *Guidelines for Professional Practice* (UKCC 1996, para.56).

vague generalisation, then it must be important to limit its application to genuine public interests exceptions.

Need to know

A principle that was originally designed to ensure that a consenting patient received the best available medical care is being gradually extended.

A conventional analysis of medical practice assumes that there will be shared information within a medical team. For example, a patient who consults a doctor impliedly consents to the doctor disclosing such information about the patient to other appropriately skilled staff, as may be necessary to enable the doctor to treat the patient.[7]

This analysis incorporates the notion of implied consent – that is what a person believes will take place when he/she consults a doctor for most aspects of physical care. It is much less clear what psychiatric patients living in the community believe, or expect, about disclosure and this notion of implied consent does not provide an answer. Consider the situation where an individual is being cared for in the community by various agencies. The user of service does not wish personal information about their case to be disclosed. Should this decision be respected? Do staff working in housing associations and the police come within the community of professionals who are allowed, or expected, to know?

Current guidance from the Department of Health assumes an enlargement of the 'need to know community' to allow the health service to function effectively and efficiently. For example, where agencies such as social service and housing authorities are 'contributing to or planning a programme of care,'[8] essential patient information may be passed, subject to the patient's consent which may be overridden where the public interest is an issue.

Another aspect of this particular qualification relates to a group of persons who at the present time mainly fall outside the need to know community. These persons are the non-professional carers who may also be parents. Should this group be afforded special treatment given the fact that they may be effectively providing the day-to-day care of patients who up until recently were being cared for in long-stay hospitals?

Recent legislation has introduced a statutory qualification to a patient's right to refuse consent to the disclosure of confidential information. Where statutory after-care under supervision is being considered, a patient's RMO may consult the patient's nearest relative who will play a 'substantial part' in the care of the patient, without the patient's consent, where the patient has a 'propensity to violent or dangerous behaviour'.[9] This qualification may signpost ways to allow carers to be provided with information in similar situations where a relative is not subject to statutory compulsion. The 1999 Code of Practice also gives guidance in this area: 'Ordinarily, information about a patient should not be disclosed without the patient's consent. Occasionally it

7   R.G. Toulson and C.M. Phipps (1996) *Confidentiality*. London: Sweet and Maxwell, p.37.
8   Protection and Use of Patient Information, paras 4.14 and 4.15.
9   Mental Health Act 1983, section 25B(3).

may be necessary to pass on particular information to professionals or others in the public interest, for instance where personal health or safety is at risk.'[10]

Disclosure on a need to know basis, like public interest, requires more thought than is normally given. To justify disclosure on this particular ground we need to be clear about:

- what information is relevant;

- to whom should it be disclosed;

- for what purpose is the disclosure required and how much information is required to be made available.

Children

It is clear from what has already been discussed that a 'pure' notion of absolute confidence is, in practice, hedged around with qualifications. In relation to children a further qualification emerges alongside 'public interest' and 'need to know'. This is the justification for disclosure 'in the best interests of the child'. This is partly signposting what information ought and needs to be shared within the need to know community:

> In child protection cases the overriding principle is to secure the best interests of the child. Therefore, if a health professional (or other member of staff) has knowledge of abuse or neglect it will be necessary to share this with others on a strictly controlled basis so that decisions relating to the child's welfare can be taken in the light of all relevant information.[11]

Cases involving children require the health professional to be proactive with the information that is available. Current official guidance makes clear that sharing of relevant information between professional staff is essential to protect children. Indeed there is a positive duty on doctors to disclose information to a third party where child abuse is suspected. Furthermore it has been argued that basic principles of negligence – the duty of care principle – require that adult psychiatrists should recognise that in certain situations confidentiality and loyalty to the adult may have to take second place to the interests of the child.[12] It is helpful to spell that out that a duty of care does exist.

The Children Act does not create a statutory obligation to disclose information and although Part III of the Children Act deals generally with the question of co-operation between statutory authorities it does not create such a legal obligation. Within Children Act proceedings the courts are moving towards a position where there should be full disclosure of all information, even where consent has not been given for its disclosure.[13] For example, if a psychiatrist sees a parent in the context of Children Act proceedings the parent must be informed that the report may be disclosed without his/her consent.

10   Mental Health Act Code of Practice 1999, para.1.8.
11   The Protection and Use of Patient Information.
12   Margaret Oates (1997) 'Patients as parents.' *British Journal of Psychiatry 170*, Supp 32.
13   Re L (Police Investigation: Privilege) [1997] 1 Family Law Report 731.

Hardly surprisingly there is an expectation, translated into guidance, that disclosure of confidential information in relation to children can be justified in much more general terms than the confidentiality qualifications that we have considered in relation to adults. Two case vignettes illustrate how rights to confidentiality have been modified in practice.

Sinclair

This is from a report published by West Kent Health Authority and Kent County Council Social Services in 1996.[13] Raymond Sinclair suffered from serious mental illness. Although never detained under the Mental Health Act he was treated both as an outpatient and inpatient by the local mental health service trust. He was discharged into the care of his 64-year-old mother. On 1 November 1994 he had a meeting with his CPN (community psychiatric nurse) where he talked of experiencing 'thoughts of frightening his mother and on one occasion killing his mother'. The CPN talked to the social worker. The social worker talked to her manager. 'The issue particularly concerning her was confidentiality. She recalls [her manager] as indicating that if risk was present then confidentiality might be overridden.' No action was taken by the social worker. The CPN wrote to Raymond Sinclair's consultant about the matter on 2 November 1998, the letter being sent on the 3 November 1998 which was received on the 8 November 1998 'to express and register my concern'. Raymond Sinclair fatally stabbed his mother on the morning the letter was sent.

Carr

This is from a report published in 1997 by Oxfordshire Health Authority.[14] In January 1994 Darren Carr was discharged into the community, after receiving inpatient psychiatric treatment in a secure unit. In January 1995 the unit social worker heard that Darren Carr was boarding locally in a household with young children, aged 6 and aged 4. The social worker, who was not a child-care specialist, 'remained troubled by questions of confidentiality' concerning the disclosing of information to others about his client, without his client's consent. So at the beginning of February 1995 the social worker spoke to his team leader, who gave him this advice: 'You have got no choice, if there is a danger to the children, that is the bottom line, let social services have that information and do what they will.' The social worker then spoke to the duty officer at the children and families team and followed up the conversation with the provision of written information about his client.

Tragically the information was not acted upon and in June 1995 Darren Carr set fire to the house killing the children and their mother.

---

13   *Report of the inquiry into the treatment and care of Raymond Sinclair* (1996) West Kent Health Authority and Kent County Council Social Services.

14   *Report of the inquiry into the treatment and care of Darren Carr* (1997) Berkshire Health Authority, Berkshire County Council, Oxfordshire Health Authority, Oxfordshire County Council.

Conclusions

In both these cases the qualifications to the obligations of confidence were understood by the professionals involved. However, the cases went wrong in the process. To deal with the process of exchanging information more effectively the following points should be considered:

1. If disclosure is to be justified on the grounds of public interest then the judge of what constitutes the public interest in each case is the practitioner.

2. Public interest in favour of disclosure cannot be automatically assumed – it must be justified in each case.

3. The scope of disclosure must be evaluated. The information to be disclosed must be *relevant*.

4. Professional guidance is given particular legal significance. In the case of *W* v. *Egdell* the judge referred approvingly, and in detail, to GMC guidance. Because of this it is important that the professional guidance in this field is clearly understood.

5. Every service needs access to clear and accessible confidentiality policy and guidance which says more than 'it may be necessary to seek legal or other specialist advice'.

6. Guidance needs to be developed in an inter-agency context in ways that individual professionals do not feel threatened by the involvement of colleagues from other agencies and cultures.

7. Guidance should be developed to assist adult psychiatrists who are treating a patient where there are child protection issues.

12

Confidentiality and Research in Mental Health

Michael Ferriter and Martin Butwell

Confidentiality lies at the heart of all clinical practice; it is present in the relationship between the physician and the patient and is necessary for the full and free transfer of information. It is as central in clinical practice as it is in the relationship between the priest and the parishioner, and between other professionals such as lawyers and their clients. The authors recognise the need for just as high standards of confidentiality in research as in clinical work. Our concern is that we now see an increasingly legalistic, rather than pragmatic, definition of confidentiality as part of a 'moral panic' about invasion of privacy. The logic of this increasing stringency appears to be based on the premise that applying more safeguards, against increasingly improbable risk, is, by definition, better, though this is done in wilful ignorance of the costs to society of these safeguards. Before developing these arguments further, we will address the general concept of confidentiality.

Confidentiality can be viewed on two levels – that of a contractual responsibility that requires the practitioner to protect the interests of their patient/client and the quite different moral and social responsibility to use the information imparted by the patient or client ethically. However, at the first level, that of a contractual dyadic relationship, the research situation is often very different from that binding clinician and patient.

There are two major current issues that are pertinent to the topic of confidentiality in mental health research. The first issue is the capacity of psychiatric patients to give informed consent – in this context, consent to widen boundaries of confidentiality beyond the patient's psychiatrist and clinical team to include the researcher. It is worth bearing in mind that widening the net of disclosure often occurs in everyday healthcare practice without the patient's formal consent, and certainly without the consent for each data transaction. There is little specific guidance on consent by the patient to widen confidentiality in a research context (to widen confidentiality in this sense means the patient giving explicit informed consent for information on his or her health to be passed on to others for research purposes). However, the issues of capacity are essentially no different from any other issues about the capacity of the mentally ill or disabled to give valid consent and will not be considered further here as there is already an excellent and extensive literature on the issues of capacity.

The second issue is the necessity for patients, psychiatric or not, to give consent for research based solely on medical records, case or disease registers. This question was given an added urgency by a recent case in the High Court in London (*Source Informatics v. Department of Health*) which raised fundamental questions on the use even of anonymised patients' records without prior consent given by the patients. However, in December 1999, the Appeal Court ruled that when using anonymised patient information for research purposes, it was not necessary to consider whether implied consent had been given (see Richards, 2000).

One summary of guidance on consent to participate in experimental research by the mentally disabled has been given by Wing (1999). In terms of treatment, where the individual is unable to give informed consent, the general principle is – would the treatment be in the person's best interest? Wing argues that such a principle is helpful in the context of therapeutic trials. In the case of non-therapeutic trials, he suggests that, in the absence of ability to consent, the following safeguards should be in place:

- there should be no more than minimal risks;

- the research is concerned only with the health problems that the participants have and cannot be carried out on competent patients;

- those involved do not indicate objections;

- that their relatives agree after being fully informed;

- the ethics committee gives its sanction and that a 'patient's friend' is appointed to provide a decision on inclusion.

It could be argued that the same principles and practices should apply in epidemiological research. Here there is no experimental procedure per se, but the consent from the patient is for widening the circle of confidentiality. In the case of incapacity due to mental disability (though it should be stressed that not all the mentally disordered are incapable of consent), should identical or similar strategies apply in a situation where, with adequate security and safeguards, no harm can occur?

Any discussion of confidentiality in medicine must acknowledge the historical importance of the Hippocratic Oath. The oath forbids the physician to procure an abortion, to practise surgery or to administer a poison; all practices that, at varying times, have been allowed by the medical profession for the perceived general good. Anyone who seeks to defend the sacrosanct nature of physician–patient confidentiality on classical grounds alone risks being accused of being selective. However, the oath is undoubtedly an important historical and emblematic reference point. What it says about confidentiality is:

> and whatsoever I shall see or hear in the course of my profession, as well as outside my profession in my intercourse with men, if it be what should not be published abroad I will never divulge, holding such things to be holy secrets. Now if I carry out this oath, and break it not, may I gain forever reputation among all men for my life and for my art;

but if I transgress it and forswear myself, may the opposite befall me. (Hippocrates 1923)

Much of this chapter is concisely and eloquently captured in the phrase 'what should not be published abroad', which of course neatly sidesteps the issue of deciding what can and should, and what should not, be published not only 'abroad' but, more specifically, to whom and how identifiable or anonymous it can be.

There are two principal arguments for confidentiality between the doctor and the patient – 'utility' and 'autonomy'. The simplest argument is that of utility. If the patient was not confident that what he or she told the doctor would remain confidential then, in certain circumstances, the patient might be reticent to pass on important information, or might not seek medical advice at all, with potentially serious consequences. One can see this argument at its clearest in sensitive situations such as HIV infection. The utilitarian argument is at its most important at the fault lines of society's moral and social reasoning. In the case of HIV, the fault lines are society's less than coherent and consistent views on sexual activity. It is less clear where the situation is not so emotive. Would we, or more importantly the patient, be particularly concerned if the patient's doctor had revealed details of diagnosis and treatment for asthma or a sprained ankle?

The autonomy argument is a moral one based on the premise of seeing the patient not as an 'object', a biological problem to be solved, but as a conscious thinking being able to take an active part in the therapeutic dialogue and, where possible, take an active part in treatment and treatment decisions. This argument is important when we review later the distinction between 'harm' and 'wrong'.

Both these arguments, developed within the clinical context, have been applied in health research and it has long been accepted that experimental research in healthcare should usually be carried out only after the participant has given informed consent. However, this simple principle may not always be possible, as in the case of research on those receiving emergency treatment or, of particular importance to us, where capacity to give consent may be compromised by a mental disorder. The principle may also be unhelpful more generally, where other factors make prior consent impossible or undesirable.

There are three forms of ethics: the ethic of virtue; the ethic of duty; and the ethic of the common good. The ethic of virtue is concerned with the inner spirit of morality that guides the action of the individual, in this case the physician. The ethic of duty guides the individual in judging whether actions are right or wrong. The ethic of common good is concerned with the nature of human communities, answering two related questions – what is the common good or goods and how should they be distributed? As Jonsen and Hellegers (1977) point out:

> The common good is not merely a separate third chapter of ethical concepts that should be glanced at from time to time whenever a 'social question' arises. Properly conceived, the theory of the common good is a third dimension in which virtues and actions take on a depth and tone that they do not have in isolation. The very meaning of virtue and action depends on its social or institutional setting. (Jonsen and Hellegers 1977, p.133)

Traditionally, the doctor–patient relationship has been viewed as a singular entity, the relationship between a doctor and a patient. The ethics of concern were the ethics of virtue and of duty, and within this singular relationship the ethic of the common good was not seen to be relevant.

In earlier times this was an unsurprising restriction of the ethical field as healthcare was almost entirely a personal, one-to-one consultation. However, times have changed and the wider good of society is now a clearer and almost ubiquitous concern in medicine. Factors that have influenced this change include:

- the growth of community medicine and practices that confer a wider benefit beyond the individual patient treated (such as vaccination and 'herd immunity');

- the growth and acknowledged value of epidemiological research;

- the widening of clinical involvement and information exchange beyond the doctor to include nurses and other health and social care professionals;

- the state funding of health systems where the tax payer or his/her agent has the legitimate right to enquire if money is being well spent;

- a growing number of exceptions to confidentiality where harm to others may occur.

As a result, doctors have long since moved into the domain where the ethic of the common good is as important as the ethics of virtue and duty.

Writing from a health economics perspective, Mooney (1992) argues that the ethic of the common good requires medical practitioners to take cognisance of efficiency as well as efficacy and effectiveness to maximise the good that can be done in a world of finite resource; therefore, issues of opportunity cost must be brought into the equation. Such reasoning has resonance for those of us who carry out research in healthcare and are fearful that the increasing trend to greater confidentiality will diminish the opportunity for research and ultimately produce a greater harm to society's future patients by the lost opportunity of research leading to new treatments. It is time that we looked at confidentiality in terms of what is lost by its strict preservation as well as what is gained. It is our view that we are reaching a point of diminishing returns where ever greater stringency buys increasingly little additional security for the patient and at a greater cost to society.

There are whole areas of observational research – epidemiological research using case notes, case registers and disease registers – which do not require direct contact with the patient and where gaining consent may be impractical, impossible or undesirable: impractical because of dealing with such large numbers; impossible because of tracing all the participants; undesirable because in seeking consent the sample may be biased; or, in gaining consent, needless anxiety may be caused to participants. Provided all reasonable safeguards are used to protect the anonymity of the patient data in terms of anonymising data, physical protection of that data and in recruiting research staff of probity (all issues that are as relevant in healthcare as in health research) there should be no risk of harm. This begs the question why participants should have to consent at all or even be aware that the research is taking place?

This question brings us immediately to a framework of autonomy and the issue of wrong. Capron (1991) argues that even in a situation where harm is not possible, such research might result in a wrong. The essence of his argument is that information about oneself, including medical information, is an aspect of oneself, and an unauthorised intrusion into this aspect of one's personal 'space' is as much a wrong as trespass. Such a trespass, he maintains, is a trespass even when the victim is not aware that the wrong has occurred. Capron argues that the principal defence against such a wrong is consent, by either participants or by a proxy method – such as peer group review (peers of the participants not the researchers).

The power of Capron's argument is achieved by two means. The first is to place his preferred position within the parenthesis of two opposite extremes, thus claiming the middle ground as the field of reason. At one extreme is the ultra-libertarian view of progress as an optional goal and that research is only warranted when those exposed to risk consent to bear the risk of experimentation. Proponents of this viewpoint, such as Jonas (1969), argue that no gain can justify the imposition of the sacrifice on others since such a sacrifice falls outside the social contract. The sacrifice in this context is the use of medical data without the patient's consent. At the other extreme is the position that researchers have not just a duty but a right to experiment. We would hope that there are few, if any, health researchers who would have any truck with either of these extremes.

The other means that Capron uses to stress the reasonableness of his case is to make only passing reference to the opposite point of view that epidemiological research is being needlessly hamstrung to the consequent detriment of the common good.

This argument has been forcefully put by Rothman (1981). In his brief but trenchant paper, Rothman reviews the history and lists some of the significant achievements of epidemiology in the twentieth century: the establishment of the link between smoking and lung cancer, the role of other substances as carcinogens and the relationship between diet and cardiovascular disease. He then charts epidemiology's decline, citing a growing public obsession, in the USA at least, with confidentiality and a significant variation in requirements between research centres which severely compromises multi-centre research. The consequent delays affect the time frame of projects and costs, which in turn has a negative effect, by way of frustration and demoralisation, on recruitment to academic careers. Talented potential recruits to the field might not see any career in an area where it is so difficult and protracted a process to undertake research. At the time Rothman wrote his paper he saw a decline in published pure epidemiological research and he perceived the role of the epidemiologist as increasingly becoming that of expert witness brought in by industry or government in what he describes as 'regulatory wars'.

Rothman's paper is undoubtedly a *cri de coeur* and it is necessary to consider whether there is any contemporary substance to his complaint. We feel there is. Walton of Detchant *et al.* (1999) have published a similar spirited defence of epidemiological research. The inconsistency of practice between ethics committees described by Rothman is still with us and research has shown this to be the case (see, for example,

Redshaw, Harris and Baum 1996). Such inconsistencies are inefficient and hard to justify on ethical grounds.

It is important to bear in mind that there are many different forms of healthcare research and the choice of method to research any given question should be based on appropriateness. Sometimes choice between different methodologies is possible, but at other times only one type of methodology will yield meaningful results and there is, of course, an ethical requirement not to place the patient at needless risk, or waste the patient's good will and society's investment by carrying out research which is valueless because the methodology is inappropriate. There may well be situations where epidemiological research is the only valid approach or where research based on case notes or registers represents the least intrusive approach. Under these circumstances, gaining consent does not, of itself, prevent any harm (though Capron's argument is that it would avoid a wrong) but of itself may result in harm in terms of needless concern to the participant as to why they have been included in such a study. Writers such as Capron assume that in the cases of large studies that have the greater statistical power, tracing all participants (let alone gaining consent) is a straightforward matter. It is not and needlessly consenting in the name of preventing a theoretical wrong is likely to deter or compromise research in areas where it is most badly needed.

Perhaps more seriously, consent can fundamentally damage research by introducing bias. On a technical level, one of the strengths of carrying out research where hitherto consent has not been needed is its freedom from many such biases. It is acknowledged that certain groups of people are more likely to consent to take part in research than others. For whatever reasons, younger patients, men and members of ethnic minorities are all less likely to consent to participate in health research. This leads to a consequent bias in research carried out, problems in generalisation to the wider population as a whole and, ultimately, to the disadvantage of people in less compliant groups. There are also groups of people whose life style is transient, who are the most difficult to locate, are most likely to be lost to follow-up but who may well be among the more needy in health terms. These people tend to fall through the conventional net of healthcare research.

There are also a number of consequences to a global requirement to gain repeated consent from the patient for each and every re-use of original data. Under these circumstances re-investigating original data may become impossible or prohibitively expensive, requiring as it would the locating and re-consenting of all participants. The only true beneficiaries, under these circumstances, would be researchers who had an interest in not having their original data re-examined, such as those presenting fraudulent results. A less sinister but perhaps more significant problem would be where important findings emerge as a by-product of the original research. It may not be possible to report such findings as they fall outside of the original contract between the researcher and the participant.

A crucial question that needs to be asked is: Has anybody ever been harmed by the use of their healthcare data in a case or disease register? Wing (1986), addressing directly the concerns of Rothman, boldly states that 'no single example of harm done to a person whose data have been entered in a research register has ever been recorded' but adds:

With the advent of commercialised data banks and the ever increasing possibilities in automated data processing the interests of the media, of politicians, and of legislators has been raised. This in turn has stirred up a great deal of unnecessary anxiety and suspicion which in the past few years has resulted in the enactment of data protection laws... In some countries, legislation has impeded important research work, especially that using case registers. (Wing 1986, p.360)

Wing had several examples in mind. The impact of the Icelandic Data Law (1981) on the Icelandic Psychiatric Register was to limit severely the transfer of data to the register and compromise its usefulness (Helgason 1986). In 1981, as a result of new data protection legislation, the Data Protection Commissioner of the Länder of Baden-Württenburg closed the Cumulative Psychiatric Case Register in Mannheim, despite the acknowledged diligence of the staff in protecting patient confidentiality and acknowledged absence of any incidents of misuse (Häfner and Pfeifer-Kurda 1986).

The sort of harm that such data protection legislation is designed to prevent is, in reality, unlikely. Even where research on patients is openly published (frequently in obscure professional journals with, to say the least, a small readership), the information is most often in aggregate form and individual identification is impossible. There is a risk in publishing the results of small cohort studies and individual case studies and there is a clear role for the appropriate ethics committee, together with the authors and the journal editors, to safeguard against such risk.

We strongly believe that alongside an absolute requirement to carry out health research ethically, there is an ethical requirement to carry out health research. In taking this view we reject, as does Capron, the two extremes he describes. We also believe that the majority of society wants health researchers to continue to carry out sound, ethical research. The inherent problem faced by all those who work in research is that, by definition, the outcome of the research is unknown at commencement and the benefit of research, if any, will be in the future. This brings us to the dimension of time and the economics of harm and benefit.

Economists are familiar with the notion of 'positive time preference' – the human phenomena whereby we place a greater value on something now than that same thing in the future. Hire purchase, mortgages and much else thrive, in fact only exist, on this principle. Those conducting research are in the thankless position of convincing participants to value a possible (though by no means certain) good in the future against a possible (though depending on the project, unlikely) harm or wrong in the present.

With this difficult task, the researcher is not working in a social or political vacuum. Creating a research culture in a society that attracts high calibre staff is a question of long-term investment with profits to society some way into the future. For example, case and disease registers rarely yield any great benefit in the first few years of existence, but may yield gold decades after they have been set up. For research to thrive and yield benefit, it must be seen as being part of the infrastructure of society, as much as roads, railways and health and welfare systems. Research thrives best in a political climate where there is consensus about investing in the future outside of any current vagaries of political and ideological disagreement.

We need, as Wing (1986) points out, to 'convince the public, the administrators and the politicians that this kind of research is essential for improvement in the health of populations and that it will constitute no danger to the rights of individuals'. How can this be achieved? Is there a way forward?

Research was not within the specific remit of the *Caldicott Report* (Department of Health 1997), but it would be foolish to ignore the recommendations of the Caldicott Committee as they are all part of a wider ethical and moral debate about how we conduct ourselves in the context of sensitive information entrusted to us by patients. The Caldicott Committee stated six principles for the protection of patient-identifiable information:

1. The purpose of using the information is justified.

2. Such information should be used only when absolutely necessary.

3. Only the minimum of information required should be used.

4. Access should be on a need to know basis.

5. All who have access should be aware of their responsibilities.

6. All who have access should understand and comply with the law.

Any debate, in the UK at least, on confidentiality and research should take cognisance of these principles.

The Medical Research Council (MRC 1999) has recently published its draft guidelines on personal information in medical research for discussion and comment and there is much here to commend. The Council clearly has concerns about the future of epidemiological research and, like Rothman, is anxious to declare the contribution of epidemiology to healthcare and provides its own list including:

• recognition of new variant CJD and its relation to the BSE epidemic;

• better understanding of newly suspected health hazards;

• reliable evaluations of new preventative measures and treatments;

• ways of reducing cot deaths;

• assessments of the healthcare needs of special groups in society and identification of adverse drug reactions.

The guidelines also point out that most international and national ethical codes do not specifically require consent for records-based research provided there is no intention to interfere in research patients' lives; the research could not lead to harm; and where the research may either benefit the participants or society as a whole. In these circumstances, the research cannot be against the patients' interests. However, the guidelines then go on to state that wherever possible it is desirable to seek consent on the grounds that it would provide reassurance that the doctor–patient relationship was being respected.

The legal situation in the UK on the use of medical information without prior consent is by no means clear and is based on Common Law, the Data Protection Acts of 1984 and 1998 and the Human Rights Act of 1998. The MRC has sought legal advice on using confidential information for research purposes without consent. The advice from the legal profession is that judgement can only be made on a case-by-case basis, but the following factors would be pertinent:

- The sensitivity of the information collected.

- The importance of the research.

- The safeguards in place to protect against leakage of sensitive information.

- The research approval of an independent body such as a local research ethics committee or multi-centre research ethics committee.

- Did alternative ways of doing the research that would have allowed consent exist?

- If explicit consent was not possible, were reasonable efforts made to inform the population involved of how their medical records were being used and, an opportunity provided to raise concerns?

The guidelines also point out that even if research is approved by an ethics committee and authorised by a health authority, individual doctors are still responsible for the use of information on their patients. The guidelines add:

> This is a controversial area of law, and the MRC is aware that there are other interpretations of Common Law, some of which would argue for freer use of personal records, and some which hold that the public interest can only justify disclosing confidential information where there is an extraordinary threat to the health of the nation or individuals.

Things are a little clearer with the Data Protection Act. The Act allows a degree of freedom for the re-use of information for research purposes. Anonymised data are also excluded from the scope of the Act and there are special exemptions, within the Act, that allow research to take place provided that it is unlikely to harm or cause distress to the data subject. However, it is important to remember that data collected for clinical purposes are covered by the Act and if such data are collected with the knowledge that they may also be used for research then the patient, the data subject, must be informed. Conversely, data collected primarily for research purposes but also used for clinical purposes are also covered by the Act. The guidelines also advise that the Human Rights Act (1998) provides for a balance between individual rights and the legitimate needs of society.

In the view of the guidelines' authors, there is one important step that could obviate a number of problems in health research. They recommend that new patients to GP surgeries and to hospital services should be informed that their clinical data may be used for future research and their consent gained. This was an original MRC recommendation that became Department of Health policy in 1996, though full implementation is some way off. Such a procedure would avoid the need for re-consenting at each new research use. However, there would still be a number of patients who would not consent and this would be unsatisfactory in those research projects that need total population figures. We also have to consider the issue of whether the process should be that the patients 'opt in' to consent to their information being used or 'opt out' of not letting their information be used. The MRC's recommendation goes a considerable way to solving a number of problems but falls short of a total solution.

The MRC guidelines contain eleven key principles (Table 12.1) which also include the situation where gaining consent may not be practicable.

Table 12.1 MRC guidelines: key principles

- Personal information of any sort which is provided for healthcare, or obtained in medical research, must be treated as confidential. Normally, clinical researchers must ensure they have consent to hold or use personal information, and in most clinical research this is practicable.

- When consent is impracticable, confidential information can be disclosed for medical research without consent: if it is justified by the importance of the study; if there is no intention to contact individuals (except to seek consent) or reveal findings to them; if there are no practicable alternatives of equal effectiveness; and if the infringement of confidentiality is kept to a minimum.

- Research must be planned with confidentiality in mind.

- All medical research using personal information – from any source – must be approved by a local research ethics committee or multi-centre research ethics committee.

- Hospitals and practices involved in research must have procedures for making patients aware that their information is used for research, and explain the reasons and safeguards.

- All personal information must be encoded or anonymised as far as is reasonably possible, and as early as possible in data processing.

- Responsibility for disclosing patient information lies with the holder of the information.

- Personal information must be handled only by health professionals or staff with an equivalent duty of confidentiality.

- Researchers must have in place procedures to minimise the risk of their research causing distress.

- Principle investigators must take personal responsibility for ensuring that training, procedures, supervision and data security arrangements are sufficient to prevent unauthorised breaches of confidentiality.

- At the outset, researchers must decide what information about the results should be available to the people involved in the study once it is complete, and agree these plans with the research ethics committee.

At the time of writing, these key principles are in draft form for consultation and we eagerly await the revised and definitive document from the MRC. Alongside the Caldicott recommendations we may be in a position to provide a framework that both protects the patient and allows potentially important work to be carried out without fear of legal action against researchers.

Acknowledgements

The authors wish to thank Felicity Ferriter for her help in proof-reading and editing this chapter and Chris Evans for his helpful suggestions for improving the original manuscript.

References

Department of Health (Caldicott Committee) (1997) *Report on the Review of Patient-Identifiable Information.* London: Department of Health.

Capron, A.M. (1991) 'Protection of research subjects: do special rules apply to epidemiology?' *Journal of Clinical Epidemiology 4*, suppl. I, 81S–89S.

Department of Health (DoH) (1996) *The Protection and Use of Patient Information.* London: DoH.

Häfner, H. and Pfeifer-Kurda, M. (1986) 'The impact of data protection laws on the Mannheim case register.' In G.H.M.M. ten Horn, R. Giel, W.R. Gulbinat and J.H. Henderson (eds) *Psychiatric Case Registers in Public Health.* Kidlington: Elsevier.

Helgason, T. (1986) 'The Icelandic experience.' In G.H.M.M. ten Horn, R. Giel, W.R. Gulbinat and J.H. Henderson (eds) *Psychiatric Case Registers in Public Health.* Kidlington: Elsevier.

Hippocrates (1923) *Hippocrates.* Trans. W.H.S. Jones. Cambridge MA: Harvard University Press.

Jonas, H. (1969) 'Philosophical reflections on experimenting with humans.' *Daedalus 98*, 219–245.

Jonsen, A.R. and Hellegers, A.E. (1977) 'Conceptual foundations for an ethics of medical care.' In S.J. Reiser, A.J. Dyck and W.J. Curran (eds) *Ethics in Medicine: Historical Perspectives and Contemporary Concerns.* Cambridge, MA: MIT Press.

Medical Research Council (1999) *Personal Information in Medical Research. Draft MRC Guidelines.* London: Medical Research Council.

Mooney, G. (1992) *Economics, Medicine and Health Care,* 2nd edn. Hemel Hempstead: Harvester Wheatsheaf.

Redshaw, M.E., Harris, A. and Baum, J.D. (1996) 'Research ethics committee audit; differences between committees.' *Journal of Medical Ethics 22*, 78–82.

Richards, T. (2000) 'Court sanctions use of anonymised patient data.' *British Medical Journal 320*, 77.

Rothman, J.R. (1981) 'The rise and fall of epidemiology 1950–2000 A.D.' *New England Journal of Medicine 304*, 10, 600–602.

Walton of Detchant, Lord, Doll, R., Asscher, W., Hurley, R., Langman, M., Gillon, R., Strachan, D., Wald, D. and Fletcher, P. (1999) 'Consequences for research if use of anonymised patient data breaches confidentiality.' *British Medical Journal 319*, 1366.

Wing, J.K. (1986) 'Data protection and problems of data confidentiality.' In G.H.M.M. ten Horn, R. Giel, W.R. Gulbinat and J.H. Henderson (eds) *Psychiatric Case Registers in Public Health.* Kidlington: Elsevier.

Wing, J. (1999) 'Ethics and psychiatric research.' In S. Bloch, P. Chodoff and S.A. Green (eds) *Psychiatric Ethics,* 3rd edn. Oxford: Oxford University Press.

13

Themes of Confidentiality in Clinical Practice

Julian Stern (with contributions from Maurice Greenberg, Rob Hale, Gill McGauley, George Szmukler and Cleo van Velsen)

I think I have taken every precaution to prevent my patient from suffering any (direct personal) injury. I … have waited four whole years since the end of the treatment and have postponed publication till hearing that a change has taken place in the patient's life of such a character as allows me to suppose that her own interest in the occurrences and psychological events which are to be related here may now have grown faint. Needless to say I have allowed no name to stand which could put a non-medical reader upon the scent; and the publication of the case in a purely scientific and technical periodical should, further, afford a guarantee against unauthorized readers of this sort. (Freud 1905)

We run the risk of essentially writing fiction if we become firm protectors of confidentiality, while we run a risk of moral transgression if we insist on a truthful presentation of our work. (Goldberg 1997, p.438)

Almost a century separates the views of Sigmund Freud and a contemporary psychoanalyst, Goldberg. They are both describing dilemmas integral to the writing and publication of case histories, and in particular how to balance, on the one hand the patient's need for and right to confidentiality, and on the other the use of such material in the interests of learning, teaching and advancing the academic study of the human psyche.

This aspect of confidentiality is only one of many, some of which are addressed in the other various chapters of this book. What will be described in this final chapter arises from a conference on 'Confidentiality and Mental Health' in Sheffield (UK), (1998), and in particular from the conference small groups. All participants were divided on two occasions into small groups to discuss and to help 'metabolise' issues arising from the conference. The dilemmas, of which both Freud and Goldberg were so aware, are refracted through the lenses of the participants in these small groups, the group convenors and memory. What follows is an attempt to distil some of the themes arising from these groups, and to describe parallels between some of the issues discussed and the group dynamics.

The group facilitators came from different backgrounds – community psychiatry, individual psychodynamic psychotherapy, group analytic psychotherapy, and forensic psychotherapy and psychiatry – and much of the flavour of a particular group was influenced by the facilitator's orientation. Thus the group led by the community psychiatrist focused on issues such as electronic record keeping, the role of the police and the community mental health team, while topics discussed in the forensic psychotherapist's group included enquiries into homicides, the protection of children and individual responsibility.

Despite the diversity of facilitators and participants, some themes recurred, in different guises, in particular:

- 'absolute' versus 'relative' confidentiality;
- boundaries and confidentiality;
- context and culture – children, the elderly and cultural subgroups and special situations;
- defences – others' and our own.

Absolute vs relative confidentiality

The stance adopted by lawyers, of absolute respect for one's clients' right to confidentiality, was contrasted with the legal and moral positions of practising psychiatrists. Psychiatrists, grappling with responsibilities – often conflicting – to patients, patients' families and the public, were much less clear about an absolute position. Examples were raised of childhood sexual abusers and of patients who threatened or had previously committed violent acts. The position of the lawyers, and criminal lawyers in particular, was envied, seemingly so clearcut and free of conflict of loyalty or interests.

Boundaries and confidentiality

Linked with the above, was the issue of boundaries. Participants in a number of the groups debated difficulties surrounding the maintenance of confidentiality in teams. An example was raised of the statutory obligations of social workers to disclose information which psychiatrists may not usually disclose. How does one obtain consent from patients under such circumstances, and to what is the patient consenting? How much of such information should then be available to other health professionals? How much should be available to other non-clinicians such as hospital managers?

Context and culture

When two consenting adults are engaged in a particular activity, most participants agreed that their right to confidentiality should be preserved. Children were the most obvious 'special group' discussed, and in one group the case of a 15-year-old Asian girl who had been sexually abused by her uncle was debated. The risks of disclosure, in terms of family discord and possible stigmatisation within her community, were weighed up against the dangers of a 'perpetrator' remaining untouched.

In a later group, the case of a medical student who was involved in an incestuous relationship with his sister was discussed, including again risks of disclosure – to their family and to his medical seniors. The complexities of this case dominated discussion – a young woman, admitted to a medical ward with bizarre abdominal and gynaecological symptoms, probably 'hysterical' in quality, disclosed that she was involved in an incestuous relationship with her brother, a medical student. He was now attending ward rounds on her ward and was about to qualify as a doctor. Was he likely to put other patients at risk? She feared family discord if the relationship came to light, and for his career; she asked for the information to be kept confidential. On the other hand, wondered group members, did the doctors caring for her have a duty towards future patients of his? And what about her well-being? Was her overt wish for confidentiality to be preserved as her only wish, or was she also 'asking' for someone to 'blow the whistle' on her brother? What was in his best interests? Intense debate and emotion ensued, and a final 'vote' as to whether to report this man to more senior figures was a 'split decision', with most participants more likely to discuss the case with professionals outside the medical student's current hospital, for example, the medical defence organisation to which one belonged.

Common to both of these examples, and to others, was the complexity of the cases, the need for senior people to whom to defer or discuss cases, and the need for professional guidelines.

Also common to the discussions was a despair at the need for external structures in lieu of the development, internally, of a sense of conscience or moral responsibility in many of the perpetrators. Thus in one group members had a strong view that if children were considered at risk, at all, there was a duty to inform those in authority. A counterview, posed by the facilitator, was that this might absolve the person's real responsibility, internally (i.e. mentally), as the essence of good treatment entails enabling the person who is posing a risk to take responsibility him/herself, both internally and externally. If reported on too quickly, then the function of being one's own internal policeman might never begin to develop.

Defences

While all these issues were being discussed, the facilitators were aware of the extent to which any such issue could be used defensively. Thus 'culture' for example, can be used to avoid a painful recognition that 'we' too (for example, Asians/Jews/doctors/therapists) might abuse our children. The wish that the perpetrator 'one day' might develop an internal sense of morality and not require an external policeman may be an idealised wish, a defence against the horror of recognition of irretrievable corruption of the personality. It may also link with one's own fantasies that 'one day' certain areas in one's own personality will be magically made better (see Akhtar 1999).

Other examples of defensive thinking included the quest for and reification of medical diagnoses; and the belief that older more senior colleagues – 'three wise men' – could be handed the problem and would deal with it; or that guidelines and protocols would do the same. ('Three wise men' refers to a traditional practice within hospitals that three senior medical staff, women or men, give advice and arbitrate on complicated ethical matters.) This is not to suggest that guidelines are not important, but they can provide a false sense of security and be used to avoid grappling with uncomfortable areas of patient care and one's own psychic reality and ethical position.

A final example of defensive thinking is described by one of the group facilitators (Greenberg): 'There was a tendency to move rapidly towards general statements of principle, with which everyone could agree, rather than explore potential areas of conflict. The fact that everyone referred their opinion as to what was "in the best interests of the patient" came across as rather banal and meaningless. Any effort to challenge felt as if it was met by a rather deadening silence.'

Confidentiality and the group processes

Some of the common themes explicitly discussed in the groups have been described, but what now follows is my own account (Stern), as one of the group facilitators, which endeavours to demonstrate, in a more detailed manner, many of the complex and intertwined issues surrounding confidentiality; how boundaries and allegiances interact; how transference and countertransference interact with issues of a forensic, legal and moral nature.

Months before the date of the meeting, I had agreed to convene a small group. My primary allegiance at this stage seemed to be to the members of the group. A few days prior to the meeting I was asked to 'write it up' for publication. My primary allegiance and responsibilities now shifted somewhat. I began to worry about whether I would remember what went on in the groups. All possibility of conducting the group 'without memory or desire' to use Bion's (1967) terminology, seemed compromised once I accepted this role. Then on the day of the conference, together with the other group facilitators, I was asked to record as much as possible of the groups and feed back to 'a professor', so that the lessons and difficulties faced by the groups and individual members within each group could help with the creation of guidelines and a protocol. Now my allegiance was once again altered – and the 'aim' of the groups was to help with policy and guidelines and professional practice as a whole. I am not suggesting that these three sets of allegiances are mutually contradictory – but with hindsight, looking back on the trajectory of events, it does seem akin to the situation faced by many of our patients who think they are seeing a doctor because the doctor will primarily want to help or care for them. They then realise (or fear), consciously or unconsciously, that they are being seen by a doctor whose primary interest may be in research, in collecting enough patients for a trial, or to publish, to help his/her career, rather than the primary or perhaps exclusive allegiance being to the patient himself.

What are the effects on a patient who senses that the doctor is not primarily interested in him/her? What are the effects on the patient's narrative? How can different hats be worn simultaneously by doctors who may want total trust from the patient, but who may act in a way which makes total trust unwise, or unviable, even in a potentially trusting patient? How does a group of professionals at a conference deal with similar issues?

The morning group

All were psychiatrists. The facilitator raised some introductory issues. 'The conference chair has asked me to consider writing this group up for publication. How do you feel about this? How will you decide whether that is appropriate? Are there any conditions that need to be applied?'

Group members were quiet, although a few mentioned it was impossible to comment at this stage as they did not know what would emerge in the group. The facilitator went on to raise the question of confidentiality in publications in general and mentioned Freud's proviso when writing up the Dora case – that the case be disguised, that a time interval lapse between the end of treatment and publication, and that the readership be relatively restricted (see Polden 1998).

The group started discussing informed consent in general, rather tentatively. The imbalance of power between professional and patient was highlighted, with mention made of the need for patients to please their doctors, and not to alienate them when they needed their doctors to care for them. An old age psychiatrist mentioned that her patients do not like being written about. A sex therapist said her patients have no problems in this regard. They are happy to be talked about having had their problems cured, after years of struggling in silence; since it has taken them so long to get help they are pleased to share the good news.

The group wondered about this difference. Was it a particularly intimate relationship with elderly patients, who are reversing generational roles and giving a nurturant role to someone the age of their own children? A group member said she would have expected the opposite; that elderly patients were brought up in a generation which respected doctors and would try to do anything to please doctors, including consenting to being 'used'.

The question of informed consent in different social classes, ethnic groups and patient populations was raised. Right at the end of the group someone expressed vague discomfort at the question of this all being written up.

The afternoon group

The atmosphere was charged right from the start. A forensic psychiatrist was angry. She was feeling 'conned'. She thought it was up to the group to decide the agenda. Why did the facilitator decide on the agenda? Had she known this was going to be the case she would have gone elsewhere. For whom was it being written? Whose idea was it?

The facilitator explained that it was the idea of the conference chair, for future publication. This seemed not to placate her. Others seemed less concerned. The facilitator tried to link the group mood with the theme of the conference. 'It is as if you are seeing a patient, and the patient suddenly feels he is being seen for your purposes, not for his/hers. This relates closely to the questions of confidentiality and power.'

The facilitator continued, explaining that the feedback was also to try to help the work of the Royal College of Psychiatrists' committee, which had the difficult task of drawing up guidelines, and in the long run to help us all as psychiatrists. Slowly, but perceptibly, the mood lightened and group members talked about their real difficulties in coping with the confidentiality issue. The feeling was increasingly of a group for the benefit of the group members, not for the benefit of an external beneficiary. Group members described, repeatedly, the sense of double bind, of being damned for disclosing too much and damned for disclosing too little. Some were attracted to the purity of the criminal barrister's position, where non-disclosure was an absolute principle, but most wistfully realised this was not possible in psychiatry.

A psychiatrist from a secure hospital mentioned how he sometimes chose not to disclose, when working with dangerous patients, as disclosure seemed so antithetical to a therapeutic alliance he has worked so hard to build up. The sex therapist described how she tells her patients 'up front' that there are only certain conditions under which she will agree to treat them, and others under which she will feel obliged to break confidentiality.

The forensic psychiatrist who was previously feeling 'conned' spoke poignantly about a group she had facilitated, in which a sex offender disclosed current acts of such a nature that she felt impelled to break confidentiality. The man was charged, convicted and imprisoned. She felt enormous guilt. She was asked about the man's emotional pain. She thought he suffered very little. The facilitator wondered out loud about the perpetrator's possible wish or need for punishment, and the interesting question as to the location of pain in her rather than in the man.

The mood continued to improve as clinical examples were described and grappled with. The facilitator, conscious of time pressure, raised the (his) issue of whether the account of the group could be published. Group members generally were in favour of this and although the question of disguise was raised, this seemed not to be necessary. As one member said, 'It is fine to disseminate it if it is for our benefit, and not for the managers.'

More and more clinical examples were raised, with a prevailing sense of clinicians working hard, having to make difficult ad hoc judgements for which there were often no hard-and-fast guidelines; and if things go wrong, each one of the group could be the subject of an inquiry. The threat of persecution from 'them' (managers, inquiries, and so on) was present, but the group did not feel paranoid. Rather, there was an overwhelming feeling of solidarity, of the group working for group members and the profession as a whole. The omnipresent tension between the rights of the individual versus those of society was evident, but the groups ended, a few minutes late, with a sense of common struggle, difficult decisions to be made, but no exaggerated persecutory anxieties.

Discussion

The above description of the two group meetings is (as always) distorted by selective memory, my own needs (probably mainly unconscious) to forget some issues, and put a particular slant on others. But what I have tried to show is how one's approach to confidentiality can affect not only one's own assumptions and attitudes in running such a group, but can also evoke different reactions among group members. The group seemed to go through various stages, from initial uncertainty, anxiety and smouldering resentment at the possibility of being 'used' to an eventual ability to focus on the explicit task of the group members.

A synthesis

What can be distilled from the groups which might help psychiatrists and other mental health professionals to think about, and then manage impasses, conflicts or anxieties around confidentiality? I make five proposals:

1. A set of guidelines regarding confidentiality, for the profession, is desirable, but it always must be borne in mind that guidelines can be used defensively by individuals and institutions, to avoid thinking and struggling with anxieties.

2. The presence of a group of senior colleagues – the so-called 'three wise men' – or women – to whom individuals can turn for advice/consultation, is desirable and should be made formal and explicit in each hospital or trust. The same proviso regarding possible defensive uses, as with guidelines above, should be borne in mind. (Incidentally, no one seems to worry much about the breaching of confidentiality implicit in the very act of discussing these matters with the so-called 'three wise men'. Are discussions of this nature to be granted an equivalent of 'diplomatic immunity'?)

3. The provision, in the training of junior psychiatrists, of formal teaching on confidentiality in particular, and ethics in general, as well as ongoing training for qualified psychiatrists and mental health professionals are essential. There is, currently, an almost total absence of such training in the formal curriculum for doctors in training, and psychiatrists.

4. Either as part of such training or separately, the provision of small group experiences such as reported above is recommended, in which these questions and dilemmas can be discussed, involving individuals in grappling with their own prejudices, fears, anxieties and sense of morality.

5. The establishment of an ongoing forum whereby legal, psychiatric, psychotherapeutic and community mental health professionals can meet and exchange ideas is once again desirable. The conference, at which these groups met, was a useful starting point and catalyst, but is not sufficient unless followed up by more permanent and ongoing structures.

Many of the recommendations derive from the explicit comments of group participants. In one group, for example (facilitated by Cleo van Velsen), participants 'commented on the lack of any real training meaning that practitioners "picked up" ideas regarding the management of confidentiality, often in an inconsistent and patchy manner. What then emerged is that people often do not consciously think about confidentiality, and act in the context of a "thinking vacuum". They tend to go along with the prevailing political pressures, which, at present, are to do with sharing information, not just to protect others, but to protect the clinicians themselves.' The recommendations above would go some way towards redressing this 'thinking vacuum'.

An afterword

Various members of one of the groups asked to see any paper which derived from the groups in which they participated. This has been done. Other members of another group were happy not to see any draft. This 'informed consent' is appreciated. I have not distributed this chapter to all members of the conference. This seemed to me to be stretching concepts of confidentiality too far – but this is my privileged and perhaps paternalistic position. And what about the rights of patients who were discussed in the groups and then disguised – is the disguise adequate? Goldberg's view, quoted at the top of this chapter, tries to steer a middle path between total disclosure with little regard for confidentiality and total non-reporting, which would make the description of the groups (and individual case histories – our 'bread and butter') impossible. What does the reader think?

Acknowledgements

My gratitude to the professional participants of all the groups, who entered into the spirit of the groups in a thoughtful and committed manner, and to the group facilitators who reported in a full and lively fashion on the group processes and themes.

References

Akhtar, S. (1999) '"Someday…" and "If only…" fantasies.' In S. Akhtar *Inner Torment: Living between Conflict and Fragmentation*. Northvale NJ: Jason Aronson.

Bion, W. (1967) 'Notes on memory and desire.' In E. Bott Spillius (ed) *Melanie Klein Today, Vol.2: Mainly Practice*. London: Routledge, 1988, pp.17–21.

Freud, S. (1905) *A Fragment of an Analysis of a Case of Hysteria*. SE7. London: Hogarth.

Goldberg, A. (1997) 'Writing case histories.' *International Journal of Psycho-Analysis 78*, 3 435–438.

Polden, J. (1998) 'Publish and be damned.' *British Journal of Psychotherapy 14*, 3, 337–347.

The Contributors

Sue Bailey is a Consultant Child and Adolescent Forensic Psychiatrist. She works in the mental health services of Salford and in the South London and Maudsley NHS Trusts. She is a senior researcher at the University of Manchester.

Christopher Bollas is a member of the British Psychoanalytic Society and in private practice in London. He is the author of many publications, most recently *Hysteria*.

Martin Butwell is the National Manager of the Special Hospitals Case Register and a member of the Department of Forensic Psychiatry, Institute of Psychiatry, London. His current interests include epidemiological research relating to Special Hospital patients and the development of evaluation packages for psychotherapeutic treatments.

Paul Cain is a lecturer in the department of professional education in community studies at the University of Reading. He works on ethical issues with students from a range of health and social care professions, including community nursing, therapeutic child care, social work and general practice.

Christopher Cordess is Professor of Forensic Psychiatry in the School of Health and Related Research at the University of Sheffield. He is an Associate Member of the British Psychoanalytical Society and is also Honorary Consultant and Director of Research at Rampton Hospital. He was formerly Honorary Senior Lecturer in forensic psychiatry at Charing Cross and Westminster Medical School.

Michael Ferriter is Research Fellow at Rampton Hospital, Honorary Research Fellow at the School for Health and Related Research at Sheffield University and Visiting Research Fellow at the University of Wales, Swansea. He is responsible for maintaining the Special Hospitals Case Register at Rampton Hospital and has researched and published on a wide range of topics including computer-aided interviewing, schizophrenia and the family, and the management and treatment of sex offenders.

Bill (KWM) Fulford is a Professor of Philosophy and Mental Health in the Department of Philosophy, University of Warwick, and Honorary Consultant Psychiatrist in the Department of Psychiatry, University of Oxford. His research interests include philosophical value theory and its applications to psychopathology and classification in psychiatry.

Maurice Greenberg is a group analyst. He is Consultant Psychiatrist at University College Hospital, London and director of the student health service at University College London.

Andrew Hall is a barrister at Doughty Street Chambers whose practice is predominantly criminal defence work with a particular interest in human rights issues. He is an member of the General Council of the Bar and sits on the Professional Standards Committee. He has written, broadcast and lectured widely on criminal law and the criminal justice system.

Rob Hale is a Consultant Psychotherapist and Psychoanalyst. He is Director of the Portman Clinic and Associate Dean for Counselling Doctors, North Thames Postgraduate Dental and Medical Education Department. His clinical interests are the treatment of perpetrators of criminal acts and his research interests include suicide. He is also responsible for organising services for Doctors in Need of Psychological Help.

Anthony Harbour is a solicitor. He is a partner in Scott-Moncrieff Harbour & Sinclair, a solicitor's firm specialising in health and social service law. He is a legal president of the Mental Health Review Tribunal.

Frank Holloway is a Consultant Psychiatrist in Community and Rehabilitation Psychiatry. He is a Clinical Director of the Croydon Directorate of the South London and Maudsley NHS Trust and an honorary Senior Lecturer in the Health Services Research Department of the Institute of Psychiatry. His clinical and research interests are focused on the needs of people with long-term severe mental illnesses.

Adarsh Kaul is a Consultant Forensic Psychiatrist at the Nottingham Forensic Service, a district and community forensic service for mentally disordered offenders and others with similar needs. He was previously a consultant forensic psychiatrist at the Regional Secure Unit in Leicester and a panel member of the Leicestershire and Rutland Public Protection panel.

Gill McCauley is Senior Lecturer in Forensic Psychotherapy at St George's Hospital medical school and honorary consultant at Broadmoor Hospital.

Roy McClelland is a Consultant Psychiatrist and Professor of Mental Health, Queen's University Belfast. He is the Chairman of the Royal College of Psychiatrists Informatics Sub-Committee and Confidentiality Working Group.

Jacki Pritchard is a qualified social worker who has worked as a practitioner in both fieldwork and hospital settings. She is currently working as a trainer, consultant and researcher focusing on abuse, risk and violence.

Julian Stern is a Consultant Psychotherapist at St Mark's Hospital, London, and the Royal London Hospital (St Clement's). He has a special interest in psychosomatic disorders, and the relationships between psychotherapy and psychiatric practice. He has recently coedited a textbook of psychiatry, *Core Psychiatry*, with P. Wright and M. Phelan.

George Szmukler is a Consultant in Community Psychiatry and Joint Medical Director of the South London and Maudsley NHS Trust. He Senior Lecturer at the Institute of Psychiatry. His current research interests focus on health services evaluation, families and carers of the mentally ill, the use of coercion in treatment, and mental health legislation.

Judith Trowell is a Consultant Child and Adolescent Psychiatrist at The Tavistock Clinic and a trained psychoanalyst and child analyst. She was formerly a psychiatric advisor with the NSPCC and senior clinical lecturer at the children's department of the Institute of Psychiatry. She is currently senior lecturer at the Royal Free and University College Hospital Medical School. She is co-organiser of legal workshops at the Tavistock Clinic and an expert witness.

Cleo van Velsen is a psychoanalyst. She is Consultant Forensic Psychotherapist at the John Howard Centre medium secure unit in Hackney, London.

APPENDIX I

Confidentiality: Protecting and Providing Information

**GENERAL
MEDICAL
COUNCIL**

*Protecting patients,
guiding doctors*

Contents

Being registered with the General Medical Council gives you rights and privileges. In return, you have a duty to meet the standards of competence, care and conduct set by the GMC.

Doctors hold information about patients which is private and sensitive. This information must not be given to others unless the patient consents or you can justify the disclosure. Guidance on when disclosures may be justified are discussed in this booklet.

When you are satisfied that information should be released, you should act promptly to disclose all relevant information. This is often essential to the best interests of the patient, or to safeguard the well-being of others.

Note Guidelines reproduced in full with the kind permission of the General Medical Council.

Glossary: This defines the terms used within this document. These definitions have no wider or legal significance.

Anonymised data: Data from which the patient cannot be identified by the recipient of the information. The name, address, and full post code must be removed together with any other information which, in conjunction with other data held by or disclosed to the recipient, could identify the patient. NHS numbers or other unique numbers may be included only if recipients of the data do not have access to the 'key' to trace the identity of the patient using this number.

Consent: Agreement to an action based on knowledge of what the action involves and its likely consequences.

Express consent: Consent which is expressed orally or in writing (except where patients cannot write or speak, when other forms of communication may be sufficient).

Health care team: The health care team comprises the people providing clinical services for each patient and the administrative staff who directly support those services.

Patients: Competent patients and parents of, or those with parental responsibility for, children who lack maturity to make decisions for themselves. (Adult patients who lack the capacity to consent have the right to have their confidentiality respected. Guidance on disclosure of information about such patients is included in paragraphs 38-39).

Personal information: Information about people which doctors learn in a professional capacity and from which individuals can be identified.

Public interest: The interests of the community as a whole, or a group within the community or individuals.

Section 1 - Patients' right to confidentiality

1. Patients have a right to expect that information about them will be held in confidence by their doctors. Confidentiality is central to trust between doctors and patients. Without assurances about confidentiality, patients may be reluctant to give doctors the information they need in order to provide good care. If you are asked to provide information about patients you should:

    - Seek patients' consent to disclosure of information wherever possible, whether or not you judge that patients can be identified from the disclosure.

    - Anonymise data where unidentifiable data will serve the purpose.

    - Keep disclosures to the minimum necessary.

You must always be prepared to justify your decisions in accordance with this guidance.

Protecting information

2. When you are responsible for personal information about patients you must make sure that it is effectively protected against improper disclosure at all times[1].

3. Many improper disclosures are unintentional. You should not discuss patients where you can be overheard or leave patients' records, either on paper or on screen, where they can be seen by other patients, health care staff or the public. Whenever possible you should take steps to ensure that your consultations with patients are private.

---

1. There are particular dangers with the storage and transfer of electronic data. Further advice is at Appendix 1 to the guidance.

Section 2 - Sharing information with patients

4. Patients have a right to information about the health care services available to them, presented in a way that is easy to follow and use.

5. Patients also have a right to information about any condition or disease from which they are suffering. This should be presented in a manner easy to follow and use, and include information about diagnosis, prognosis, treatment options, outcomes of treatment, common and/or serious side-effects of treatment, likely time-scale of treatments and costs where relevant. You should always give patients basic information about treatment you propose to provide, but you should respect the wishes of any patient who asks you not to give them detailed information. This places a considerable onus upon health professionals. Yet, without such information, patients cannot make proper choices, as partners in the health care process. Our booklet *Seeking Patients' Consent: The Ethical Considerations* gives further advice on providing information to patients.

6. It is good practice to give patients information about how information about them may be used to protect public health, to undertake research and audit, to teach or train medical staff and students and to plan and organise health care services.

Section 3 - Disclosure of information

Sharing information with others providing care

7. Where patients have consented to treatment, express consent is not usually needed before relevant personal information is shared to enable the treatment to be provided. For example, express consent would not be needed before general practitioners disclose relevant personal information so that a medical secretary can type a referral letter. Similarly, where a patient has agreed to be referred for an X-ray physicians may make relevant information available to radiologists when requesting an X-ray. Doctors cannot treat patients safely, nor provide the continuity of care, without having relevant information about the patient's condition and medical history.

8. You should make sure that patients are aware that personal information about them will be shared within the health care team, unless they object, and of the reasons for this. It is particularly important to check that patients

understand what will be disclosed if it is necessary to share personal information with anyone employed by another organisation or agency providing health or social care. You must respect the wishes of any patient who objects to particular information being shared with others providing care, except where this would put others at risk of death or serious harm.

9. You must make sure that anyone to whom you disclose personal information understands that it is given to them in confidence, which they must respect. Anyone receiving personal information in order to provide care is bound by a legal duty of confidence, whether or not that they have contractual or professional obligations to protect confidentiality.

10. Circumstances may arise where a patient cannot be informed about the sharing of information, for example because of a medical emergency. In these cases you should pass relevant information promptly to those providing the patients' care. ·

Section 4 - Disclosure of information other than for treatment of the individual patient

Principles

11. Information about patients is requested for a wide variety of purposes including education, research, monitoring and epidemiology, public health surveillance, clinical audit, administration and planning. You have a duty to protect patients' privacy and respect their autonomy. When asked to provide information you should follow the guidance in paragraph 1, that is:

    - Seek patients' consent to disclosure of any information wherever possible, whether or not you judge that patients can be identified from the disclosure.

    - Anonymise data where unidentifiable data will serve the purpose.

    - Keep disclosures to the minimum necessary.

12. The paragraphs which follow deal with obtaining consent, and what to do where consent is unobtainable, or it is impracticable to seek consent.

Obtaining consent

13. Seeking patients' consent to disclosure is part of good communication between doctors and patients, and is an essential part of respect for patients' autonomy and privacy.

Consent where disclosures will have personal consequences for patients

14. You must obtain express consent where patients may be personally affected by the disclosure, for example when disclosing personal information to a patient's employer. When seeking express consent you must make sure that patients are given enough information on which to base their decision, the reasons for the disclosure and the likely consequences of the disclosure. You should also explain how much information will be disclosed and to whom it will be given. If the patient withholds consent, or consent cannot be obtained, disclosures may be made only where they can be justified in the public interest, usually where disclosure is essential to protect the patient, or someone else, from risk of death or serious harm.

Consent where the disclosure is unlikely to have personal consequences for patients

15. Disclosure of information about patients for purposes such as epidemiology, public health safety, or the administration of health services, or for use in education or training, clinical or medical audit, or research is unlikely to have personal consequences for the patient. In these circumstances you should still obtain patients' express consent to the use of identifiable data or arrange for members of the health care team to anonymise records (see also paragraphs 16 and 18).

16. However, where information is needed for the purposes of the kind set out in paragraph 15, and you are satisfied that it is not practicable either to obtain express consent to disclosure, nor for a member of the health care team to anonymise records, data may be disclosed without express consent. Usually such disclosures will be made to allow a person outside the health care team to anonymise the records. Only where it is essential for the purpose may identifiable records be disclosed. Such disclosures must be kept to the minimum necessary for the purpose. In all such cases you must be satisfied that patients have been told, or have had access to written material informing them:

- That their records may be disclosed to persons outside the team which provided their care.

- Of the purpose and extent of the disclosure, for example, to produce anonymised data for use in education, administration, research or audit.

- That the person given access to records will be subject to a duty of confidentiality.

- That they have a right to object to such a process, and that their objection will be respected, except where the disclosure is essential to protect the patient, or someone else, from risk of death or serious harm.

17. Where you have control of personal information about patients, you must not allow anyone access to them for the purposes of the kind set out in paragraph 15, unless the person has been properly trained and authorised by the health authority, NHS trust or comparable body and is subject to a duty of confidentiality in their employment or because of their registration with a statutory regulatory body.

Disclosures in the public interest

18. In cases where you have considered all the available means of obtaining consent, but you are satisfied that it is not practicable[2] to do so, or that patients are not competent to give consent, or exceptionally, in cases where patients withhold consent, personal information may be disclosed in the public interest where the benefits to an individual or to society of the disclosure outweigh the public and the patient's interest in keeping the information confidential.

19. In all such cases you must weigh the possible harm (both to the patient, and the overall trust between doctors and patients) against the benefits which are likely to arise from the release of information.

20. Ultimately, the 'public interest' can be determined only by the courts; but the GMC may also require you to justify your actions if we receive a complaint about the disclosure of personal information without a patient's consent.

---

2. For example where records are of such age and/or number that reasonable efforts to trace patients are unlikely to be successful; where the patient has been or may be violent, or where action must be taken quickly (for example in the out-break of some communicable diseases) and there is insufficient time to contact patients.

Section 5 - Putting the principles into practice

21. The remainder of this booklet deals with circumstances in which doctors are most frequently asked to disclose information, and provides advice on how the principles in paragraphs 14 – 20 should be applied.

Disclosures which benefit patients indirectly

Monitoring public health and the safety of medicines and devices including disclosures to cancer and other registries

22. Professional organisations and government regulatory bodies[3] which monitor the public health or the safety of medicines or devices, as well as cancer and other registries, rely on information from patients' records for their effectiveness in safeguarding the public health. For example, the effectiveness of the yellow card scheme run by the Committee on Safety of Medicines depends on information provided by clinicians. You must co-operate by providing relevant information wherever possible. The notification of some communicable diseases is required by law (see also paragraph 43), and in other cases you should provide information in anonymised form, wherever that would be sufficient.

23. Where personal information is needed, you should seek express consent before disclosing information, whenever that is practicable. For example, where patients are receiving treatment there will usually be an opportunity for a health care professional to discuss disclosure of information with them.

24. Personal information may sometimes be sought about patients with whom health care professionals are not in regular contact. Doctors should therefore make sure that patients are given information about the possible value of their data in protecting the public health in the longer-term, at the initial consultation or at another suitable occasion when they attend a surgery or clinic. Patients should be given the information set out in paragraph 16: it should be clear that they may object to disclosures at any point. You must record any objections so that patients' wishes can be

---

3.   Such as the Medicines Control Agency, the Committee on Safety of Medicines, the Medical Devices Agency, the Drug Safety Research Unit and the Public Health Laboratory Service.

respected. In such cases, you may pass on anonymised information if asked to do so.

25. Where patients have not expressed an objection, you should assess the likely benefit of the disclosure to the public and commitment to confidentiality of the organisation requesting the information. If there is little or no evident public benefit, you should not disclose information without the express consent of the patient.

26. Where it is not practicable to seek patients' consent for disclosure of personal information for these purposes, or where patients are not competent to give consent, you must consider whether disclosures would be justified in the public interest, by weighing the benefits to the public health of the disclosure against the possible detriment to the patient.

27. The automatic transfer of personal information to a registry, whether by electronic or other means, before informing the patient that information will be passed on, is unacceptable save in the most exceptional circumstances. These would be where a court has already decided that there is such an overwhelming public interest in the disclosure of information to a registry that patients' rights to confidentiality are overridden; or where you are willing and able to justify the disclosure, potentially before a court or to the GMC, on the same grounds.

Clinical audit and education

28. Anonymised data will usually be sufficient for clinical audit and for education. When anonymising records you should follow the guidance on obtaining consent in paragraphs 15-17 above. You should not disclose non-anonymised data for clinical audit or education without the patient's consent.

Administration and financial audit

29. You should record financial or other administrative data separately from clinical information, and provide it in form, wherever that is possible.

30. Decisions about the disclosure of clinical records for administrative or financial audit purposes, for example where health authority staff seek access to patients' records as part of the arrangements for verifying payments, are unlikely to bring your registration into question, provided that, before allowing access to patients' records, you follow the guidance in

paragraphs 15-17. Only the relevant part of the record should be made available for scrutiny.

Medical research

31. Where research projects depend on using identifiable information or samples, and it is not practicable to contact patients to seek their consent, this fact should be drawn to the attention of a research ethics committee so that it can consider whether the likely benefits of the research outweigh the loss of confidentiality. Disclosures may otherwise be improper, even if the recipients of the information are registered medical practitioners. The decision of a research ethics committee would be taken into account by a court if a claim for breach of confidentiality were made, but the court's judgement would be based on its own assessment of whether the public interest was served. More detailed guidance is issued by the medical royal colleges and other bodies.

Publication of case-histories and photographs

32. You must obtain express consent from patients before publishing personal information about them as individuals in media to which the public has access, for example in journals or text books, whether or not you believe the patient can be identified. Express consent must therefore be sought to the publication of, for example, case-histories about, or photographs of, patients. Where you wish to publish information about a patient who has died, you should take into account the guidance in paragraphs 40-41 before deciding whether or not to do so.

Disclosures where doctors have dual responsibilities

33. Situations arise where doctors have contractual obligations to third parties, such as companies or organisations, as well as obligations to patients. Such situations occur, for example, when doctors:

- Provide occupational health services or medical care for employees of a company or organisation.

- Are employed by an organisation such as an insurance company.

- Work for an agency assessing claims for benefits.

- Provide medical care for patients and are subsequently asked to provide medical reports or information for third parties about them.

- Work as police surgeons.

- Work in the armed forces.

- Work in the prison service.

34. If you are asked to write a report about and/or examine a patient, or to disclose information from existing records for a third party to whom you have contractual obligations, you must:

    - Be satisfied that the patient has been told at the earliest opportunity about for the purpose of the examination and/or disclosure, the extent of the information to be disclosed and the fact that relevant information cannot be concealed or withheld. You might wish to show the form to the patient before you complete it to ensure the patient understands the scope of the information requested.

    - Obtain, or have seen, written consent to the disclosure from the patient or a person properly authorised to act on the patient's behalf. You may, however, accept written assurances from an officer of a government department that the patient's written consent has been given.

    - Disclose only information relevant to the request for disclosure: accordingly, you should not usually disclose the whole record. The full record may be relevant to some benefits paid by government departments.

    - Include only factual information you can substantiate, presented in an unbiased manner.

    - The Access to Medical Reports Act 1988 entitles patients to see reports written about them before they are disclosed, in some circumstances. In all circumstances you should check whether patients wish to see their report, unless patients have clearly and specifically stated that they do not wish to do so[4].

35. Disclosures without consent to employers, insurance companies, or any other third party, can be justified only in exceptional circumstances, for example, when they are necessary to protect others from risk of death or serious harm.

---

4. In some cases other bodies give patients access to reports, for example, the Department of Social Security gives all claimants access to reports made in connection with state benefits. In such cases it is not necessary for you to check patients' wish to see the report

Disclosures to protect the patient or others

36. Disclosure of personal information without consent may be justified where failure to do so may expose the patient or others to risk or death or serious harm. Where third parties are exposed to a risk so serious that it outweighs the patient's privacy interest, you should seek consent to disclosure where practicable. If it is not practicable, you should disclose information promptly to an appropriate person or authority. You should generally inform the patient before disclosing the information.

37. Such circumstances may arise, for example:

    • Where a colleague, who is also a patient, is placing patients at risk as a result of illness or other medical condition. If you are in doubt about whether disclosure is justified you should consult an experienced colleague, or seek advice from a professional organisation. The safety of patients must come first at all times. (Our booklet Serious Communicable Diseases gives further guidance on this issue.)

    • Where a patient continues to drive, against medical advice, when unfit to do so. In such circumstances you should disclose relevant information to the medical adviser of the Driver and Vehicle Licensing Agency without delay. Fuller guidance is given in Appendix 2.

    • Where a disclosure may assist in the prevention or detection of a serious crime. Serious crimes, in this context, will put someone at risk of death or serious harm, and will usually be crimes against the person, such as abuse of children.

Children and other patients who may lack competence to give consent

38. Problems may arise if you consider that a patient is incapable of giving consent to treatment or disclosure because of immaturity, illness or mental incapacity[5]. If such patients ask you not to disclose information to a third party, you should try to persuade them to allow an appropriate person to be involved in the consultation[6]. If they refuse and you are convinced that it is essential, in their medical interests, you may disclose relevant information

---

5. Guidance on assessing patients' capacity to make decisions is provided in our booklet Seeking Patients' Consent: The Ethical Considerations.

6. In some cases disclosures will be required for example under some sections of the Mental Health Act 1983, or under the Adults with Incapacity (Scotland) Act 2000.

to an appropriate person or authority. In such cases you must tell the patient before disclosing any information, and, where appropriate, seek and carefully consider the views of an advocate or carer. You should document in the patient's record the steps you have taken to obtain consent and the reasons for deciding to disclose information.

39. If you believe a patient to be a victim of neglect or physical, sexual or emotional abuse and that the patient cannot give or withhold consent to disclosure, you should give information promptly to an appropriate responsible person or statutory agency, where you believe that the disclosure is in the patient's best interests. You should usually inform the patient that you intend to disclose the information before doing so. Such circumstances may arise in relation to children, where concerns about possible abuse need to be shared with other agencies such as social services. Where appropriate you should inform those with parental responsibility about the disclosure. If, for any reason, you believe that disclosure of information is not in the best interests of an abused or neglected patient, you must still be prepared to justify your decision.

Disclosure after a patient's death

40. You still have an obligation to keep personal information confidential after a patient dies. The extent to which confidential information may be disclosed after a patient's death will depend on the circumstances. These include the nature of the information, whether that information is already public knowledge or can be anonymised, and the intended use to which the information will be put. You should also consider whether the disclosure of information may cause distress to, or be of benefit to, the patient's partner or family.

41. There are a number of circumstances in which you may be asked to disclose, or wish to use, information about patients who have died. For example:

- To assist a Coroner, Procurator Fiscal or other similar officer in connection with an inquest or fatal accident inquiry. In these circumstances you should provide relevant information (see also paragraph 19 of *Good Medical Practice*).

- As part of National Confidential Enquiries or other clinical audit or for education or research. The publication of properly anonymised case studies would be unlikely to be improper in these contexts.

- On death certificates. The law requires you to complete death certificates honestly and fully.

- To obtain information relating to public health surveillance. Anonymised information should be used unless identifiable data is essential to the study.

42. Particular difficulties may arise when there is a conflict of interest between parties affected by the patient's death. For example, if an insurance company seeks information in order to decide whether to make a payment under a life assurance policy, you should release information in accordance with the requirements of the Access to Health Records Act 1990 or with the authorisation of those lawfully entitled to deal with the person's estate who have been fully informed of the consequences of disclosure. It may also be appropriate to inform those close to the patient.

Section 6 - Disclosure in connection with judicial or other statutory proceedings

43. You must disclose information to satisfy a specific statutory requirement, such as notification of a known or suspected communicable disease.

44. You must also disclose information if ordered to do so by a judge or presiding officer of a court. You should object to the judge or the presiding officer if attempts are made to compel you to disclose what appear to you to be irrelevant matters, for example matters relating to relatives or partners of the patient, who are not parties to the proceedings.

45. You should not disclose personal information to a third party such as a solicitor, police officer or officer of a court without the patient's express consent, except in the circumstances described at paragraphs 36-37, 39 and 41.

46. You may disclose personal information in response to an official request from a statutory regulatory body for any of the health care professions[7], where that body determines that this is necessary in the interests of justice

---

7. For example, the General Medical Council, the General Dental Council, the United Kingdom Central Council for Nursing, Midwifery and Health Visiting, the Council for Professions Supplementary to Medicine; the General Optical Council, the General Osteopathic Council and the General Chiropractic Council.

and for the safety of other patients. Wherever practicable you should discuss this with the patient. There may be exceptional cases where, even though the patient objects, disclosure is justified.

If you decide to disclose confidential information you must be prepared to explain and justify your decision.

Appendix 1

Electronic processing

1. You must be satisfied that there are appropriate arrangements for the security of personal information when it is stored, sent or received by fax, computer, e-mail or other electronic means.

2. If necessary, you should take appropriate authoritative professional advice on how to keep information secure before connecting to a network. You should record the fact that you have taken such advice.

3. You must make sure your own fax machine and computer terminals are in secure areas. If you send data by fax you should satisfy yourself, as far as is practicable, that the data cannot be intercepted or seen by anyone other than the intended recipient.

4. When deciding whether, and in what form to transmit personal information, you should note that information sent by e-mail through the may be intercepted.

Appendix 2

Disclosure of information about patients to the Driver and Vehicle Licensing Agency (DVLA)

1. The DVLA is legally responsible for deciding if a person is medically unfit to drive. The Agency needs to know when driving licence holders have a condition which may now, or in the future, affect their safety as a driver.

2. Therefore, where patients have such conditions you should:

    •   Make sure that patients understand that the condition may impair their ability to drive. If a patient is incapable of understanding this advice, for example because of dementia, you should inform the DVLA immediately.

    •   Explain to patients that they have a legal duty to inform the DVLA about the condition.

3. If patients refuse to accept the diagnosis or the effect of the condition on their ability to drive, you can suggest that the patients seek a second opinion, and make appropriate arrangements for the patients to do so. You should advise patients not to drive until the second opinion has been obtained.

4. If patients continue to drive when they are not fit to do so, you should make every reasonable effort to persuade them to stop. This may include telling their next of kin.

5. If you do not manage to persuade patients to stop driving, or you are given or find evidence that a patient is continuing to drive contrary to advice, you should disclose relevant medical information immediately, in confidence, to the medical adviser at the DVLA.

6. Before giving information to the DVLA you should try to inform the patient of your decision to do so. Once the DVLA has been informed, you should also write to the patient, to confirm that a disclosure has been made.

Subject
Index

Author Index